Learning and Teaching in Physical Education

Learning and Teaching in Physical Education

Edited by

Colin A. Hardy and Mick Mawer

UK   Falmer Press, 1 Gunpowder Square, London, EC4A 3DE
USA   Falmer Press, 325 Chestnut Street, 8th Floor, Philadelphia, PA 19106

First published in 1999

A catalogue record for this book is available from the British Library

ISBN 0 7507 0875 1 cased
ISBN 0 7507 0874 3 paper

Library of Congress Cataloging-in-Publication Data are available on request

Jacket design by Caroline Archer

Typeset in 10/12pt Times by
Graphicraft Limited, Hong Kong

Printed in Great Britain by Biddles Ltd., Guildford and King's Lynn on paper which has a specified pH value on final paper manufacture of not less than 7.5 and is therefore 'acid free'.

Every effort has been made to contact copyright holders for their permission to reprint material in this book. The publishers would be grateful to hear from any copyright holder who is not here acknowledged and will undertake to rectify any errors or omissions in future editions of this book.

Contents

v

Contents

Figures and Tables

Introduction

Colin A. Hardy and Mick Mawer

The last 20 years has witnessed a rapid expansion in research and knowledge concerning the many factors that influence learning and teaching in physical education. These include such issues as the context in which physical education teachers work, what teachers think about when they are teaching and planning their teaching, and the knowledge they require to teach effectively. However, it is only in recent years that research has begun to provide an insight into what physical education teachers feel about their role and their lives in teaching, and what pupils themselves feel about the physical education they experience in schools. In fact, research that actually focuses on the pupils, their feelings, their thought processes, what motivates them, and how they respond to the instruction provided by the teacher has only recently attracted limited research interest. That is why we have emphasized pupil *learning* in both the title of this book, and in the placement of the chapters. It is not that we see research on *teaching* as having less importance, but that we feel that the time is ripe to focus as strongly on research into pupil learning and motivation in physical education as on research into teaching, teachers and the context of teaching. As Merlin Wittrock (1986) has pointed out, the study of pupils' thought processes brings a distinctive perspective to the understanding of teachers' effects on learning, and:

> . . . emphasises the critical role that student background knowledge, perceptions of instruction, attention to the teacher, motivation and attribution for learning, affective processes, and ability to generate interpretations and understandings of instruction play in teaching and in influencing student achievement'. (p. 297)

The purpose of this book is three-fold:

- to draw together the research and implications of research on topics that influence the learning and teaching of physical education;
- to provide a relatively new insight into recent research findings on such topics as pupil cognition, learning and motivation in physical education, and their implications for teaching;
- to provide some suggestions for future research into the factors that may influence the learning and teaching of physical education.

'Learning and teaching in physical education' is a complex area of study and one that needs to be examined from a variety of perspectives. However, in attempting this task we have naturally had to be selective in our choice of topics and have chosen areas of study on the basis of their particular prominence and relevance at this point in time. Although the majority of contributors come from a physical education background, they do offer the individuality and variety of theoretical positions that provide both width and depth to any discussion of learning and teaching as a field of study. In an educational world that is becoming increasingly competency-based, and where measurement takes precedence over process, it is hoped that this particular text may help pre-service teachers, experienced practitioners and administrators to 'stand back' and reflect upon their professional work. The overall aim is to provide an up to date account of the breadth of research approaches in this field, and to highlight those topics that many feel have a particular influence on the effective teaching of physical education. The topics chosen are grouped into five parts relating to the context in which physical education teachers work, pupil learning in physical education, topical issues relating to the teaching of physical education, and those areas of research that are concerned with understanding physical education teachers, their knowledge, expertise, thought processes and sense of self. The final part offers an 'eye to the future', and raises issues about the values that will sustain and develop the sports pedagogy research community in order that it might further influence the teaching of PE in schools.

John Evans, Brian Davies, and Dawn Penney 'kick off' this tome by centring attention on the political context of teaching and learning in PE in the UK, and consider how socio-political and cultural influences bear upon, and perhaps define, not only the nature of teaching in schools, but also what is to count as 'learning', 'worthwhile knowledge' and being 'able' in PE. This opening chapter draws attention to changes that have occurred in the curriculum and teaching in state schools in the UK in recent years; and the authors believe these changes have been driven by the politics of the 'new right' and have been refined, but essentially re-instated, by 'new Labour'. The authors draw upon the theoretical work of Basil Bernstein, and examine ways in which the relationships between actions inside classrooms and the wider socio-cultural and political influences can be conceptualized. They consider that unless these connections are made, our understandings of how teachers teach and what children learn in PE will remain partial and incomplete.

Part 2 focuses on the pupil, and in Chapter 2 Richard Fisher and Chris Laws explore the reality of PE from the pupils' perspective. They examine some of the issues of power that may exist within the interactions of pupils and teachers at the operational level of the curriculum, particularly related to the structure, knowledge and rituals that exist in physical education. This, they argue, is very different to the assumptions that exist based on ideological principles and the formal curriculum they generate. They report on research that has used children's stories as a means of helping them explain and interpret their experiences, how physical education is viewed in relation to other subjects, and how important it is for teachers to understand the frameworks that pupils use to interpret the subject if they are to implement an effective curriculum that is relevant to pupils' lives.

In their chapter on 'pupils' metacognition and learning' Ian Luke and Colin Hardy note how metacognition refers to the knowledge and control that pupils have of their cognitive functioning. They attempt to clarify the term by utilizing a metacognitive ability conceptual framework where the distinctions and the connections between the three major concepts of metacognitive knowledge, metacognitive strategies and metacognitive experiences are highlighted. These three components are developed separately and related to physical education events. The implications of metacognitive ability research in physical education is then discussed with the suggestion that there are some signs that pupils could be guided in their development of metacognitive ability. However, Ian and Colin stress that development of this ability should be continuous and incremental and form a way of life in physical education lessons and that it should not be assumed that this development is automatically taking place.

In their chapter on 'cognitive strategies' Ian and Colin suggest that pupils' cognitive strategies can significantly influence learning ability in physical education although they recognize the complexity of cognitive strategy development. They explain the difficulties in defining cognitive strategy, they examine the connection between cognitive style combinations, cognitive strategies and cognitive tactics and consider the initiation and control of cognitive strategies. The implications of strategy development for teaching physical education are explored and, in particular, whether teaching should match or mismatch pupils' tendencies in cognitive style combinations and cognitive strategies. The importance of having efficient metacognitive ability for effective development and utilization of cognitive strategies, and understanding interactions between pupils' cognitive strategies and their knowledge base, personal attributes and contextual variables are also discussed. In conclusion, Ian and Colin emphasize that teachers of physical education must not only look at the content and organization of their lessons, but also to the cognitive strategies deemed necessary to make pupils' learning more meaningful.

Part 3 examines four topics related to the teaching of physical education, concentrating specifically on issues concerned with teaching approaches, instruction, motivation and class management and control. Recent research developments concerning teaching styles and teaching approaches in physical education are reviewed by Mick Mawer in Chapter 5, with particular emphasis on the nature and results of studies examining Mosston's Spectrum of Teaching Styles, approaches to teaching critical thinking skills in physical education, direct and indirect approaches to teaching games, and cooperative teaching and learning in physical education.

Why are some young people motivated to succeed in physical education and sport whereas others see physical education as a source of stress and failure and endeavour to avoid physical education lessons? In order to enhance the motivation of pupils in physical education teachers need to understand the complexity of pupil motivation and how they might apply this knowledge in their teaching. In Chapter 6 Stuart Biddle suggests approaches to understanding motivation based on three specific contemporary motivational research areas: how pupil attributions of success and failure are related to pupil confidence and emotional reactions, and how maladaptive attributions may be changed; pupil achievement goal orientations and how they define success; the establishment of a motivational climate for learning in physical education that is oriented towards mastery rather than normative performance; and the creation of an autonomy-supporting environment in physical education as opposed to one based on coercion and control. Throughout the chapter Stuart explains how these various perspectives on pupil motivation have implications for the teacher of physical education.

Colin Hardy's chapter on pupil misbehaviours and teachers' responses examines the occurrence of pupil misbehaviour, the relevance of gender and time of day to pupil misbehaviour, the manner of teachers' responses and the reasons behind particular pupil misbehaviours and teacher responses. With the limited number of physical education studies in the area Colin has concentrated mainly on explaining and commenting upon the results of four investigations. However, although he accepts that such an examination of pupil misbehaviour in physical education classes cannot do justice to the very complex area of control and discipline in schools, he suggests it can provide evidence for teacher reflection and a platform from which to develop further research.

In Chapter 8 Judith Rink discusses the teaching of motor skills from a learning perspective, and focuses on learner needs, learning theory, and the critical variables and principles of quality instruction such as: providing opportunities to respond, communication skills, selecting and developing content, guidance and feedback, and the provision of an environment that will facilitate learning. In particular, Judith discusses the question of whether there is a single theory of learning that can be applied to all situations and therefore a single approach to instruction, or whether instruction should be matched to specific objectives and specific learner outcomes.

In Part 4 the emphasis is on understanding the teacher of physical education — what they think about and how their knowledge and thoughts may influence their effectiveness as teachers. In Chapter 9 Andrew Sparkes focuses attention on the apparent neglect of the 'lived body' in attempting to understand PE teachers, their experiences and their sense of self. Andrew draws upon life history data from two PE teachers, Rachael and David, in order to highlight the dilemmas that some PE teachers face in maintaining a coherent sense of self and contentment with their bodies when their body projects are interrupted by specific critical moments in their lives, and how this image of themselves influences their choice of teaching as a career and their role as teachers. Andrew also goes beyond the lives of these two teachers to discuss issues that are raised concerning the 'body stories' that circulate around the PE community, and how important it is to understand them if we are to develop a real insight into the behaviour and lives of PE teachers.

What do we mean when we talk about teachers' *knowledge* in PE? As a profession we do seem to be unsure about the knowledge that distinguishes us as teachers. There has been a lot of recent interest in identifying knowledge *for* teaching, but it is knowledge *about* teaching physical education that Tony Rossi and Tania Cassidy focus on in Chapter 10. They begin with a discussion of the traditions of research into physical education teachers' knowledge, and how they feel recent quantitative research approaches have 'balkanized', or broken up and reassembled our concept of effective pedagogy. They then take a more holistic view of teachers' knowledge and discuss the concept of 'knowledgeable teachers', and the notion of 'knowledgeability' being related to such issues as self-identity, practical consciousness, and the day to day routines and regimes of PE teachers. They argue that the sum of the parts of the PE teachers knowledge do not equal the whole, because certain discourses dominate what is taught in PE and how it is taught. They, therefore, advocate a much broader view of knowledge, with teacher identity being a crucial feature in teachers' knowledge. This approach, they argue, may provide a more secure, although not necessarily complete, view of teachers' knowledge in physical education.

Research on teacher thinking has emerged as an important educational topic in recent years, and David Griffey and Lynn Housner trace these research developments in physical education in Chapter 11. Dave and Lynn concentrate specifically on such topics as teacher cognition, decision-making, teachers' beliefs and sense of purpose, planning for instruction, teachers' perceptions of the instructional environment, and how these issues influence effective teaching and the making of appropriate decisions about how to facilitate pupil learning. Comparisons are made between the thinking and decision-making of beginning and experienced teachers, and suggestions put forward for those working in teacher education. Finally, they argue that knowing what teachers value and how this influences their decision-making processes in the classroom will enable us to improve teacher instruction in physical education lessons.

In Chapter 12 Patt Dodds provides a thought-provoking finale to this book with her views concerning the future of research in learning and teaching in physical education. Patt suggests that those interested in learning and teaching in physical education, and constituting a loosely structured research learning community, should attempt to extend the research reviewed in this book by gradually accumulating research-based knowledge, through progressive research programmes, rather than constantly look for 'silver bullets'. Such a community, Patt argues, needs to create learning opportunities to improve research practice, take a life long view of learning research, and to share practice-oriented goals in order to really influence how physical education is taught in our schools.

Reference

WITTROCK, M. (1986) 'Students' thought processes', in WITTROCK, M. (ed.) *Handbook of Research on Teaching*, New York, MacMillan, pp. 297–314.

Part 1

The Context in Which Physical Education Teachers Work

1   The Social Construction of Teaching and Learning: The Politics of Pedagogy

John Evans, Brian Davies and Dawn Penney

The Political Context of Teaching and Learning

We write this paper at a time when teachers, teacher educators, the nature of teaching in schools and in Initial Teacher Education (ITE) in England and Wales are in the public eye. While to some extent this is true 'worldwide', many of the phenomena to which we refer in this paper are particularly evident in New Zealand and Australia. In the UK, the 'new Labour' government elected in 1997 has made 'education' a priority manifesto commitment and is pressing forward with a number of policy initiatives aimed both at 'increasing opportunity' and 'raising standards in schools'. Its Conservative predecessors viewed the latter task largely, though never solely, in terms of manipulating and defining *what* was to be taught to all pupils in all state funded schools in England and Wales, that is to say, as a *curriculum issue*. New Labour, while retaining elements of the Conservative project (for example, in its emphasis on the teaching of the three Rs in schools and ITE), seems increasingly bent, discursively and materially, on directing attention away from the content of the curriculum towards issues of *how* pupils and students are to be effectively taught in schools and ITE. Government appointed 'experts', with an apparent wanton disregard for the dangers and difficulties of cross-cultural comparison purportedly have discovered in the more didactic pedagogies of schools in south Asia, better ways of ensuring that pupils and students in the UK will learn — especially in the 'core' subjects of science, technology and maths. The associated implications heavily lace the mantras of the Secretary of State and his ministers: other subject areas should note that the more didactic the teaching methodology, the better the education and the more students and pupils will learn and retain. Yet the evidence to support such a claim is very difficult to discern.

If nothing else, the attention given by politicians in recent years to what, and how students are taught in schools has provided a salutary reminder to teachers and researchers wherever they may be located, and brought to the surface the 'fact' that teaching and learning are now, as they have been historically, socio-cultural and political as well as educational processes and are, therefore, always and inevitably contested domains. They are never arbitrary, value free, or independent of the ideologies and driving interests of those, often powerful, others, individuals, associations, interests groups (e.g. politicians, or appointed spokespersons who may operate within and outside schools) who may hold strong views relating not only to how and what children and young people should learn from the content of the curriculum but also what they, as 'good citizens', really ought to be. It is therefore unsurprising that debates about the nature of teaching are often deeply emotive affairs; they are 'contests' concerning the nature of the individual, of discipline and authority, social order and control.

Understanding Teaching: Form and Content Matter

Recent debates about curricula and teaching methods have, however, revealed more than the socio-cultural and political aspects of teaching PE. They have also highlighted the dangers of conceptually separating teaching from curriculum content in any quest to understand *how* and *what* it is that pupils learn (or should learn) in schools. Much of our research evidence suggests that children may learn as much from the manner or mode of transmitting knowledge (i.e. from the styles and/or techniques that teachers use) as from the 'contents' of the curriculum. For example, our studies of teaching PE have suggested that girls are more likely, and have more opportunity, to learn independence and problem solving skills in PE than boys because of the frequent maintenance of the pattern of female teachers teaching girls while male teachers teach boys, and then the tendency for female teachers to use child-centred teaching techniques more often than their male counterparts, who routinely subject their pupils mainly to didactic teaching modes. Pupils learn from the pedagogical mode as well as or even instead of the content that teachers intend or want them to receive. In essence, there is no such thing as a content-only curriculum. In the act of teaching, teachers socialize pupils as they skill them. Indeed, there would hardly be the heated debates surrounding the nature of teaching methods in schools and ITE (usually framed in terms of crude and unhelpful dichotomies, or 'which is better' arguments, e.g. 'informal' or 'formal', child or teacher centred methods) if this were not so. Bernstein (1996) has articulated more eloquently than most how this complex relationship between education and socialization is simultaneously embedded in the act of teaching. In his view, pedagogic discourse is a 'rule which embeds two discourses'; a 'discourse of skills of various kinds and their relation to each other', which he refers to as 'instructional discourse' (ID), and a discourse of social order, which he calls 'regulative discourse' (RD). 'Instructional discourse is always embedded in regulative discourse, and the regulative discourse is the dominant discourse' (p. 46). Thus there can be no transmission of skills without the transmission of values. All theories of teaching, therefore, *ipso facto*, embrace issues of social control.

Moreover, any study of teaching and learning in PE in schools and ITE needs to address, not only the instructional and regulative aspects of the methodologies used to make knowledge available to pupils and students in classrooms, but also those transmitted by the systems of assessment and evaluation used to monitor student progress and by the intentions of the overt and hidden curriculum. All three message systems — *pedagogy, curriculum and evaluation* (see Bernstein, 1996) both independently and together are likely to have a powerful bearing not only on how and what pupils learn but also on the prior determination of *who* can learn and gain access to knowledge and understandings and, therefore, who succeeds, gains status and is valued in contexts of education and PE. While we elaborate on the dynamic of these processes below, the point we stress here is that to talk of the social construction of teaching and learning is, on the one hand, to acknowledge that teaching and learning in PE are socio-political and cultural acts (in both process and outcome) and, on the other, to recognize that these processes are always constructed relationally, that is to say, as the products of the volitional actions of teachers in interaction with pupils inside classrooms and schools, and the frames (discursive and material) set *for* them by factors which may have origins outside schools at sites or levels of decision making and action which are not always either accessible, immediately apparent, or easily observed (Evans, 1985; Penney and Evans, 1999). The actions of teachers thus always *frame* pupils learning opportunities and possibilities and are themselves framed, for example, by the products of contemporary policies, initiatives, ideological interests and influences, as well as by those factors that have been established historically by the actions and decisions of those that have gone before. Teaching has to be viewed as a complex social process/practice, always created, in part, by teachers and taught inside classrooms and schools but not always in conditions of either material and human resourcing or curricular practice, of their own making and over which they may have little or no control. Much of our research on policy, teachers and teaching in the UK has illustrated this and revealed that the balance of power between agency and structure, between teachers' capacity to decide what and how to teach and being told what to do, has shifted in recent years in the direction of powerful agencies of central government and the state outside schools. The professional autonomy of teachers has been significantly eroded as a direct result of Conservative education policies, particularly the introduction of a National Curriculum in England and Wales. Teachers now have far fewer opportunities to determine for themselves what is to be taught to pupils in state schools and, increasingly, how and when pupils should learn PE (Evans and Penney, 1995a and b; Penney and Evans, 1998) than they previously enjoyed.

While we have outlined the social or policy context of teaching in PE in schools and ITE in the UK in some detail elsewhere (Evans, Davies and Penney, 1996; Penney and Evans, 1997) we now seek to further explore the means of conceptualizing teaching as a social process in such a way as to capture its relational qualities, regardless of whether it occurs in the UK or elsewhere. We stress that although on this occasion our attention centres on the framing of relationships inside classrooms and the connections between teaching and teacher and student identity, rather than the framing of the curriculum and teaching by factors outside schools (Penney and Evans, 1999), these phenomenon can not be separated in any study of teaching in any meaningful or helpful way. We must explore a way of conceptualizing teaching and learning in a way that allows us to capture the connections both between what teachers do in classrooms (how they teach) and what pupils learn in terms of their physical capabilities, their senses of social and cultural 'distinction' or difference, and their individual sense of self, value and worth and a recognition of how these processes connect with wider socio-cultural, political and economic processes of globalization and changes in physical culture ongoing outside schools. It should also allow us to address the 'active' role of pupils in pedagogical relations while recognizing that the degree to which they are able to shape pedagogical processes is similarly framed by not only teachers but wider socio-cultural and political contexts. For us, the key concepts for achieving these ends are provided by the post-structuralist social theory of Michael Foucault (1972, 1980) alongside the inspirational work of Basil Bernstein (1971, 1996) on pedagogy and symbolic control.

Framing Teaching and Learning: Language and Identity

Teaching, of course, is quintessentially a discursive act. It is constructed in and through language. In PE it is expressed both linguistically and physically/corporeally, in contexts defined as appropriate. Teachers enter PE with pedagogical perspectives and discursive orientations (ways of seeing, thinking and speaking about education, children, and so on, which define appropriate teaching and learning) which have been formed, influenced and more or less strongly framed by the nature and range of discursive practices and the texts which they generate (for example, defining worthwhile education, physical education, learning) that they have experienced in ITE and, before that, in their own schooling. These discourses are not arbitrary but themselves selections from the range of discursive possibilities that are potentially available for expression. In ITE for example, institutions of Higher Education may 'choose' to privilege particular elements of sports science, physiology rather than pedagogy, or purvey a view that child-centred rather than teacher-centred teaching is the more valued pedagogy, or that sport, rather than dance or other forms of physical recreation, should be dominant in the curriculum of PE. Students tend to leave college imbued with particular ways of thinking about teaching, what counts as worthwhile knowledge, 'proper' learning and ways of behaving as a teacher and as a child. Such views are embedded and, literally, embodied in and through the teaching of PE. In the enactment of these discursive tendencies in schools and PE, teachers are themselves 'positioned' and position themselves as professionals of one kind or another, in turn positioning pupils as one kind or another (able, less able, athlete or dancer for instance), according to whether or not they can, or are able, to meet the hidden and explicit requirements of their adopted pedagogical modes or codes. The work of Foucault provides a majestic means of understanding discursive practice; how the thinking and actions of teachers and pupils are framed by wider 'regimes of truth' relating, for example, to the scientific, physical, political, educational, economic and other knowledge and ideological domains of contemporary society and which are selected and recontexualized in ITE and schools. But it does not help us explore the whole story, especially the detail of pedagogic discourse and practice, or the means by which such discourses are mediated within and through sites of educational practice, ultimately expressed in classrooms and help frame teaching and the identities of teachers and pupils. It is to the work of Bernstein that we have turned to advance our understandings in these terms.

For example, Bernstein (1996) suggests that contemporary pedagogic discourses are not arbitrary but constituted by a variety of theories drawn either from linguistics and the social and psychological sciences, or from more behaviourist and vocational perspectives and interests. He refers to the former properly, though rather disturbingly, to our ears tuned to the ways in which the term has been co-opted and inverted by the more technicist practices of central government and its agencies in recent years, as 'competency' modes, and the latter, 'performance' modes. These theories contain implicit models of the social, of communication, of interaction and of the subject. Both generate very different uses of time, space, discourse, forms of evaluation, notions of the acquirer (child, pupil, student), of autonomy and economy in contexts of education and PE. Competency theories (e.g. derived from Chomsky, Piaget, Levi-Strauss, Garfinkle) assume an 'in-built procedural democracy, an in-built creativity, an in-built virtuous self-regulation' (p. 56). The focus is likely to be on the potential 'within' the child, of what the child is and can become. They are also predicated on 'similar to' relations, that is to say, on recognizing what individuals, their communities, or class and cultures have in common rather than on what sets them apart, while acknowledging 'difference' as a positive characteristic rather than as a negative 'deficit'. By contrast, performance models place 'emphasis upon the specific outputs of the acquirer, upon a particular text the acquirer is expected to construct, and upon specialised skills necessary to the production of this specific output, text or product' (pp. 57–8). The focus is upon the explicit, surface features of learning and on what the individual needs to acquire in order to 'become' and achieve. Performance models are based on 'different from' relations, that is to say they are geared towards the separation of categories, the identification and recognition of what sets individuals apart. 'All competence modes, despite oppositions, share a preoccupation with the development (liberal/progressive), the recognition (populist) and change (radical) of consciousness' (p. 68). Performance modes 'focus on something that the acquirer does not possess, upon an absence, and as a consequence place the emphasis upon the text to be acquired and so upon the transmitter' (p. 71). Pedagogically, the former are consequently student-centred, the latter, teacher-centred, in focus. While both modes of competence and performance are evident in PE pedagogies, the latter, we suggest, has long dominated the subject, being reflected especially in the actions of male teachers of PE. Bernstein also makes the point that which model is appropriated for transmission in ITE or schools depends upon the dominant ideology in what he calls the official recontextualizing field (ORF) and of the relative autonomy of the pedagogic recontextualizing field (PRF). Our research has shown how performance theories have been privileged in the making of the National Curriculum PE by individuals and central government agencies operating in the ORF, while those educationalists and teachers in the PRF have been largely either excluded or ignored in the decision-making process relating to the curriculum and teaching.

However, it is the concept of *frame* which, in our view, permits us to address these matters, along with more general and enduring issues in empirical and theoretical work within the sociology of education concerning the relationship between action and social and organizational structure, agency and structure, power and control. Indeed, our research has embodied a strong reaction against studies of teaching and classroom life which pay little attention to the connections between individual teacher and pupil intentions and action and to the organizational and wider social contexts in which they are found. The concept of frame, drawn from Bernstein, 1971; Lundgren, 1972, 1977; Douglas, 1966, 1973; Evans, 1985; Penney, 1994; Penney and Evans, 1999, to identify and examine specific educational factors and to connect them with various levels and contexts of decision-making inside and outside schools, provided our work with a flexible way of indicating how specific factors of classroom life and the outside are interrelated. It has allowed us to show how different combinations of educational factors become differently framed and how they are both constructed by, and for, teachers and pupils. We suggest that, at the school organizational level, three *major* aspects of framing can be delineated. The first is the *curriculum* which defines for teachers and pupils the organization and the content of what is to be taught. In the UK these requirements have increasingly been set for teachers and pupils by interest groups and political agendas operating outside schools. The second is the *timetable* which puts groups of pupils together with teaching and staff and resources within designated curriculum for specific periods of time. It is this which generates planned diversity in the context of order. It decides the social and physical space of pupils, subjects and teachers. Time is not evenly distributed amongst subject disciplines or to areas of activity within the curriculum. This necessarily acts as a limit upon the actions of teachers and has implications for how they and their subject are perceived. In the UK PE tends to receive significantly less time than other 'core' subjects (such as maths, English and science). The third factor, *schooling*, reaches out to what we have recently referred to as the discursive frames of schooling (see Penney, 1994; Penney and Evans, 1999) and is a more complex phenomenon. In our view, it is not synonymous with all that goes on inside schools. The view we take is that to be schooled normally entails having the cognitive, emotional, socio-cultural attributes/ resources (the 'habitus') and discursive resources that are prerequisite to learning in large classes and the different modes of transmission (methods of making knowledge available to children and young people) within them. Whether there are discursive processes, affective and cognitive skills and attitudes which are constantly required by pupils to facilitate access to curriculum content (whatever their measured 'ability' or 'skill') should be of primary interest to any study of teaching and learning in contexts of PE. In essence, we need to make much more complex our ideas of what it is to be 'skilled' and 'able', or otherwise, in school and contexts of PE. Decisions taken in policy contexts outside school (see Penney and Evans, 1999) or in the broader school context concerning the timetable, curriculum and 'schooling' can thus be seen as frames forming limits or possibilities for the actions of teachers and pupils. Figure 1.1 may help to clarify this conceptual scheme.

Figure 1.1:   *Organizational frame factors and teaching process*

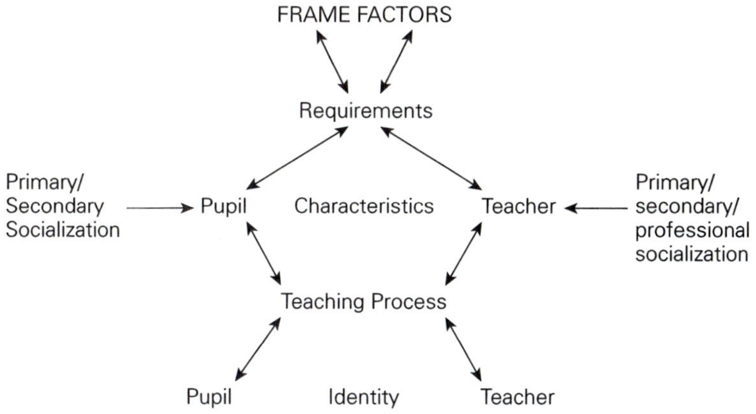

Source: from Evans, 1985, p. 12

The Social Construction of Learning and Identity

We can thus look at the classroom as a context of transmission which is constituted by the interrelation of frame factors — *what* is made available to pupils (content frames), *how* it is made available (transmission frames), *when* it is made available (pacing frames) and the relationships between teacher and pupils (disciplinary or schooling frames), along with those of resource (physical and human). These factors, constructed for, and by, teachers and pupils, define the parameters for teacher–pupil interaction. As frame factors they define what is to be required of pupils and teachers by way of skills, understandings and social competencies if a successful performance as a pupil or teacher within the classroom is to be achieved. At the intersection of these factors with the characteristics with which teacher and pupils are predisposed occurs a process and a structure of communication in which pupil–teacher identity is constructed. Teachers and pupils enter into this context with attitudes, interests, expectations and abilities which form the action and interpretation of the problems and possibilities which schooling presents. Pupils arrive with expectations of what constitutes a proper lesson, a good teacher, real learning. They are likely to deploy strategies to negotiate an acceptable existence. Cultural influences may be a prominent feature of strategies. These may be established in the broader context, peer group sub-cultural relationships, professional training which may build on and sediment personal experiences of schooling, or within the school itself. According to the characteristics that teachers and pupils have, frames may be differently experienced as limits, constraints, or possibilities.

In order to learn successfully in this context, pupils must be able to meet the requirements given by a complex interaction of frame factors (see Figure 1.2).

They must be able to cope with a content which is often abstract and culturally discontinuous or disruptive and even too difficult (factor i). They meet this context

Figure 1.2: *Frame factors and learning requirements*

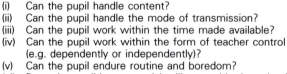

FRAME FACTORS

Requirements

(i)	Can the pupil handle content?	+	–
(ii)	Can the pupil handle the mode of transmission?	+	–
(iii)	Can the pupil work within the time made available?	+	–
(iv)	Can the pupil work within the form of teacher control (e.g. dependently or independently)?	+	–
(v)	Can the pupil endure routine and boredom?	+	–
(vi)	Does the pupil have a social milieu outside the school supportive of these characteristics?	+	–

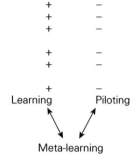

Source: from Evans, 1985, p. 48

in specific pedagogic modes (for example, in case of whole class method, with strong emphasis on closed question and answers) (factor ii), and time frames, experienced mainly as pacing (factor iii). Moreover, to manage learning successfully, they must willingly enter into the teachers' frame of control and 'pay attention' to teacher talk, which is usually the primary mode of transmission (factors iv and ii). This willingness or ability may itself be related to previous school experience and perhaps the social milieu outside the schools (factor vi), as well as immediate interpretations of the adequacy of subject content and teacher. They must do all this within the limits of time imposed by the teacher, or the pace defined by pupils (factor iii). Moreover, an ability to meet certain requirements, e.g. (i) and (ii) may, of course, contribute to a pupil's willingness or otherwise to meet other requirements such as those of (iv). Those pupils least able to cope with these requirements tend to be the greatest victims of routine and boredom (factor v).

Class teaching, ubiquitous in PE, tends to involve few pupils and to create a spurious appearance that the class as a whole is successfully progressing through and comprehending subject content. In fact, many of the pupils may be engaged in what Lundgren has elsewhere referred to as *piloting*, the strategy whereby a teacher avoids problems by simplifying them so that students are able to solve them by answering a simple chain of questions (1977, p. 200) or following a simple range of physical activities. It creates the illusion that learning is occurring. Collective piloting occurs when the teacher works this effect in front of the whole class. For those pupils who lack the prerequisite necessary for learning in large groups and in limited time, collective teaching tends, inevitably, to become mere collective piloting. In these circumstances, some pupils learn only that while they have received instruction, they still have not understood. They meta-learn, learn about their own 'learning', in this case about merely their (in) ability to comprehend instruction in Physical Education. As time goes on, given the cumulative nature of subject teaching, some pupils are unable to take part altogether. Teachers have to choose between recovering content which pupils failed to understand or to progress to new content. Discipline problems emerge as the process becomes more and more meaningless for some pupils. Thus the interplay of frames generate a structure of communication. The notion of structure does not refer to linguistic structure but, in a similar way to Lundgren (1977), to a pattern of who communicates with whom about what in what situation, a structure which itself gives rise to hierarchies of social relation and 'ability', as some meet the requirements of the context while others fall outside the curriculum, content and pedagogical mode of transmission and their needs cannot be met in the available time.

Consider here the experiences of the pupils involved in PE in the classrooms of Mrs M. and Mr T. (see Evans, Davies and Penney, 1996). Both teach in Llanwerin, a co-educational comprehensive school in a rural location in Wales. Both are experienced teachers. The context is framed by the 'flexibility' offered by the requirements of the National Curriculum that permits either dance or gymnastics at Key Stage 3 (age 11–14), the constraints of the timetable, and very limited resources; and an ITE experience which did not equip Mr T. to teach dance. They combine to ensure that boys and girls experience a sex differentiated curriculum where boys have no access to the educational experience of dance. In this context, girls generally were positioned as 'the other' in relation to boys and often considered as less active than they. In this context 'ability' seems to have been constructed particularly, by the men, first with reference to the putative needs of the nation and a particular team game (Rugby), rather than those of the children who do not necessarily 'support' or have an ability to play it. So positioned, many feel alienated not only from their bodies but also from any desire to explore their physical potential and to take up the opportunities for leisure that feature in the immediate and wider terrain. Within these contexts, the frames established not only position boys in relation to girls, but create intra-group hierarchies of achievement and ability in PE. For example, consider Rhys, male, 13 years of age and keen on physical activity. The son of a farmer, he likes nothing better than to fish, ride and walk the hills around his farm. He does not like team games and prefers to engage in outdoor activities, given the chance. He is bored with PE, finds it remote from his experience of physical recreation and dislikes Mr T. telling him what to do all the time, never listening properly, especially since he is given lots of responsibility by his parents at home on his farm. His 'ability', it seems, has little relevance or meaning within criteria framed by the requirement of pursuing the NCPE and the interests of the national team game. Consequently, in lessons he seems, to Mr T., to be 'unable' and/or unwilling either to learn or behave properly, that is to say, to enter into his frame of control and relate to the content of the games of the NCPE. In Mr T.'s terms Rhys, like so many boys these days, is deemed not 'fit' and 'underachieving', which he puts down to farm technology, too little manual labour and too much TV, rather the limits of his pedagogy or the NCPE. By contrast Sioned, female, 13, is seen by Mrs M. as an 'able' child. Taken by her parents to ballet and dance out of school she is easily able to meet the requirements of the pedagogical frames established in the teaching of dance and educational gymnastics, the individualized pedagogical modes that Mrs M. provides. She is equally comfortable at games and meeting the requirements of the more performance centred frames, the visible hierarchies and disciplines of games teaching. Her friend Ruth, however, although an able athlete, dislikes the context of schooling which Mrs M. defines for PE, that does not always tell them clearly or directly either what to do or when to do it, especially in dance and gym, activities that she knows that she could do well at but cannot access because of the way in which Mrs M. expects her to behave. She thinks Mrs M. weak, unable to control and make her work. However, while defined as weak in dance, she is seen as an able child in the context of games. At least she has the possibility, given Mrs M.'s capacity to mix performance and competency modes of teaching, of being defined as 'able' in some aspects of PE, those where there are strong performance codes. Boys, because of the dominance of a performance mode in male PE, in contrast, have far fewer opportunities than girls to be defined as able and achieve success.

Appreciating the Complexity of Teaching

It should be noted that these examples are merely 'fictional' caricatures, composite cases built from the limited data that we have on children in contexts of PE and from interviews with teachers. They are not in that sense 'real' people, but constructed 'types' used here only to illustrate how children's identities are constructed and framed in classrooms by rules and requirements, some of which are invisible, others explicit and which are established routinely both by the mode of transmission and the content of the curriculum of PE. Individual students are differently predisposed to be 'able' or 'willing' to meet such rules and requirements and so achieve success or failure in contexts of PE. This indicates that 'ability' in PE is as much a social construct as it is a physical construct, and that these two elements, inseparable and inextricably related, are compounded corporeally, in the act of becoming 'a pupil' (successful or otherwise) in the processes of PE. Figure 1.2 is in this spirit intended only as a heuristic device to help begin exploration of the ways in which teaching, learning and identity are framed (constrained and facilitated) inside classrooms and by wider contexts of decision making and influence inside and outside schools. We have very little research work to date in classrooms and schools constructed in terms of it. The performance mode privileged in recent British curricular, pedagogic and assessment policies is inimical to it and unless new Labour accept that questioning structures (of belief and institution) is a precondition of widening opportunity, we shall continue to spin in the mindless universe of 'raising standards' because we do not know any better.

References

BERNSTEIN, B. (1971) 'On the classification and framing of knowledge', in YOUNG, M.F.D. (ed.) *Knowledge and Control*, London: Collier Macmillan, pp. 47–70.

BERNSTEIN, B. (1996) *Pedagogy, Symbolic Control and Identity*, London: Taylor and Francis.

DOUGLAS, M. (1966) *Purity and Danger*, London: Routledge and Kegan Paul.

DOUGLAS, M. (1973) *Natural Symbols*, London: Barrie and Jenkins.

EVANS, J. (1985) *Teaching in Transition: The Challenge of Mixed Ability Grouping*, Buckingham: Open University Press.

EVANS, J., DAVIES, B., BASS, D. and PENNEY, D. (1997) 'Playing for position: Education policy, Physical Education and nationalism in Wales', *Journal of Education Policy*, **12**, 4, pp. 285–302.

EVANS, J., DAVIES, B. and PENNEY, D. (1996) 'Teachers, teaching and the social construction of gender relations', *Sport, Education and Society*, **1**, 2, pp. 165–83.

EVANS, J. and PENNEY, D. (1995a) 'Physical Education, restoration and the politics of sport', *Curriculum Studies*, **3**, 2, pp. 183–96.

EVANS, J. and PENNEY, D. (1995b) 'The politics of pedagogy: Making a national curriculum physical education', *Journal of Education Policy*, **10**, 1, pp. 27–44.

FOUCAULT, M. (1972) *The Archaeology of Knowledge* (SHERIDAN-SMITH, A. Trans), New York: Harper and Row.

FOUCAULT, M. (1980) Power/knowledge, in GORDON, C. (ed.), GORDON, C., MARSHALL, L., MEPHAM, J. and SOPER, K. (Trans), New York: Pantheon.

LUNDGREN, U. (1972) *Frame Factors and the Teaching Process*, Stockholm: Almquist and Wiksell.

LUNDGREN, U. (1977) *Model Analysis of Pedagogical Process*, Stockholm: Almquist and Wiksell.

PENNEY, D. (1994) 'No change in a new era?', The impact of the ERA (1988) on the provision of PE and sport in schools, PhD Thesis, University of Southampton.

PENNEY, D. (1998) 'School subjects and structures: Reinforcing traditional voices in contemporary "reforms" of education', *Discourse*, **19**, 1, pp. 5–17.

PENNEY, D. and EVANS, J. (1997) 'Naming the game: Discourse and domination in physical education and sport in England and Wales', *European Physical Education Review*, pp. 21–33.

PENNEY, D. and EVANS, J. (1999) *Politics, Policy and Practice in Physical Education and Sport*, London: Routledge.

Part 2

Learning in Physical Education

2   Pupils' Interpretations of Physical Education

Christopher Laws and Richard Fisher

Introduction

In many ways this chapter was born some years ago in two separate research projects. In one school a 15-year-old pupil was being interviewed about games in the physical education (PE) curriculum, in the course of which he declared a preference for rugby rather than football. When prompted he reasoned that it took place on the lower pitch and was, therefore, less windy and cold; in fact he hated all PE including the ethos and smell of the changing room and the intimidation provided by those who were good at it. Further pupil interviews provided entry into what is effectively another world in which pupils exercise their own, often complex, sets of interpretations about PE which have relevance within their own frame of reference and which may or may not be available to the teacher. Whilst pupils' attitudes towards, and opinions about, PE and related contexts has received fairly wide attention, there has been much less emphasis on the pattern of constructions underpinning pupils' interpretations of PE even though an appreciation of the pupils' world has great significance for those who structure the context in which it takes place. In another school a group of adolescent girls were expressing their wish for greater equality of opportunity within the PE curriculum, including access to the so called boys' games. In fact they did not wish to participate in most of these activities and it proved to be more than a simple issue of equality, of having other activities available to them. It was more a matter of having the opportunity to say 'no', of being able to exercise some power which, in spite of the emphasis on individualism in the curriculum, is something which has received relatively little attention among the profession.

Observing the behaviour of children in the PE context may indicate what their experience might be, but it is unlikely to suffice in determining what their experience actually is. Visible evidence may actually belie what is really happening as far as the individual is concerned. In this instance it is necessary to identify the feelings and reasons for those emotions that the child has as a result of engaging in such activity; a physical display of hesitancy may emanate from a lack of actual skill, a perceived lack of skill, a fear of the individual or group they are competing against, or any combination of such factors. The intangible perceptions that the child has of the PE programme clearly need to be identified in order that a distinction may be made between what we *believe* to be happening, as portrayed by behaviour, and what we may come to *know* of the child's experience through actually asking them. It is interesting that educational research to date has largely failed to give an internal view of the child since they, as the very subjects of investigation are, ironically, largely excluded from active contribution to the research process. Dyson (1995) suggests that whilst students are central to the educational process they are rarely consulted and where they have been there has been a tendency to treat their views as almost incidental. The focus has been largely on responses to questionnaires which makes information quantifiable and easily accessible, but inadequate in identifying the 'human condition' in the situations concerned. Power of expression has largely been accorded to 'legitimate' adults and the inferences of researchers, almost as though we do not consider children to have the ability to interpret their own situation. Failure to involve the child proactively in educational research may rest superficially in the belief that the child may be unable to articulate their feelings or more significantly in a feeling that they may in fact misinterpret what is actually happening. Here lies a danger that we, as 'adults' believe that our 'truth' carries greater significance than the child's. What is real for the child and how they allocate meaning are at least of equal consequence to any inferences we may make. This chapter seeks to explore the reality of PE as far as pupils are concerned and to examine some of the issues of power which arise from this examination of the way that pupils and teachers interact at an operational level in the curriculum as opposed to assumptions based on ideological principles and the formal curricula they generate.

Pupils and Physical Education

If we are seeking to identify children's experiences of PE it is essential that we take a back seat and accept the child's version of reality without imposing upon it our own parameters of interpretation. Significantly, an individual's perception of events may differ from what is observed and, therefore, be deemed to be 'untrue' by the outsider. However, if the person relating a situation believes something to have happened in a certain way, with relationships unfolding in a certain sequence and emotions in a certain pattern, then that for them is their experience. The exploration of this subjective experience of reality requires sensitive and subtle approaches. Dyson (1995) pointed out that the techniques most widely used to uncover pupils' views of PE have too frequently relied on more positivistic approaches which, though useful, offer a rather sanitized and tidy perspective of what is actually a complex system of personal meanings about the world. It can be argued then that the way to attain an understanding of children's experiences of the PE, is to literally allow them to 'tell their stories'. Children's stories provide, in fact, theories, which help explain and interpret phenomena. The stories that children tell may be deemed to function in terms of a particular setting, together with the characters and action that play a part in the setting, all of which provide the framework for their experience. According to Gilbert (1991, cited in Oliver, 1998, p. 224) '. . . stories show whose voices are heard, and whose are silenced; whose histories are valued, and

Figure 2.1: *Pupils' interpretations of Physical Education*

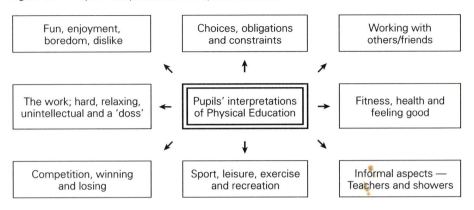

whose are devalued.' Of particular significance in interpreting the meaning behind children's stories is the language utilized in their telling. What does the use of one particular term allow us to infer? For example Carlson (1995, p. 467) suggests that use of a term such as 'boring' to describe a feeling towards PE could actually imply that the activity lacks meaning for the child. This kind of inference may be taken one stage further in identifying the presupposition that a particular statement assumes. Bruner (1986) has identified certain triggers used in literature to pinpoint specific presuppositions without overtly stating fact. Similar methods may be used by the child in narrative to indicate certain perceptions they are uncomfortable about or are unable to identify directly. What is of importance here is to be mindful that we do not always say what we mean nor mean what we say and it is necessary to rely on the complexities of the narrative to elucidate what it really means to the individual or group.

The work of Laws (1997) with pupils at Key Stages 3 and 4 provides us with signposts into children's interpretations of PE and guides this exploration of what PE might mean to pupils. The point is not to assume generality in all PE contexts but to indicate likely frames of reference which might be employed by pupils, although Fisher (1996) has shown that some common frames of reference can be reasonably assumed not only between different schools but even different national cultures. The diagram in Figure 2.1 represents pupils' interpretations of PE. Data arose from a three-year case study at one 11–16 co-educational comprehensive school, anonymously referred to as Hutton (Laws, 1997). The study attempted to understand some of the underlying assumptions, nature, purpose and process of the realities of teaching and learning in PE. What is reported is one small element of the study. The various dimensions of pupils' interpretations of PE are examined, although naturally there is considerable overlap since all of them constitute what for each pupil is a coherent system of constructions which enable them to deal with the world as it confronts them. The only people for whom this picture has to be coherent are the pupils themselves and this pattern of interpretations is necessarily presented tentatively.

Fun, Enjoyment — Boredom, Dislike

The most commonly recurring expression from pupils across the age range was that of 'fun' and 'enjoyment'. For the pupils, these words seemed to encapsulate all that was positive or 'good' about PE at Hutton. Other work by Fisher (1996) and Goudas and Biddle (1993) has shown that fun and enjoyment are important parts of the frame of reference for pupils in PE and physical activity in general. Equally significantly they define the boundaries between real work, in other words what goes on in classrooms and is mostly 'boring', and the chance to relax and enjoy themselves, an idea which is explored further in the next section. Pupils reiterate these experiences with words like 'good', 'OK', 'brilliant', 'magnificent', 'cool', 'satisfying', 'exciting', 'interesting', 'enjoyable' and 'excellent'. However it is not easy to get beneath these words and find out what pupils meant by 'fun'. One attempt to ascertain the meanings attached to these experiences is contained in the following discussion with Alex (Yr 7, age 12).

> PE is fun because it's fun . . . it's the experience of it . . . because what you do is fun in PE.

It was very clear to Alex what 'fun' meant, but he found it hard to express exactly what it was and an exploration of what was not fun led to:

> Standing around in the cold . . . or getting told off . . . and when the lessons aren't good . . . when the teachers don't make it fun or enjoyable . . . it's boring then.

As with many of the other interviews and discussions with pupils, the theme of 'fun' was repeated with value-terms. These were expressed with conviction, but often remain unclassified although frequently involving such things as 'having a good laugh' and 'having a break'. Alternatively, statements in antithesis to 'fun' were candid and described exactly why PE was 'boring', 'a waste of time', 'unfair', or 'horrible'. These statements usually seem to be in the minority but are often associated with ability or being ridiculed and teased:

> I'm not being nasty, but they can't do it very well . . . they're not very good at it. Yr 11 (Female — F)

> Yes, but some get laughed at — that's not nice . . . it's because I'm quite slow. Yr 9 (Male — M)

> Because you can't get very good and help your team. Yr 7 (F)

Explanations for boredom and dislike were also expressed in terms of particular teachers (see later) or activities, for example:

> PE is something I enjoy on Thursday but not on Tuesday. Yr 7 (F) (Jenny)

For Jenny, Thursdays meant hockey and Tuesdays meant gym.

Hard Work, Relaxing, Unintellectual and a 'Doss'

Responses to the 'work' in PE were expressed as respite from academia, relaxation, and more negatively as boring, a waste of time, or of low intellectual status. Being away from the classroom and the structures it imposes is a reference point for many pupils, particularly those in Years 10 and 11 (ages 15/16). They are aware of increasing academic workloads in the run-down to General Certificate of Secondary Education (GCSE) examinations and typically would indicate that:

> You really need it sometimes. It's different from normal lessons — it gets you out. You're going all the time and the lessons have a lot of activities . . . and less brainache! Yr 11 (Male age 16)

However, interpretations can vary with age and might reflect changes in the delivery of the curriculum, for example in games the development from work on key skills and strategies at younger ages to more of a 'playing the game' approach in later years. In the earlier years this can be reflected in such comments as:

> They (the staff) worked us real hard then (Yrs 7, 8 and 9, age 12, 13, 14) 'cos we were all learning like. We *had* to do all the warm-ups . . . and we *had* to work real hard or else they'd tell us off. Now it's all sort of relaxed. Yr 11 (Female age 16)

> You've got to work hard . . . concentrate on what you're doing . . . not messing around . . . using your brain and thinking of ideas as you go along. Yr 7 (Male age 12)

The notion of 'relaxation' rarely seems to be made by pupils in Years 7, 8 or 9 (age 12, 13 and 14). However, just as pupils in Years 10 and 11 (age 15 and 16) used 'relaxation' as their term of release, so those in Years 7, 8 and 9 often substitute words like 'letting off steam', 'getting puffed', or even 'exhausting' as their release. Predominantly, ideas of PE being 'non-academic' seems to be a positive feature for many of the younger pupils:

> It's quite good in a way because you don't have to write anything and I'm not very good at writing. Yr 7 (Male age 12)

> It saves the brain for other subjects. Yr 9 (Male age 14)

Fisher (1996) found similar views expressed by German pupils and in some respects PE might be seen as an aside to the academic subjects, so that individuals could return to class relaxed and refreshed. In some respects this can be seen as a useful aspect of the subject but amongst the older pupils referred to above it also fostered a denigrating attitude to PE — 'you don't have to think — you just do it,' and:

> You can get away with being thick or not knowing what to do in PE . . . you can't in maths or science . . . it's a doss really. Yr 11 (Male age 16)

This has to be seen in the context of a large increase in recent years in the number of pupils taking public examinations in PE at GCSE (16) and Advanced ('A') level (post 16), which is generally thought by teachers and pupils to have increased the status of the subject and has almost certainly led to increases in the time available for PE.

Choices, Constraints and Obligations

Choices seem to be important to most pupils and this reflects aspects of the power debate that were referred to above. Deciding what to do, when and where can be seen as a big feature of children's experiences of PE. Being able to choose how hard to work, what physical movements to make, whether to play for the after school teams, being able to talk, where to stand on the field or sports hall seem to give PE a credibility that in many children eyes, other subjects do not have:

> It's much more fun. In lessons (non-PE) you have to listen to teachers going on and on. You can talk more to your friends more than in lessons and you can do your own thing. Yr 7 (Female age 12)

> You have loads of choices . . . like when you're playing tennis, you can decide whether to hit the ball or leave it. You can choose whether to apply for the team . . . if you're the captain for a team you have to make decisions, like say, 'you're substitute, you play in mid-field, you play defence, you go in goal' or whatever. Yr 8 (Male age 13)

Nevertheless, pupils are also aware that their choices exist only within a certain framework — namely those placed on them by teachers. This becomes increasingly apparent as pupils achieve ever more freedom and individual responsibility in their lives in general and seek to exercise this in PE:

> PE is compulsory — you have to do it. You can't always choose who you want to work with 'cos the teacher puts you into teams . . . they say we can choose what we want to do, but we can't do the stuff like girls' rugby. Yr 10 (Female age 15)

Even the choices that pupils make are often determined by the teacher. For example, in discussion about gymnastic sequences one pupil commented on the final product:

> Well you choose which moves you want which the teacher has already told you . . . then you use them . . . so I guess you make more of a guided choice . . . especially when she says 'you can't use this and you can't use that piece of apparatus. . . .' Yr 8 (Male age 13)

Apart from providing some insight into the reality of choice for pupils, it also reveals that pupils can have relatively sophisticated levels of thinking if they are allowed to express them. Most departments would probably point out that pupils in the lower school are restricted in the choice of activities, but that choice is widened with the older pupils in order to offer, as the report to the governors in this school pointed out, 'a range of activities representative of those available in post-school life'. They would also point to obvious restrictions in the resources and time available to many PE departments.

Physical Education as Working with Others/Friends

The influence of peer groups and having freedom within them is fundamental to PE. The issues involved can probably be contained within four types of responses: 'talking to people you don't normally talk to/making new friends', 'working with my mates in a team', 'cooperating to win', and 'sharing ideas with the rest'. The significance of these experiences to pupils can be underscored by the emerging emphasis at all levels of education (see Department for Education and Employment, 1998 for example) on developing key skills such as communication and developing the ability to work with others. This is clearly apparent to pupils:

> It's hard to work on your own. When you grow up, when you get into jobs you're gonna have to work with somebody . . . it might make you do better and . . . you'll meet new people. Yr 7 (Male age 12)

Relevance beyond school-life was important to a Yr 8 pupil also:

> In PE, I can learn to play more games and that means I can have a better social life with my friends. Yr 8 (Female age 13)

One of the key issues to arise in the comparative study of Fisher (1996) was the importance as far as pupils were concerned as to whether subjects were relevant to 'me and my life'. Most departments would reinforce the idea that team games are not only valuable in developing skills but also as an 'arena for social and emotional development'. Teachers comments in this regard would be articulations for an educational audience and reflect one of the curriculum's key aims, but pupils seem to hold similar views although the messages might be conveyed in less sophisticated terms.

Competition — Winning and Losing

With sport, particularly team games, having increased prominence in curriculum development in PE in many schools, competition is often an integral part of what goes on in lesson time — whether it is intended or not. The idea of winning and losing is frequently portrayed as a positive feature, often in the sense that it is good to win and to learn to lose well, or as long as you play well it does not matter whether you win or lose, and winning and losing and many other such sentiments can be shared as a team. For pupils as well winning seems to be something worth reporting and conversations with pupils often reveal accounts of how many games have been won and who had scored goals. It is not difficult to find statements such as:

> I like it when we play football and you win. Yr 7 (Male age 12)

However, it is not difficult to find a wide divergence on this issue between pupils. O'Neill (1993) discovered in a school athletics lesson that winning and performing well were what the 'good ones' do. For the bulk of female pupils in O'Neill's study success was interpreted as getting in a legal jump — taking off from the board and landing properly in the pit. Positive comments about competition often tend to come from pupils of higher physical ability and those who play for school teams.

> It's really important to try hard and do your best to win. I get really annoyed when some of them don't bother. Yr 9 (Male, basketball and football player)

and

> It's great when we have a game with Mr X. It makes it much more tense and exciting. I think we learn more. Yr 9 (Female, hockey player)

The opposite view can be seen in the comments of one pupil:

> It's really silly, I can't see what's all the fuss is about; I don't care if we lose. Yr 8 (Female age 13)

Even so, conventional wisdom can also be found among pupils who are quite capable of accepting or rehearsing the view that winning and losing can be useful experiences in general:

> You have to learn to lose; sometimes it's good for you. Yr 10 (Male age 15)

> It's what PE is all about. Having a game, winning and losing, it's good for you providing you don't take it too seriously and get carried away. Yr 10 (Female age 15)

It is doubtful though whether the deeper ramifications of winning and losing have really been teased out and appreciated properly. It is not difficult to find numerous examples of personal embarrassment related to public displays during competition, sometimes associated with letting other team members down and sometimes with having one's incompetence highlighted for all to see. Lee's (1993) analysis of what children value in sport is useful in itself but it is also an example of the potential to develop the negative aspects of competition; mastery and winning can be cheating, intimidation and fear in another guise if we are not careful.

Physical Education as Fitness, Health and Feeling Good

Pupils consistently gave justification for PE under the theme of health and generally accept the idea that it is useful to be fit. For younger pupils in particular, 'being able to run around . . . and get puffed out', 'exhausted' or just 'hot and sweaty' are usually synonymous with 'getting fit'. When asked why he thought he had to do PE James (Yr 9 age 14) said:

It's good for the old ticker . . . keeps you in shape.

Like the statements about 'fun', however, the notion of health can be ambiguous. Enquiries about what PE has to do with 'health' typically invoke the reply that:

It keeps you fit . . . it's exercise and running about . . . energetic and hard work.
Yr 9 (F)

Older pupils actively involved in Health Related Exercise lessons are often more specific about the health input and capable of talking about such things as suppleness, stamina and strength, muscles, respiration, learning about injuries, diet, heart disease, specific contributions of particular sports to types of fitness. It is worth remembering, however, that Cale (1996) stressed the importance of the messages about physical activity that teachers convey to young people in their lessons and highlighted the significant influence that experiences at school have on participation outside school.

Informal Aspects: Teachers and Showers

To this point, pupil references have implied interpretations of PE emerging from lesson content and organization. The more informal aspects of what happens in PE and how these are construed constitute priorities for many pupils. The notion that pupils' interpretations of PE can be influenced more by whether they are in the warm, wearing acceptable clothing and with their friends than by the nature of the curriculum delivered to them can be a shock. Pupils in Years 7, 8 and 9 can be seen to communicate a 'hidden curriculum' shaped around changing, showers, wearing the correct kit, the merit of particular sports and degrees of teacher input. Changing and showers were the strongest image of PE for Mark (Yr 8):

I object to the changing rooms and showers . . . I don't bother with them — they just make you late for the next lesson . . . it's a waste of money.

When asked if there was anything good about having showers he gave access to a hidden pupil culture:

> Well, kids don't mind it when they're 'head of the showers' . . . they're the people who chuck your shoes in there. PE would be all right if we didn't have the showers.

Many girls report that the worst thing about PE is having to wear the school PE kit and compulsory showers. Comments such as the following were commonplace;

> It would be much better if we could wear shorts, they're much more fashionable than those stupid skirts we have to wear. Yr 10 (Female age 15)

> I really hate showers, it's so embarrassing. Yr 9 (Female age 14)

> I can't see the point in having a shower. If I was at home I wouldn't have to rush around showering and getting dressed in five minutes. It's ridiculous. Yr 10 (Male age 15)

Cale (1996) stressed the importance of teachers conveying positive messages to pupils about activity, especially to girls for whom key issues concerned the organization of lessons, regulations concerning kit/clothing, changing/showering routines and, crucially, the relevance of the curriculum within the context of their lifestyle. Pupils also seem to be acutely aware of teacher input and the level of attention directed on them or on something else, most notable if the teacher seems distracted by other matters. Some of the responses during interviews revealed that:

> I don't think it was worthwhile because we never had nobody watching us. Yr 7 (Female)

> For most of the first lesson Mr X and Mr Y talked about the game of cricket they played after school. Yr 9 (Male)

> Mr X is really good, not like . . . Mr Y . . . he never shouts at you and makes you look small. Yr 9 (Female)

> He doesn't show you up or force you to shower. Yr 10 (Male)

> He's not strict . . . but we don't muck about . . . we talk all the time . . . he often talks with us. Yr 9 (Female)

Praise and approval expressed by staff leaves pupils with images of 'feeling good about the lesson' because it is '*important to work hard, not just for yourself, but your teacher too*' (Yr 9 Male). Some of the Upper School pupils, when asked 'what kind of pictures do you get in your mind when someone says PE?' tended to respond with teachers' names:

> (Laughing) Mr . . .)!! ranting and raving!! . . . Yeah, a lot depends on what the teacher's like. Enjoyment tends to be on what teacher you have. Yr 11 (Female age 16)

Sport, Leisure, Exercise, Recreation and Physical Education

When discussing PE pupils often appear to have difficulty in distinguishing between PE, sport, exercise and leisure and tend to use these terms interchangeably.
For some, PE is sport and leisure rolled into one. Those who recognize that there is
not total freedom in their PE experiences can distinguish between PE and leisure.
Pupils who are members of school teams are more likely to agree that PE was
'sport'. In the main research reported here (Laws, 1997) the pupils that called to
mind their Health Related Exercise lessons tended to reject PE being just sport:

> It has other areas than sport — it's educational . . . learning how the body works . . .
> diet . . . about how to treat injury . . . Yr 11 (Male age 16)

Pupils who admitted to watching much media sport commented that 'PE is not
a lot like sport' though it was part of it. All pupils, after discussion of the terms,
decided that the parent term was 'sport' because this had a high representation in
both PE and leisure. In reflecting on how pupils spoke of their experiences in PE it
is worth considering Sparkes' (1987) findings at Branstown, much of which focused
on the more public discourses of educationalists. He talks of 'strategic rhetoric':

> the use of everyday language of concepts borrowed from educational theory such
> as 'developing the whole child', 'core experiences', 'relevant life skills'. (Sparkes,
> 1987, p. 40)

At Branstown this 'lip service' was used to legitimize, in other words to:

> . . . create an illusion as the teacher attempts to present a certain self to a selected
> audience. (Sparkes, 1987, p. 40)

On the other hand, we feel that the pupil interpretations were sophisticated
and meaningful — more so than among the staff in some cases, because they were
not obliged to make PE credible or 'special' and subsequently did not rely on the
discursive practice of rhetoric. They just spoke what they felt.

In terms of the research examined here, it is possible to suggest a framework
of the way that pupils interpret PE, which seem to unfold along a continuum of
expressions respective of particular ages and degrees of experiences in PE. The
more 'emotive specifics' of lower school pupils and the 'general descriptiveness'
of the upper school pupils can be placed against the more analytical justifications
offered by staff. In many respects these demonstrate an increasing complexity of
conceptualization of PE as the respondents advance, not necessarily in age, but
in cumulative experience of PE. For example, lower school pupils seem to focus
more on attributes of PE that are specific to the moment such as: whether the
teacher lets them choose who to work with, how they feel at the end of a busy day,
whether it is cold outside, if the teacher and/or activity is liked, whether showers
are compulsory, what is happening after school etc. They do not display a unitary,

straightforward view of PE and interpret the subject as consisting of a mass of experiences which might only be expressed in bits and pieces, which in turn represent elements of an overall personal framework which makes sense only within their own system of construing the subject and its related elements.

Older pupils have more developed ideas of what constitutes physical education but frequently reduce the subject into all embracing concepts such as 'character development' or 'fitness'. In general pupils still equate PE lessons with ability and stereotyped images of what activities are more suitable for boys and girls although it has not been possible to fully reflect all these issues here. As a result, hierarchical placements related to gender and ability are still visible within the apparent philosophy of equal worth and value.

Teachers, Pupils and Physical Education

Ultimately the reality of the PE curriculum exists in what happens in lessons and the way that two sets of frameworks relate to each other, those of pupils and teachers. PE is not something that happens to the child; rather it is an interactive process, ongoing in terms of the child's relationship with the subject material, significant others affecting the learning context and their own experiences and personal agency. A child's experience will inevitably depend upon their personal beliefs/values/ideology and their power to actualize them in a learning situation. Thus, where there is conflict between the child and 'curriculum', they may resist the power that in theory is being exercised over them. Whilst it is clear that teachers hold 'legitimate' power of authority over the child, their power is not absolute and 'teachers not only control pupils, they too are controlled by pupils' (Dyson, 1995, p. 395) and the child may well determine the direction of a lesson. Additionally, children are themselves afforded such roles of 'legitimate' authority over one another through taking on a variety of roles, e.g. . . . *coach, official* as suggested in the National Curriculum for PE (Department for Education and Employment, 1995). Power relationships in PE is a factor that is evident, often implicitly, in the analysis presented in the previous section but in general has received little emphasis thus far in research. It would seem to be worthy of much closer attention.

In terms of the curriculum itself, the research presented here suggests that consideration be given to two different ideas, the physical and the educational. Teachers found the word 'physical' to be significant because it is an umbrella term; it describes what they mostly do, it is concrete, descriptive and on the surface. 'Education' takes on a deeper, larger and less generally agreed meaning because it '. . . *cannot be dissociated from prevailing societal values and ideologies*' (Arnold, 1988, p. 2). Pupils seem to feel that they can actually point to 'physical' but are not sure how to identify education. Although staff place a heavy initial reliance on educational concepts they still seemed committed to the discourse of the 'physical' — it is part of the everyday working language — 'movement, 'coordination', 'doing', 'action/activity'. Even the language used in lessons to communicate with classes tends to be rigidly physical; 'sit down', 'move', 'be quiet', 'run' etc. Statements common amongst teachers like 'they learn to do' justify PE in terms of the intel-lectual (where doing is a consequence of 'learning'). Similarly, it communicates a priority with outcomes — they all learn to 'do' the same thing. However, consider the phrase 'they do to learn', this puts children first and facilitates more plural outcomes and the manifold realities children bring to school. For pupils and teachers whether PE is a 'subject', an 'aspect of learning', 'the physical' or 'a process' depends on the particular priorities and values individuals hold, which often deter-mine, and are determined by, the context they work within. There is a pervasive rhetorical discourse in PE which suggests certain generally agreed values regarding PE but at times these can be spurious and there can easily be a lack of coherence between what is said and what is done and experienced.

Conclusion

PE pedagogy requires carefully defined goals and structure. Without this many children may have a distorted view of everyday life in PE and their experiences may not reflect their teachers' intentions. This process of defining has several implications for teachers and teacher educators as well as for PE pedagogical con-tent knowledge. Wilson, Shulman and Richert (1987) suggest that for successful teachers pedagogical content knowledge cannot simply be an intuitive understand-ing of subject matter. We would support their argument that:

> Successful teachers cannot simply have an intuitive or personal understanding of a particular concept, principle, or theory. Rather, in order to foster understanding, they must themselves understand ways of representing the concept for students. They must have knowledge of the ways of transforming the content for the pur-poses of teaching. (Wilson, Shulman and Richert, 1987, p. 110)

The knowledge to teach effectively, to match intentions and outcomes is elusive to clarify. Cochran, Deruiter and King (1993) have provided a useful description within which to locate the implications of knowing more about pupils' interpretations of PE:

> Pedagogical content knowledge differentiates expert teachers in a subject area from subject area experts. Pedagogical content knowledge concerns the manner in which teachers relate their subject matter knowledge (what they know about what they teach) to their pedagogical knowledge (what they know about teaching) and how subject matter knowledge is part of the process of pedagogical reasoning. (p. 263)

The descriptions of pupil experiences might suggest a need for teachers to consider the nature of their pedagogical content knowledge, indeed the general thrust of their curriculum. In this context it is worthwhile relating the significance of pupils' experiences at school to future life, utilizing Laporte et al.'s (1993) study of over 1,000 Belgian university students, based on earlier work by Crum (1986)

Christopher Laws and Richard Fisher

and Underwood (1988). They investigated the students' interpretations of what they had learned in their school PE programmes in terms of four domains — technical/skill, socio-motor, affective and cognitive/reflective. They discovered that students felt that they had not learned a great deal during their school PE programmes but the largest amount of what they had learned was located in the technical/skill aspects of PE and in the affective area. The largest deficiency was in the cognitive/reflective area, involving understanding and personal exploration of learning concepts and knowledge about PE. However, those programmes that had emphasized such an approach to PE resulted in students who felt that they had learned more. More PE tended to provide selective gains in learning, mostly in the technical/skill areas, and programmes that were based on recreational or 'fitness related' approaches appeared to lead to less efficient learning. On its own this may mean something or nothing, but it is interesting in view of Hardman's (1996) analysis of the rather parlous state of PE worldwide and an interesting example from Canada (Janzen, 1995) where the Minister of Education for Manitoba claimed that despite massive investment in PE:

> ... the attitudes of society had not been positively affected by their physical education experience within the school system. (p. 8)

Whatever perspective we take of the state of PE at the end of the twentieth century it is clear that an understanding of the frameworks that pupils use to interpret the subject is crucial to teachers' ability to implement an effective curriculum. Most significant would seem to be the need to provide a curriculum that pupils interpret as relevant to them and their lives, one which they feel they can carry forward into the rest of their lives.

References

ARNOLD, P. (1988) *Education, Movement and the Curriculum*, London: Falmer Press.
BRUNER, J. (1986) *Actual Minds, Possible Worlds*, London: Harvard University Press.
CALE, L. (1996) 'An assessment of the physical activity levels of adolescent girls: Implications for physical education', *European Journal of Physical Education*, **1**, 1, pp. 46–55.
CARLSON, T.B. (1995) 'We hate gym: Student alienation from Physical Education', *Journal of Teaching in Physical Education*, **14**, pp. 467–71.
COCHRAN, K.F., DERUITER J.A. and KING, R.A. (1993) 'Pedagogical content knowing: An integrated model for teacher preparation', *Journal of Teacher Education*, **44**, 4, pp. 263–72.
CRUM, B.J. (1986) 'The use of learner reports for exploring teaching effectiveness in physical education', in PIÈRON, M. and GRAHAM, G. (eds) *Sport Pedagogy*, Champaign, IL: Human Kinetics, pp. 97–102.
DEPARTMENT FOR EDUCATION AND EMPLOYMENT (DFEE) (1995) *Physical Education in the National Curriculum*, London: HMSO.
DEPARTMENT FOR EDUCATION AND EMPLOYMENT (DFEE) (1998) *The Learning Age*, London: HMSO.

DYSON, B.P. (1995) 'Students voices in two alternative elementary physical education programmes', *Journal of Teaching in Physical Education*, **14**, pp. 394–407.

EVANS, J. and PENNEY, D. (1995) 'The National Curriculum for physical education: Entitlement for all?', *British Journal of Physical Education*, **26**, 4, pp. 6–13.

FISHER, R. (1994) 'Physical education in England and Germany: A tale of two schools', Unpublished PhD Thesis: University of Surrey.

FISHER, R. (1996) 'A comparative study of teachers' and pupils' interpretations of Physical Education', *Journal of Comparative Physical Education and Sport*, **18**, 2, pp. 50–6.

GOUDAS, M. and BIDDLE, S. (1993) 'Pupil perceptions of enjoyment in physical education', *Physical Education Review*, **16**, 2, pp. 145–50.

HARDMAN, K. (1996) 'The fall and rise of school physical education in international context', Paper presented to the Pre-Olympic Scientific Congress, Dallas, 10–14 July.

JANZEN, H. (1995) 'The status of physical education in Canadian public schools', *CAHPERD Journal*, **61**, 3, Autumn, pp. 5–9.

KIRK, D. (1993) *The Body, Schooling and Culture*: Deakin University.

LAPORTE, W., MUSCH, E. and VERMEESCH, M. (1993) 'Perceived learning results of physical education lessons in secondary schools by the learner: A report', *Proceedings of the ICHPER 36th. World Congress*, Yokohama, Japan, pp. 437–44.

LAWS, C. (1997) 'Physical education, curriculum change and individualism', Unpublished PhD Thesis: University of Southampton.

LEE, M. (1993) *Coaching Children in Sport: Principles and Practice*, London: E. and F.N. Spon.

OLIVER, K.L. (1998) 'A journey into narrative analysis: A methodology for discovering meanings', *Journal of Teaching in Physical Education*, **17**, pp. 244–59.

O'NEILL, J. (1993) 'National Curriculum athletics: Teaching children first', *British Journal of Physical Education*, **24**, 1, Spring, pp. 15–17.

SPARKES, A. (1987) 'Strategic rhetoric: A constraint in changing the practice of teachers', *British Journal of Sociology of Education*, **8**, 1, pp. 37–54.

UNDERWOOD, G. (1988) *Teaching and Learning in Physical Education: A Social Psychological Perspective*, London: Falmer Press.

WILSON, S., SHULMAN, L. and RICHERT, A. (1987) '"150 different ways" of knowing: Representations of knowledge in teaching', in CALDERHEAD, J. (ed.) *Exploring Teachers Thinking*, London: Cassell, pp. 104–24.

3   Pupils' Metacognition and Learning

Ian Luke and Colin A. Hardy

Introduction

While metacognition has been discussed in educational research for some years, Physical Education has been slow to acknowledge and adopt the ideas emerging from such research. There is a distinct lack of Physical Education research in this area even though it has been argued that metacognition may be the pivot or key to pupils' learning processes (Nisbet and Shucksmith, 1986) if learning is viewed as active and strategic (Luke and Hardy, 1996). It is reported that by having efficient metacognitive ability pupils are able to learn material faster, understand it better and retain it for longer (Derry and Murphy, 1986; Pressley, Goodchild, Fleet, Zajchowski and Evans, 1989). Furthermore, the development of metacognitive ability may increase pupils' control and responsibility over their own learning processes (Nisbet and Shucksmith, 1986).

Metacognitive Ability

Metacognition refers to the knowledge and control that pupils have of their cognitive functioning, that is, what they know about their cognitive activity and how they regulate their cognitive activity during learning (Flavell, 1979; Garofalo, 1987). Unfortunately, literature has often lacked clarity in the definition and explanation of metacognition, interchanging and confusing terms such as metacognition, metacognitive knowledge, metacognitive strategies and metacognitive experiences. Metacognition is rather a generic and vague term overseeing all concepts deemed to be metacognitive. However, metacognitive knowledge, metacognitive strategies and metacognitive experiences are specific and distinct concepts and, while it has been acknowledged that they all interact, literature has often failed to clarify the connections and interactions between them. Thus, in order to highlight both the distinctions and the connections between each metacognitive concept, it was considered necessary to develop a conceptual framework based around the concept of metacognitive ability (Luke, 1998).

The two key referents in any definition of metacognition, the knowledge of cognitive activity and the effective control and regulation of that cognitive activity (Campione, 1987), are structured within the concepts of metacognitive knowledge and metacognitive strategies respectively (Flavell, 1979). Pupils who have developed the necessary levels of metacognitive knowledge and have developed efficient metacognitive strategies, and utilize this information for specific learning tasks, are claimed to have efficient metacognitive ability in those tasks. From the model (Figure 3.1) developed by Luke (1998) it can be recognized that the utilization of metacognitive knowledge and metacognitive strategies underpins metacognitive ability. Pupils' metacognitive knowledge and metacognitive strategies interact strongly with each other and may be either conscious or unconscious. If this combination of metacognitive knowledge and metacognitive strategies is made conscious, either from a deliberate consideration of it or due to a triggering event in the learning situation, the pupils are believed to undergo metacognitive experiences which may be either cognitive or affective in nature. That is, pupils may have conscious thoughts or feelings concerning the learning situation. Whether the combination of metacognitive knowledge and metacognitive strategies is conscious or unconscious, only when pupils efficiently utilize this information will they develop efficient metacognitive ability.

To clarify the concept of metacognitive ability, each component involved in it, metacognitive knowledge, metacognitive strategies and metacognitive experiences, will be discussed separately within the conceptual framework of metacognitive ability (see Figure 3.1).

Metacognitive Knowledge

Metacognitive knowledge consists of the knowledge and beliefs about the factors which interact to affect the course of cognitive outcomes. Flavell (1979) suggested three major categories, task, person and strategy, and Flavell and Wellman (1977) also included a further category which they referred to as interactions. The importance of such knowledge was emphasized when it was '... found that students' general metacognitional knowledge for classroom learning was significantly related to students' achievement' (Peterson, 1988, p. 8).

Task

Metacognitive knowledge of task variables includes knowledge concerning the information available to pupils during a cognitive activity, such as the desired outcomes of a task (Weinstein, 1988), information concerning the context in which the task is taking place (Ramsden, 1988), the abundancy and the organization of information (Brown, 1984), and information regarding the demands of the activity (Weinstein, 1988). Nisbet and Shucksmith (1986) have suggested that pupils frequently lack metacognitive knowledge of task variables and that the knowledge they do have is far from reliable. Baird (1992, p. 41) also noted that '... many students seemed to have little idea of the answers to such questions as "Why were you doing the topic?"' Lee and Solmon (1992) stated that, in the complex Physical Education environment, pupils' perceptions of a task will be a critical variable but it would seem, from recent Physical Education research, that many 11–14-year-old pupils lack an awareness of task purpose and fail to appreciate teachers' aims of

Figure 3.1: The metacognitive ability conceptual framework

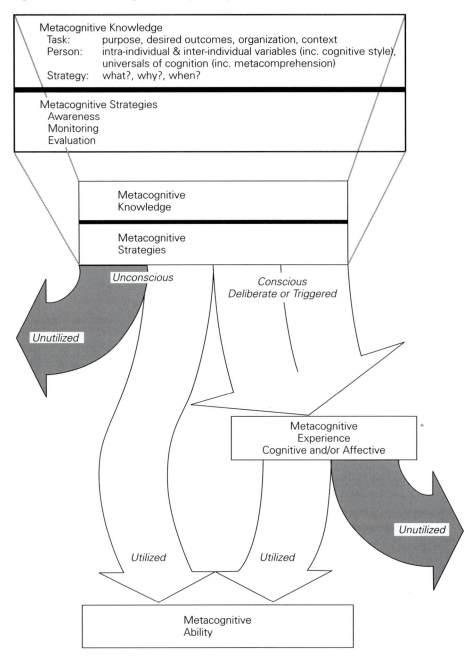

developing physical and mental abilities even if teachers overtly refer to these abilities and feel that they have structured the tasks appropriately (Luke, 1998). Pupils appear able to describe tasks but struggle to explain the purpose behind doing them (Luke, 1998) and, as Weinstein (1994, p. 258) simply stated, 'It is impossible to know if you have reached a goal if you are not clear about the nature of the goal.' Pupils have also struggled to show an insight into the influences upon the tasks in Physical Education (Lee, Landin and Carter, 1992), failing to fully appreciate the physical and mental influences upon tasks, both from an intrinsic and extrinsic perspective (Luke, 1998). Singer and Chen (1994) suggested that only when pupils learn how to analyse task conditions will they show an adequate insight into learning efficiently.

Marton (1988) noted that pupils sometimes struggle in differentiating between superordinate and subordinate characteristics of a text and can fail to understand procedural aspects of common tasks such as how to select the important ideas and information in a textbook. Pupils can often be influenced by the presentation of material or by class organization, rather than being influenced by events related to specific variables which are being forced upon them by the teacher (Edwards and Mercer, 1987: cited in Clayden, Desforges, Mills and Rawson, 1994; Eylon and Linn, 1988). Chemistry pupils often failed to differentiate between the behaviour of single molecules and the interactions of many molecules in trying to explain chemical processes due to textbooks repeatedly showing pictures of single molecules (Eylon and Linn, 1988). A class of 10-year-old pupils stated that the pendulum experiment that they were given had four main variables involved in it because the teacher had established four groups (Edwards and Mercer, 1987: cited in Clayden, Desforges, Mills and Rawson, 1994). Therefore, if pupils do examine and connect the presentation and organization of a task for an insight into the nature or number of learning points, it may be that there is some support for the principles underpinning the 'Teaching Games for Understanding' approach in Physical Education; for example, when faced with long, thin badminton courts pupils may consider why the teacher has presented and organized the environment in such a way and, therefore, may be encouraged to consider the long-short gameplay strategy that is available. However, it is also possible that the intensity of the focus on the presentation and organization may mean that pupils fail to appreciate the interactions between an exaggerated or a modified game and a complete game, and, if the examination of presentation and organization occurs on a superficial basis, pupils could believe that the long, thin courts are created due to problems such as a lack of space. While the connection between presentation, organization and task purpose may seem obvious to teachers, it may not be so obvious to pupils. From recent research (Luke, 1998, p. 407) it was noted that during health-related exercise lessons pupils have been more concerned with the music and general words of encouragement offered by the teacher as opposed to the ability of pacing themselves, during hockey lessons pupils have suggested that the purpose behind each task was '. . . to improve your passing skills and erm . . . your tackling skills' even though the lesson only really contained reference to passing and control, and during cricket lessons pupils have prioritized '. . . the other person that's going in next has got a bat' and organizing the team in order to avoid any arguing rather than the development of any physical or mental techniques. Thus, pupils of Physical Education can struggle to organize and prioritize information, and they can develop superficial or misdirected views upon what information is important (Luke, 1998). Teachers and researchers cannot assume that pupils understand why a specific presentation and organization is selected and, therefore, teachers and researchers cannot assume that structuring practice and game situations will inevitably lead pupils to the purpose of tasks. In succinct terminology, if pupils lack metacognitive knowledge of task variables and do not understand the purpose of a task, even with time and effort, efficient learning may not occur (Weinstein, 1988).

Person

Metacognitive knowledge of person variables can be subdivided into beliefs about intra-individual variables, inter-individual variables and universals of cognition. Nisbet and Shucksmith (1986) argued that the knowledge of person variables should also include the knowledge of transient processes and states, that is the 'here-and-now' experiences, both cognitive and affective, which can emerge during learning. However, following the example of previous literature (e.g. Flavell, 1979, 1987), and with reference to Luke's (1998) Model (Figure 3.1), such here-and-now experiences are incorporated with metacognitive experiences.

Knowledge of intra-individual variables may be seen as knowledge about personal skills, strengths, weaknesses, preferences, better and worse times of the day and goals (Flavell and Wellman, 1977; Schmeck, 1988a; Weinstein, 1994). A simple example may be that pupils appreciate that they can learn a gymnastic move better if they watch it being performaned rather than listening to someone explaining the technique. Interestingly, Torrance and Rockenstein (1988) have suggested that pupils' awareness of their abilities may be potentially dangerous as some pupils may form self-limiting views as a result of this awareness. Pupils' perceptions of themselves seem to be responsible for their willingness to try new ideas and their tendency to evaluate ideas (Eylon and Linn, 1988) and, therefore, if pupils develop negative views of themselves it could potentially hinder their learning processes. However, Weinstein (1988) believed that personal awareness is extremely important and helps pupils to know the kinds of resources or assistance they will need to perform efficiently and effectively. From recent Physical Education research it would seem that appreciation of intra-individual awareness is relatively scarce amongst pupils between 11 and 14 years of age, especially with regards to their mental abilities (Luke, 1998). Such findings are worrying as it is acknowledged that the quality of pupils' thoughts are related to the quality of their practice (Lee, Landin and Carter, 1992) and that pupils '... play an active role in their motor learning through their cognitive processes' (Lee and Solmon, 1992, p. 67).

Knowledge of inter-individual variables refers to any knowledge concerning the people involved in the learning situation, such as peers or teachers. Thus, a pupil may realize that a friend is more socially sensitive than another or a pupil may understand the type of behaviour that a teacher desires. Unfortunately, pupils may consider that teachers simply want them '. . . to come up with the right answers to the questions' (Marton, 1988, p. 79) and they may be able to satisfy such criteria without efficient understanding of the task (MacLure and French, 1980). Furthermore, although it is undesirable, the development of metacognitive knowledge of person inter-individual variables may enlighten pupils to the task-avoidance participation patterns (Griffin, 1984, 1985) and coping strategies (Portman, 1995) that have been evident in Physical Education lessons. Luke (1998) noted, for example, that during health-related exercise lessons many pupils were aware that the teacher was wandering around the gymnasium timing and verbally motivating pupils, and it was common for pupils to simply stand still until the teacher came near to them and then to burst into action and be complimented for the determination that they were showing in the task. Thus, it may be that these pupils did have a degree of metacognitive knowledge of person inter-individual variables but utilized it negatively; they utilized their knowledge of the teacher to be seen to do well on the tasks and cope with the lesson as opposed to trying to develop an awareness of the purpose of the task and lesson. Nevertheless, pupils must have knowledge of inter-individual variables if they are to appreciate the learning situation that they face; as a basic example, tennis players are more likely to learn how to defeat their opponent if they understand the opponent's strengths and weaknesses.

Interestingly, it appears that at the heart of the person intra-individual and inter-individual variables is the complex concept of learning styles and, more specifically, cognitive style combinations.[1] Weinstein (1988) suggested that learners should know and understand their preferred cognitive style combinations if they are to learn efficiently. The importance of acknowledging pupils' cognitive style combinations in Physical Education has been recognized (Luke and Hardy, 1996), but while it would seem that pupils of Physical Education may have some awareness of their cognitive style combinations, pupils' awareness can vary considerably in depth and understanding (Luke, 1998).

Knowledge of the universals of cognition may be seen as a recognition that there are various degrees and kinds of understanding and, therefore, that every individual can vary in their degree of understanding with respect to a specific task. Pupils need to be able to distinguish between illusory understanding and accurate understanding before they take any necessary corrective action (Brown, 1980; Flavell, 1979; Weinstein, 1994). If pupils can appreciate their personal level of understanding it is argued that they must have a level of metacomprehension i.e. a knowledge of what and when they understand. It has been suggested in both classroom and Physical Education research that pupils can overestimate their understanding of tasks (Flavell, 1979; Lee, Landin and Carter, 1992; Luke, 1998) implying that many pupils are often under the illusion of knowing (Glenberg, Wilkinson and Epstein, 1982). As an example, Luke (1998) noted how pupils in a volleyball lesson were convinced that they had enough information to complete and understand all of the tasks established by the teacher, but when they were questioned further they were unaware of even the purpose of most tasks and the most basic influences upon those tasks.

The interactions between these three subdivisions of person variables are also important; for example, pupils must be willing to admit the potential existence of better options and to '. . . be aware that one's knowledge is always open to refutation or modification from the vantage point of a different perspective' (Ranson and Martin, 1996, p. 17). As such, a pupil must understand intra-individual variables, appreciating that one has potential limitations in one's knowledge, while also appreciating, from inter-individual variables and the universals of cognition, that there may be different ways of approaching the same problem and different degrees of understanding a problem. As an example, a defender in a football game may appreciate that he or she is slower than the attacker whom he or she is responsible for marking. Thus, the defender may begin to close the attacker down to avoid any chance of the attacker running with the ball. This would seem to be a reasonable course of action. However, as the game progresses the attacker begins to receive the ball to the feet and is able to spin away from the defender easily. The defender notices that one team-mate is coping with a similar problem by hanging or floating away from the attacker and anticipating passes and runs. Thus the defender acknowledges the different approach and understanding of the problem and reacts accordingly; in turn also being successful in halting the attacker.

Strategy

Weinstein (1988) claimed that there is a need for metacognitive knowledge of cognitive strategies so that they can be used to guide learning or can be called upon when a comprehension problem is encountered. Garner (1988) implied that metacognitive knowledge of cognitive strategies includes declarative (what strategy), procedural (how to use the strategy) and conditional (why use the strategy) variables. In short, an individual must be able to judge the appropriateness of the cognitive strategy for a given task (Borkowski, Estrada, Milstead and Hale, 1989).

The problem is that pupils are not sufficiently aware of the importance of strategic factors (Matlin, 1994) or, in Physical Education, pupils' cognitive strategies may be performance oriented rather than learning oriented (Singer and Chen, 1994). It has appeared that pupils of Physical Education who are requested to play a game or demonstrate a skill in front of others may use this situation to focus on performance and outcome thoughts as opposed to learning and process thoughts (Luke, 1998). Obviously, games-based or demonstration tasks are important, especially as they may provide the opportunity for pupils to evaluate their learning, however, it should be acknowledged that during such tasks pupils can lose sight of the task purpose and the learning processes that are actually being focused upon in the lesson. Furthermore, pupils can know cognitive strategies and fail to utilize them, having the declarative knowledge of the cognitive strategy variables but lacking the procedural and conditional knowledge of the strategy variables (Cavanaugh and Perlmutter, 1982). Pupils can fail to appreciate that some cognitive strategies are more effective than others (Matlin, 1994) and they may view cognitive strategies as simply extra content (Biggs, 1985). Younger pupils are often reluctant to abandon their usual cognitive strategies even if the strategies are ineffective or if the task is altered (Crowley and Siegler, 1993) and, at the other extreme, younger pupils can randomly swap their cognitive strategies even if the same problem or task is given to them twice within a short space of time (Siegler, 1989). In the latter case, this does not mean that the pupils are making progress in their cognitive strategy as they are just as likely to switch from a more advanced to a less advanced strategy (Siegler, 1989). Thus, in gymnastics pupils may fail to abandon the analogy of a fast forward walkover to help them improve their handspring technique even though this proves unsuccessful and the teacher offers different advice. Or, indeed, the pupils may attempt to utilize a more analytical approach and focus on the push through the shoulders (the 'shrug' of the shoulders) on take-off. Although this would be of benefit, the pupils may not initially be successful and, therefore, return to the analogy of a fast forward walkover for their following attempts.

However, the problem does not only concern the selection of cognitive strategies, because as Crowley and Siegler (1993) noted, without efficient metacognitive knowledge of cognitive strategies any further developed strategies may be illegitimate. Furthermore, without metacognitive knowledge of a specific cognitive strategy, it is only likely to be used in the short term with pupils often quickly reverting back to their initial habits even if there was some immediate success gained (Martin and Ramsden, 1986: cited in Biggs, 1988). Pupils can often be in the position of being encouraged to use cognitive strategies that they do not fully understand (Crowley and Siegler, 1993) or they are only able to use a cognitive strategy when explicitly told to do so (Derry and Murphy, 1986; Luke, 1998; Schmeck, 1988a). Thus, conditional variables or knowing why to use a strategy are as important as procedural variables or knowing how to use a strategy (Garner, 1988). Flavell (1979) noted how pupils may know of relevant cognitive strategies but demonstrate a production deficiency in that they lack the awareness of how to utilize them and how to adapt them to a specific situation when they are appropriate. Brown and Smiley (1978: cited in Armbruster and Brown, 1984), noted that pupils who were induced to utilize cognitive strategies, such as underlining important parts of the text, did so more randomly than those pupils who spontaneously used such strategies. Reading researchers have argued that pupils who do not use cognitive strategies independently and effectively also exhibit a lack of metacognitive appreciation of the value of cognitive strategies and how to use them (Paris and Oka, 1986); in other words, the pupils remain blind to the strategies (Brown, Campione and Day, 1981; Campione, Brown and Ferrarra, 1982). Luke (1998) noted how pupils, during a task intended to help to coordinate the movement phases in a discus throw, remained blind to the specific cognitive strategy of rhythmically counting as the teacher initiated and directed the counting. While the pupils seemed to follow the teacher's counting during the lesson they failed to appreciate, or even to recall, the cognitive strategy following the lesson.

To summarize, successful learners have a range of cognitive strategies from which they are able to select appropriately and to adapt flexibly to meet the needs of a specific situation (Nisbet and Shucksmith, 1986). Without thoughtful selection of cognitive strategies the learning processes could be hindered (Gitomer, 1984: cited in Alexander and Judy, 1988).

Interaction

Brown, Campione and Day (1981) reported that pupils must be aware of the nature of the material to be learned, what their unique characteristics and limitations are and what learning activities are appropriate. In other words, individuals must have metacognitive knowledge of task, person and strategy variables. Problems can occur within each of these separate categories (Butler and Winne, 1995; Goos and Galbraith, 1996); for example, pupils may misperceive task conditions and thus mismatch their choice of cognitive strategies. 'The essence of sophisticated meta-cognitive activity is the ability to juggle and balance these aspects interactively' (Nisbet and Shucksmith, 1986, p. 40). Therefore, successful learners are more likely to be those who are perceptive of the requirements of a learning task and who have developed a range of cognitive strategies which they can apply accordingly[2] (Nisbet and Shucksmith, 1986). Thus faced with a basketball jump shot, pupils may realize that they prefer to gain a holistic impression of the action and, there-fore, utilize a cognitive strategy such as an analogy to help in the development of the shot. However, if the task is changed to a lay-up shot these pupils may want to change their cognitive strategy to a rhythmical counting to aid in the action. As Flavell (1987) noted, given their particular cognitive make-up and a particular task, pupils develop intuitions about which cognitive strategies are better.

Metacognitive Strategies

As already stated, it is important for a pupil to have metacognitive knowledge of cognitive strategies including knowing what the strategy involves (declarative knowledge), how to use it (procedural knowledge) and why to use it (conditional knowledge). However, whereas cognitive strategies aim to make cognitive progress, metacognitive strategies aim to monitor, evaluate, and regulate it (Flavell, 1979). These metacognitive strategies may be consciously or unconsciously utilized. Al-though little is known about the nature of secondary pupils' metacognitive strategy use, and how these metacognitive strategies are applied during learning (Goos and Galbraith, 1996), it is suggested that they form the executive control which frames and guides more specific knowledge and strategies. Weinstein and Mayer (1986) suggested that metacognitive strategies can result in better integration of new mater-ial with prior content and personal knowledge. Similarly, Schoenfeld (1987) noted that once metacognitive strategies were hinted at, a group of mathematics pupils, who had struggled at a task without success, completed it with few problems. It appeared that the executive control which the metacognitive strategy offered per-mitted them to access the necessary knowledge and procedures. However, some Physical Education research suggested that very few pupils between 11 and 14 years of age appear to acknowledge or utilize any efficient form of metacognitive strategy (Luke, 1998).

There appears to be agreement concerning the components incorporated into metacognitive strategies. Firstly, pupils must have an awareness of their own personal cognitive activities. Awareness involves the recognition of implicit as well as explicit information (Haller, Child and Walberg, 1988) and, therefore, includes the pupils' metacognitive knowledge of task, person and strategy variables that influence performance (Pintrich, 1990). Flavell (1987) suggested that awareness may be encouraged through practices such as prediction, for example, skimming a text before reading it may provide a pupil with some awareness of the work that lies ahead and, therefore, how that pupil should approach the reading passage depending upon the purpose of the exercise. In Physical Education, a tennis player may play a friendly match on a grass court prior to a competition on grass courts in order to gain an insight into the task, the problems that he or she may personally face and the cognitive and gameplay strategies that could be utilized to overcome them.

Secondly, pupils must be able to monitor their learning processes. Monitoring checks comprehension and, therefore, may include the checking of understanding through self-questioning, paraphrasing or summarizing (McCombs, 1988). Monitoring understanding can be as simple as trying to paraphrase the content being learned or as complex as trying to analyse and evaluate how it fits in with a pupil's prior knowledge (Weinstein, 1994). 'Checking on understanding is an important part of strategic learning that fosters self regulation. Students must be aware of their problems in understanding, or gaps in knowledge, before they can do something about it' (Weinstein, 1994, p. 268). As such, monitoring can provide the 'triggering mechanism' which signals whether there is a failure in comprehension and, potentially, prompt a corrective strategy (Brown, 1980). 'As a specific example, consider a child faced with the task of remembering 10 items. If he or she believes that the items can be readily remembered (and overestimates his or her span), there is no reason for engaging any specific learning activity, even if one were available. Further, if the learner did not monitor performance on recall trials, he or she would not become disabused of the original notion' (Campione, 1987, p. 123). However, the importance and the implications of monitoring do not end here; Campione (1987, p. 123) continued, '. . . if instruction is provided, and if performance improves, it is reasonable to expect that the learner will continue to employ that strategy only if he or she monitors its use and notes that it has actually helped; if no such monitoring takes place, it is not surprising that transfer is limited.' Furthermore, monitoring is not just about how well you understand something, but, also, how much you ought to believe it or do what it says (Flavell, 1979). The interest here for Physical Education is that pupils can become so inflexible and fixed to gameplay strategies that little monitoring of situations occurs, there may not be any personal examination of the validity of the gameplay strategies for various contexts and pupils can robotically drift through games. Monitoring and evaluation encourage flexibility when pupils are considering the demands of task and material, and such flexibility is a necessary requirement in Physical Education. Taking the example of games, surely flexibility is required to encourage the movement from the mere artisan, capable only of skilled mechanical responses, to a player who matches skills to the demands of the game and threatens the unexpected (Read, 1989). Kirby and Teasdale (1987: cited in Kirby, 1988) suggested that most pupils are capable of cognitive monitoring but appear to choose not to do so in standard reading situations. Importantly, Garner (1990) suggested that certain situations are more likely to elicit cognitive monitoring than others; for example, when pupils do not need to act on instructions or descriptions, or if their memory resources are strained or if they view a task as unimportant, they are unlikely to monitor cognitions rigorously. Various studies suggest pupils can vary in whether they can sense if they have allocated sufficient time and effort to a learning task and, therefore, vary in their level of monitoring of a learning situation (Flavell, Friedrichs and Hoyt, 1970; Masur, McIntyre and Flavell, 1973). However, Flavell (1979, 1987) suggested that, in general, pupils do relatively little monitoring of their own memory, comprehension and other cognitive enterprises. Similar findings emerged from research concerning pupils in Physical Education lessons (Luke, 1998).

The third component incorporated into metacognitive strategies concerns the evaluation and regulation of the learning processes. The idea of evaluation is to examine the success of the learning processes, checking the effectiveness of cognitive strategies and to ascertain whether an adequate level of comprehension has been achieved. Regulation consists of compensatory strategies to redirect and bolster faltering comprehension; for example, in the case of reading, these compensatory strategies may include re-reading or a comparison between any main ideas and specific details from the text (Haller, Child and Walberg, 1988). Regulation of cognition consists of self-regulatory mechanisms such as planning, checking strategy outcomes, monitoring the effectiveness of any attempted action, and testing, revising and evaluating strategies for learning (Armbruster and Brown, 1984). Often the problem is not that pupils fail to understand but that, prior to a deliberate analysis, those pupils may fail to realize that they have not understood (Markman, 1979). When learners do not fully understand how to evaluate their learning, they may not detect failure (Garner, 1990). Baker (1984) demonstrated that readers, particularly younger and poorer readers, often rely on a single criterion for textual understanding and that this criterion is the understanding of single words. Pupils can continue reading, ignoring text-level miscomprehension, as long as each single word makes sense. Pupils of Physical Education are no different as it has been suggested that pupils are quite willing to carry on with a task whether or not they appreciate or understand why they are doing it (Luke, 1998). As an example, most of the pupils from three swimming classes failed to identify the purpose behind the breaststroke leg and arm action tasks from their lessons, although they continued with the tasks quite happily (Luke, 1998).

The interaction of metacognitive knowledge with the evaluation component of metacognitive strategies has been suggested from several sources; for example, Markman (1979) noted that the repetition of material, even by a child, is not enough to improve comprehension and understanding as this only occurs after evaluation and after inferences are drawn. Pupils must evaluate the task and their personal learning requirements if they are to improve their metacognitive knowledge of task and person variables. Furthermore, evaluating the processes of learning can help pupils to build up a repertoire of cognitive strategies that can be called upon more automatically in the future when a similar situation arises (Weinstein,

1994). As an example in Physical Education, pupils may strongly evaluate the take-off phase of their somersault action, possibly utilizing a stretch-jump analogy to help in this evaluation. As this take-off action is common in gymnastics such evaluation may be worthwhile as the analogy may be called upon automatically in other movements and actions. However, Flavell (1979) has suggested that continuous evaluation of any cognitive enterprise could actually prove debilitating leaving too little a focus upon cognitive progress. Continuing the example of gymnastics, it is possible to imagine pupils excessively evaluating the long flight of their handsprings when their next planned progression could be a linked movement with forward rotation which would involve shortening the flight phase of the handspring. Nevertheless, Flavell (1979) concluded that while continuous evaluation could prove a hindrance to cognitive progress, there is generally far too little than too much. It would appear that metacognitive strategies encourage learners to be more self-regulating, and 'theoreticians seem unanimous — the most effective learners are self-regulating' (Butler and Winne, 1995, p. 245).

Metacognitive Experiences

Flavell (1979) stated that metacognitive experiences are any conscious, cognitive or affective experiences which are concerned with an intellectual venture. As noted by Luke (1998), metacognitive experiences utilize metacognitive knowledge and would be encouraged by the use of metacognitive strategies (Figure 3.1). Flavell (1979) suggested that metacognitive knowledge and metacognitive strategies may be activated as a result of a deliberate, conscious search of mind; for example, a pupil may make a conscious effort to think of an effective cognitive strategy. Schmeck (1988b) agreed, stating that learning can be improved if skills are used more intentionally and responsibly. However, metacognitive experiences cannot be constantly deliberate or learners could never learn because of thinking about learning (Nisbet and Shucksmith, 1986). Thus, as well as being intentionally used, metacognitive knowledge can be used automatically or unconsciously (Armbruster and Brown, 1984; Flavell, 1979; Palincsar and Brown, 1984) until some triggering event alerts that pupil to a problem (Brown, 1987). The most common of these triggering events is the retrieval of cues from the task situation (Flavell, 1979); there could be confusion about the purpose of a task, an expectation may not have been confirmed, or unfamiliar concepts are encountered too frequently for the learners to remain tolerant of their ignorance (Palincsar and Brown, 1984). Whatever the nature of the triggering event, learners slow down and allot extra processing to the learning situation, entering a controlled and strategic state that takes time and effort (Brown, 1987; Palincsar and Brown, 1984). As an example, a powerful server in tennis may find that his or her opponent is beginning to read and return the service forcing the server to consciously consider the placement and action of the service in order to confuse the opponent.

Nisbet and Shucksmith (1986) argued that because young pupils are often unaware of what or when they know, triggering does not always occur and results in pupils failing. The implication here is that pupils require efficient metacomprehension i.e. knowledge of what and when they know. Thus, returning to the handspring example, pupils may actually know that certain actions and techniques need to change in order to link them to other movements. However, if pupils fail to acknowledge or utilize such knowledge, they may not change the technique of their handspring when they are attempting to link it with a movement of forward rotation, even if they are repeatedly unsuccessful. Through metacomprehension pupils are able to appreciate what they need to do and how they need to react within a learning situation. Only when pupils acknowledge what they do or do not understand can a triggering event occur when necessary. Therefore, metacomprehension may well be '. . . the key which enables us to gain new knowledge and strategies' (Nisbet and Shucksmith, 1986, p. 45). However, even if a pupil is motivated, concerned and cooperative, that pupil can still have poor metacomprehension (Markman, 1979). Flavell (1979) noted, when metacognitive knowledge or metacognitive strategies rise to the consciousness, it is a metacognitive experience. Brown (1980: cited in Derry and Murphy, 1986) suggested that knowing what types of comprehension failures there are might help some pupils to have metacognitive experiences. It appears that pupils who cannot provide detailed explanations of their comprehension problems tend to do poorly on achievement tests (Garner, 1988; Peterson, 1988) and, interestingly, Flavell (1981: cited in Mayo, 1993) noted that learning disabled pupils did not exhibit metacognitive experiences. Therefore, metacognitive experiences, and their strong interaction with metacomprehension, may be significant in the learning processes.

Flavell (1979) viewed metacognitive experiences as any conscious, cognitive or affective experiences which accompany or relate to an intellectual activity. Therefore, while they may include the area of metacomprehension they may also include such feelings as despair, frustration or excitement which can emerge during learning. As McCarthy and Schmeck (1988) claimed, awareness and acceptance of personal thoughts, memories and feelings are essential for learning flexibility to develop. It has appeared that some pupils of Physical Education can either lack metacognitive experiences or fail to acknowledge them (Luke, 1998); as a basic example, up to 50 per cent of a Physical Education class were unable to recall any feelings that they experienced with regard to the learning tasks initiated during the lesson (Luke, 1998). Nevertheless, it would seem that metacognitive experiences may possibly add to, delete from, or revise metacognitive knowledge (Flavell, 1979); that is, if pupils were to experience either positive or negative thoughts and feelings during a learning situation it could be assumed that their metacognitive knowledge of relevant task, person and strategy variables could be influenced. To clarify the point, if pupils experience excitement after successfully completing a tumble turn in swimming, this feeling could understandably affect the pupils' confidence and, thus, their knowledge of intra-individual person variables, especially with regard to swimming.

Interestingly, '. . . metacognitive experiences are especially likely to occur in situations that stimulate a lot of careful, highly conscious thinking . . . in novel roles or situations, where every major step you take requires planning beforehand

and evaluation afterwards; where decisions and actions are at once weighty and risky; where high affective arousal or other inhibitors of reflective thinking are absent' (Flavell, 1979, p. 908). The implication is that metacognitive experiences are triggered in situations creating cognitive conflict, that is, a situation which makes learners reconsider their habitual way of delimiting the phenomenon in question (Marton, 1988). Indeed, Physical Education teachers are often encouraged to create such situations and 'Teaching Games for Understanding' appears to strongly utilize the idea of triggering metacognitive experiences through cognitive conflict. Referring to the earlier badminton example, pupils may be asked to play on a long, thin court so as to make them realize that hitting the shuttlecock at one length all of the time is not very effective for winning points (Thorpe, Bunker and Almond, 1986). However, even if a situation does trigger an awareness, it does not automatically lead to learning; for example, pupils may realize that something needs to be corrected in their flic flac technique because they are travelling away from the straight or centre line. However, these pupils may still not improve with this awareness no matter how much they want to or try to. The metacognitive experience needs to be transformed into knowledge and usable cognitive strategies and, as this will not inevitably happen, the cognitive strategies may need to be explicitly instructed (Nisbet and Shucksmith, 1986). Thus, the pupils need to understand that the mistake in their flic flac technique could be that they are throwing their arms to one side and, therefore, going over one shoulder as opposed to throwing their arms squarely over their heads. Such knowledge could then be transformed into a cognitive strategy or tactic, possibly the analogy of throwing a ball with straight arms directly over the head, which may enhance the pupils' learning of the flic flac technique. In summary, although metacomprehension and other metacognitive experiences are important to learning, they do not inevitably lead to it. As Flavell (1987) noted, young pupils may have such metacognitive experiences but do not understand how to interpret them or how to react to them effectively.

Recent Physical Education Research

Luke (1998) investigated the metacognitive ability that pupils showed in Physical Education lessons, the influences upon pupils' metacognitive ability and the effects of pupils' metacognitive ability. Furthermore, there was an attempt to guide the development of pupils' metacognitive strategy through intervention treatments that suggested a self-questioning metacognitive strategy (King, 1991; Seifert and Wheeler, 1994).

It appeared that a large percentage of pupils between 11 and 14 years of age struggled to develop efficient metacognitive ability in their Physical Education lessons, and it seemed that with a lack of such metacognitive ability pupils may have been controlled by, and at the mercy of, a range of contextual variables (Luke, 1998).

Numerous variables emerged as potential influences upon pupils' metacognitive ability; age variables, covert school variables (the school and the school ethos, the

Physical Education Department and the Physical Education Department ethos), overt school variables (the teacher, the class, the lesson events) and pupil variables (pupils' perceptions of the purpose of Physical Education, their motivational orientation, their self-efficacy, their volitional control and their locus of control) all seemed to have some form of influence upon the development of pupils' metacognitive ability. Importantly, it was suggested that these variables did not act individually, but it was the combination and interaction of these variables that proved influential (Luke, 1998). It appeared that if these variables interacted to encourage pupils to take responsibility, to experiment and, therefore, to appreciate their learning, there was a greater opportunity for pupils to develop efficient metacognitive ability. Taking the example of lesson events, pupils appeared to benefit from the opportunity to experiment with a technique before and after instruction as opposed to having all technique and attempts initiated and controlled by the teacher (Luke, 1998).

The effects of efficient or inefficient metacognitive ability were evident in terms of pupils' perceptions and appreciation of task, person and strategy variables, but also in their content knowledge. As an example, those pupils who implied that they had poor metacognitive ability seemed to have learning goals that contradicted the intentions of the teacher and the tasks, they failed to appreciate the organization and prioritization of task information, they assumed they had learned information when they had not, and they failed to appreciate any need to consider strategic action. In addition, it seemed from the reciprocal relationship of metacognitive ability with pupil variables that metacognitive ability was not only influenced by, but could also affect pupils' perceptions of motivational orientation, their self-efficacy, their volitional control and their locus of control (Luke, 1998).

The effectiveness of a short intervention was limited; as Meloth (1990, p. 796) stated, in a natural classroom setting, '. . . it may be unreasonable to expect immediate, dramatic improvements in the knowledge of cognition'. Nevertheless, there were some signs that pupils could be guided in their development of metacognitive ability (Luke, 1998), although the authors stress that the development of metacognitive ability should be continuous and incremental and form a way of life in Physical Education lessons.

Conclusions and Implications for Physical Education

The development of metacognitive ability relies upon the utilization of metacognitive knowledge and metacognitive strategies. Pupils' metacognitive knowledge and metacognitive strategies interact strongly and the utilization of these two concepts may occur consciously or unconsciously.

For pupils to understand and learn efficiently, as opposed to simply and robotically perform, in Physical Education, the authors suggest that efficient metacognitive ability should be developed. With reference to classroom subject areas, it has been implied that the development of efficient metacognitive ability would enable pupils to learn information faster, understand it better and retain it for longer (Derry and Murphy, 1986; Pressley, Goodchild, Fleet, Zajchowski and Evans, 1989) while also potentially enhancing pupils' problem solving performance (Swanson, 1990). Thus, metacognitive ability would seem to increase pupils' control and responsibility over their learning processes (Nisbet and Shucksmith, 1986), a desirable aim in Physical Education (Tousignant, Brunelle, Laforge and Turcotte, 1990).

With specific reference to Physical Education, Schwager and Labate (1993, p. 25) suggested that metacognitive ability, and the critical thinking it involves, '. . . can heighten students' awareness of their own thinking and the degree to which their thinking skills can be effective in helping them become more skilful, fit, and knowledgeable about physical activity'. Furthermore, metacognitive ability may not only enhance the development of individual skills and cognitive strategies, but may also enhance the development of gameplay strategies. As an example, a pupil may be faced with the problem of moving down a basketball court and being closely marked. In this instance, the pupil will need to analyse the situation on court, selecting a possible course of action, predicting which actions or movements may prove successful, and finally evaluating the outcome of the choice made (Schwager and Labate, 1993). In this basic example, the efficient utilization of metacognitive knowledge and metacognitive strategies is required for a successful result. Importantly, the utilization of such metacognitive knowledge and metacognitive strategies will not always be conscious. Brown (1987) acknowledged how perceptual motor activities are notoriously difficult to describe or explain and that many sports people can perform a great deal that they cannot describe. As an example, asking an expert gymnast to consider every aspect of a double twisting, double straight back somersault could initially hinder the gymnast's performance. However, this does not mean that metacognitive ability is not present, it may have become intuitive. Nevertheless, it could be argued that such metacognitive ability should also be retrievable to consciousness when necessary (Nisbet and Shucksmith, 1986). Returning to the example of the gymnast, if a mistake naturally keeps occurring, that gymnast should be aware of the movement requirements and be able to analyse the action, either holistically or analytically, in order to discover and correct the fault.

The problem within most school subject areas, and Physical Education is no exception, is that there seems to be an assumption that metacognitive ability, or aspects of metacognitive ability, are being developed. Schwager and Labate (1993), for example, questioned how 'Teaching Games for Understanding' is assumed to encourage critical thinking even though pupils have not necessarily learned, or indeed, have ever been taught how to think critically. Recent research in Physical Education (Luke, 1998) suggested that as pupils' perceptions and thought processes often vary considerably from each other and, more importantly, often differ from those of the teacher, pupils' learning processes cannot be assumed. While the National Curriculum Physical Education (DfE, 1995) now states that pupils should have the ability to monitor, evaluate and self-direct their learning, and OFSTED (Office for Standards in Education) inspectors are keen to endorse their point, there appear to be too many assumptions that these abilities are being developed in Physical Education lessons. To imply that a teaching approach such as guided discovery will always and inevitably lead to specific learning outcomes such as an understanding of task principles (Mosston and Ashworth, 1990; Williams, 1996) appears too simple (Luke, 1998). Importantly, the metacognitive ability conceptual framework may provide the foundation from, or around, which to consider pupils' learning processes more effectively. By utilizing the metacognitive ability conceptual framework, Luke (1998) was able to identify some common areas of pupil mis-understanding and pupil weaknesses in Physical Education lessons that undoubtedly would have implications for teaching and learning approaches in Physical Education; for example, as it appeared that pupils were frequently unaware of the main purpose behind various tasks, teachers would seemingly need to re-consider how to develop pupils' awareness of task information.

Thus, to summarize, pupils in Physical Education need to develop efficient metacognitive ability. The influences upon the development of pupils' metacognitive ability are both complex and vast, but it would appear that if pupils can be guided in their development of metacognitive knowledge and metacognitive strategies, their learning processes may be enhanced (King, 1991; Luke, 1998).

Definition of Terms

- Metacognitive ability
  The utilization, be it conscious or unconscious, of metacognitive knowledge and metacognitive strategies for a given task.
- Metacognitive knowledge
  The knowledge that individuals have concerning their cognitive processes and products, or anything related to them (Flavell, 1976). It is suggested that there are three major categories of metacognitive knowledge; task, person and strategy categories (Flavell, 1979).
- Metacognitive strategies
  Metacognitive strategies refer to an individual's awareness, monitoring and evaluation of a learning situation and, as such, they are closely connected with an individual's metacognitive knowledge.
- Metacognitive experiences
  Metacognitive experiences are any conscious, cognitive or affective experiences during a learning task (Flavell, 1979). Therefore, metacognitive experiences occur when metacognitive knowledge and/or metacognitive strategies become conscious.

Notes

1 The concept of cognitive style combinations in Physical Education is elaborated upon further in the article entitled, Differentiation: A Consideration of Pupils' Learning Preferences in Physical Education Lessons (Luke and Hardy, 1996).
2 It would also seem that pupils' choice of cognitive strategy or tactic is also influenced by their cognitive style combination, although this is elaborated upon further in the chapter on cognitive strategies.

References

ALEXANDER, P.A. and JUDY, J.E. (1988) 'The interaction of domain-specific and strategic knowledge in academic performance', *Review of Educational Research*, **58**, 4, pp. 375–404.

ARMBRUSTER, B.B. and BROWN, A.L. (1984) 'Learning from reading: The role of metacognition', in ANDERSON, R.C., OSBORN, J. and TIERNEY, R.J. (eds) *Learning to Read in American Schools: Basal Readers and Content Texts*, Hillsdale, NJ: Lawrence Erlbaum Associates, pp. 273–81.

BAIRD, J.R. (1992) 'Collaborative reflection, systematic enquiry, better teaching', in RUSSELL, T. and MUNBY, H. (eds) *Teachers and Teaching: From Classroom to Reflection*, London: Falmer Press, pp. 33–48.

BAKER, L. (1984) 'Children's effective use of multiple standards for evaluating their comprehension', *Journal of Educational Psychology*, **76**, pp. 588–97.

BIGGS, J.B. (1985) 'The role of metalearning in study processes', *British Journal of Educational Psychology*, **55**, pp. 185–212.

BIGGS, J. (1988) 'The role of metacognition in enhancing learning', *Australian Journal of Education*, **32**, 2, pp. 127–38.

BORKOWSKI, J.G., ESTRADA, M.T., MILSTEAD, M. and HALE, C.A. (1989) 'General problem-solving skills: Relations between metacognition and strategic processing', *Learning Disability Quarterly*, **1**, 1, pp. 57–70.

BROWN, A.L. (1980) 'Metacognitive development in reading', in SPIRO, R.J., BRUCE, B.C. and BREWER, W.F. (eds) *Theoretical Issues in Reading Comprehension*, Hillsdale, NJ: Lawrence Erlbaum Associates.

BROWN, A.L. (1987) 'Metacognition, executive control, self-regulation, and other more mysterious mechanisms', in WEINERT, F.E. and KLUWE, R.H. (eds) *Metacognition, Motivation, and Understanding*, Hillsdale, NJ: Lawrence Erlbaum Associates, pp. 65–116.

BROWN, A.L., CAMPIONE, J.C. and DAY, J.D. (1981) 'Learning to learn: On training students to learn from texts', *Educational Researcher*, **10**, 2, pp. 14–21.

BROWN, G. (1984) 'Metacognition: New insights into old problems', *British Journal of Educational Studies*, **32**, 3, pp. 213–19.

BUTLER, B.L. and WINNE, P.H. (1995) 'Feedback and self-regulated learning: A theoretical synthesis', *Review of Educational Research*, **65**, 3, pp. 245–81.

CAMPIONE, J.C. (1987) 'Metacognitive components of instructional research with problem solvers', in WEINERT, F.E. and KLUWE, R.H. (eds) *Metacognition, Motivation, and Understanding*, Hillsdale, NJ: Lawrence Erlbaum Associates, pp. 117–40.

CAMPIONE, J.C., BROWN, A.L. and FERRARRA, R.A. (1982) 'Mental retardation and intelligence', in STERNBERG, R.J. (ed.) *Handbook of Human Intelligence*, Cambridge: Cambridge University Press, pp. 392–490.

CAVANAUGH, J.C. and PERLMUTTER, M. (1982) 'Metamemory: A critical examination', *Child Development*, **53**, pp. 11–28.

CLAYDEN, E., DESFORGES, C., MILLS, C. and RAWSON, W. (1994) 'Authentic activity and learning', *British Journal of Educational Studies*, **42**, 2, pp. 163–73.

CROWLEY, K. and SIEGLER, R.S. (1993) 'Flexible strategy use in young children's tic-tac-toe', *Cognitive Science*, **17**, pp. 531–61.

DERRY, S.J. and MURPHY, D.A. (1986) 'Designing systems that train learning ability: From theory to practice', *Review of Educational Research*, **56**, 1, pp. 1–39.

DfE (1995) *Physical Education in the National Curriculum*, London: HMSO.

EYLON, B.S. and LINN, M.C. (1988) 'Learning and instruction: An examination of four research perspectives in science education', *Review of Educational Research*, **58**, 3, pp. 251–301.

FLAVELL, J.H. (1976) 'Metacognitive aspects of problem solving', in RESNICK, L.B. (ed.) *The Nature of Intelligence*, Hillsdale, NJ: Lawrence Erlbaum Associates.

FLAVELL, J.H. (1979) 'Metacognition and cognitive monitoring: A new area of cognitive-developmental inquiry', *American Psychologist*, **34**, 10, pp. 906–11.

FLAVELL, J.H. (1987) 'Speculations about the nature and development of metacognition', in WEINERT, F.E. and KLUWE, R.H. (eds) *Metacognition, Motivation and Understanding*, Hillsdale, NJ: Lawrence Erlbaum Associates, pp. 21–9.

FLAVELL, J.H., FRIEDRICHS, A.H. and HOYT, J.D. (1970) 'Developmental changes in memorization processes', *Cognitive Psychology*, **1**, pp. 324–40.

FLAVELL, J.H. and WELLMAN, H.M. (1977) 'Metamemory', in KAIL, R.V. and HAGEN, J.W. (eds) *Perspectives on the Development of Memory and Cognition*, Hillsdale, NJ: Lawrence Erlbaum Associates, pp. 3–34.

GARNER, R. (1988) 'Verbal-report data on cognitive and metacognitive strategies', in WEINSTEIN, C.E., GOETZ, E.T. and ALEXANDER, P.A. (eds) *Learning and Study Strategies: Issues in Assessment, Instruction, and Evaluation*, San Diego: Academic Press Inc., pp. 63–76.

GARNER, R. (1990) 'When children and adults do not use learning strategies: Toward a theory of settings', *Review of Educational Research*, **60**, 4, pp. 517–29.

GAROFALO, J. (1987) 'Metacognition and school mathematics', *Arithmetic Teacher*, **34**, May, pp. 22–33.

GLENBERG, A.M., WILKINSON, A.C. and EPSTEIN, W. (1982) 'The illusion of knowing: Failure in the self-assessment of comprehension', *Memory and Cognition*, **10**, pp. 597–602.

GOOS, M. and GALBRAITH, P. (1996) 'Do it this way!: Metacognitive strategies in collaborative mathematical problem solving', *Educational Studies in Mathematics*, **30**, pp. 229–60.

GRIFFIN, P. (1984) 'Girls' participation patterns in a middle school teams sports unit', *Journal of Teaching in Physical Education*, **4**, 1, pp. 30–8.

GRIFFIN, P.S. (1985) 'Boys' participation styles in a middle school physical education team sports unit', *Journal of Teaching in Physical Education*, **4**, 2, pp. 100–10.

HALLER, E.P., CHILD, D.A. and WALBERG, H.J. (1988) 'Can comprehension be taught?: A quantitative synthesis of "metacognitive" studies', *Educational Researcher*, **17**, 9, pp. 5–8.

KING, A. (1991) 'Effects of training in strategic questioning on children's problem-solving performance', *Journal of Educational Psychology*, **83**, 3, pp. 307–17.

KIRBY, J.R. (1988) 'Style, strategy, and skill in reading', in SCHMECK, R.R. (ed.) *Learning Strategies and Learning Styles*, New York: Plenum Press, pp. 229–74.

LEE, A., LANDIN, D. and CARTER, J. (1992) 'Students' thoughts during tennis instruction', *Journal of Teaching in Physical Education*, **11**, pp. 256–67.

LEE, A.M. and SOLMON, M.A. (1992) 'Cognitive conceptions of teaching and learning motor skills', *Quest*, **44**, 1, pp. 57–71.

LUKE, I.T. (1998) 'An examination of pupils' metacognitive ability in physical education', Unpublished doctoral thesis: Loughborough University, Leicestershire.

LUKE, I.T. and HARDY, C.A. (1996) 'Differentiation: A consideration of pupils' learning preferences in physical education lessons', *The Bulletin of Physical Education*, **32**, 2, pp. 36–44.

MacLure, M. and French, P. (1980) 'Routes to right answers: On pupils' strategies for answering teachers' questions', in Woods, P. (ed.) *Pupil Strategies: Explorations in the Sociology of the School*, London: Croom Helm, pp. 74–93.

Markman, E.M. (1979) 'Realising that you don't understand: Elementary school children's awareness of inconsistencies', *Child Development*, **50**, pp. 643–55.

Marton, F. (1988) 'Describing and improving learning', in Schmeck, R.R. (ed.) *Learning Strategies and Learning Styles*, New York: Plenum Press, pp. 53–82.

Masur, E.F., McIntyre, C.W. and Flavell, J.H. (1973) 'Developmental changes in apportionment of study time among items in a multi-trial free recall task', *Journal of Experimental Child Psychology*, **15**, pp. 237–46.

Matlin, M.W. (1994) *Cognition*, Fort Worth: Harcourt Brace Publishers.

Mayo, K.E. (1993) 'Learning strategy instruction: Exploring the potential of metacognition', *Reading Improvement*, **30**, 3, pp. 130–3.

McCarthy, P. and Schmeck, R.R. (1988) 'Students' self-concepts and the quality of learning in public schools and universities', in Schmeck, R.R. (ed.) *Learning Strategies and Learning Styles*, New York: Plenum Press, pp. 131–56.

McCombs, B.L. (1988) 'Motivational skills training: Combining metacognitive, cognitive, and affective learning strategies', in Weinstein, C.E., Goetz, E.T. and Alexander, P.A. (eds) *Learning and Study Strategies: Issues in Assessment, Instruction, and Evaluation*, San Diego: Academic Press Inc., pp. 141–69.

Meloth, M.S. (1990) 'Changes in poor readers' knowledge of cognition and the association of knowledge of cognition with regulation of cognition and reading comprehension', *Journal of Educational Psychology*, **82**, pp. 792–8.

Mosston, M. and Ashworth, S. (1990) *The Spectrum of Teaching Styles: From Command to Discovery*, New York: Longman Press.

Nisbet, J. and Shucksmith, J. (1986) *Learning Strategies*, London: Routledge and Kegan Paul.

Palincsar, A.S. and Brown, A.L. (1984) 'Reciprocal teaching of comprehension-fostering and comprehension-monitoring activities', *Cognition and Instruction*, **1**, 2, pp. 117–75.

Paris, S.G. and Oka, E.R. (1986) 'Children's reading strategies, metacognition, and motivation', *Developmental Review*, **6**, pp. 25–56.

Peterson, P. (1988) 'Teachers' and students' cognitional knowledge for classroom teaching and learning', *Educational Researcher*, **17**, 5, pp. 5–14.

Pintrich, P.R. (1990) 'Implications of psychological research on student learning and college teaching for teacher education', in Houston, W.R. (ed.) *Handbook of Research on Teacher Education*, London: Macmillan Publishing Company, pp. 826–53.

Portman, P.A. (1995) 'Coping behaviours of low-skilled students in physical education: Avoid, announce, act out, and accept', *The Physical Educator*, **52**, 1, pp. 29–39.

Pressley, M., Goodchild, F., Fleet, J., Zajchowski, R. and Evans, E.D. (1989) 'The challenges of classroom strategy instruction', *The Elementary School Journal*, **89**, pp. 301–42.

Ramsden, P. (1988) 'Context and strategy: Situational influences on learning', in Schmeck, R.R. (ed.) *Learning Strategies and Learning Styles*, New York: Plenum Press, pp. 159–84.

Ranson, S. and Martin, J. (1996) 'Towards a theory of learning', *British Journal of Educational Studies*, **44**, 1, pp. 9–26.

Read, B. (1989) 'Artisans, players and gods: A reflection on the teaching of games', *Physical Education Review*, **12**, 2, pp. 134–7.

SCHMECK, R.R. (1988a) 'Individual differences and learning strategies', in WEINSTEIN, C.E., GOETZ, E.T. and ALEXANDER, P.A. (eds) *Learning and Study Strategies: Issues in Assessment, Instruction, and Evaluation*, San Diego: Academic Press Inc., pp. 171–91.

SCHMECK, R.R. (1988b) 'Strategies and styles of learning: An integration of varied perspectives', in SCHMECK, R.R. (ed.) *Learning Strategies and Learning Styles*, New York: Plenum Press, pp. 317–47.

SCHOENFELD, A.H. (1987) 'What's all the fuss about metacognition?', in SCHOENFELD, A.H. (ed.) *Cognitive Science and Mathematics Education*, Hillsdale, NJ: Lawrence Erlbaum Associates, pp. 189–215.

SCHWAGER, S. and LABATE, C. (1993) 'Teaching for critical thinking in physical education', *Journal of Health, Physical Education, Recreation and Dance*, **64**, 5, pp. 24–6.

SEIFERT, T.L. and WHEELER, P. (1994) 'Enhancing motivation: A classroom application of self-instruction strategy training', *Research in Education*, **51**, pp. 1–9.

SIEGLER, R.S. (1989) 'Strategy diversity and cognitive assessment', *Educational Researcher*, **18**, 9, pp. 15–20.

SINGER, R.N. and CHEN, D. (1994) 'A classification scheme for cognitive strategies: Implications for learning and teaching psychomotor skills', *Research Quarterly for Exercise and Sport*, **65**, 2, pp. 143–51.

SWANSON, H.L. (1990) 'Influence of metacognitive knowledge and aptitude on problem solving', *Journal of Educational Research*, **82**, 2, pp. 306–14.

THORPE, R., BUNKER, D. and ALMOND, L. (1986) *Rethinking Games Teaching*, Loughborough University: Loughborough University Press.

TORRANCE, E.P. and ROCKENSTEIN, Z.L. (1988) 'Styles of thinking and creativity', in SCHMECK, R.R. (ed.) *Learning Strategies and Learning Styles*, New York: Plenum Press, pp. 275–90.

TOUSIGNANT, M., BRUNELLE, J., LAFORGE, M. and TURCOTTE, D. (1990) 'Getting students to take responsibility for their learning: A concern of primary importance for dance teachers', AIESEP World Convention: Loughborough University, E. and F.N. Spon.

WEINSTEIN, C.E. (1988) 'Assessment and training of student learning strategies', in SCHMECK, R.R. (ed.) *Learning Strategies and Learning Styles*, New York: Plenum Press, pp. 291–316.

WEINSTEIN, C.E. (1994) 'Strategic learning/strategic teaching: Flip sides of a coin', in PINTRICH, P.R., BROWN, D.R. and WEINSTEIN, C.E. (eds) *Student Motivation, Cognition, and Learning: Essays in Honour of Wilbert J. McKeachie*, Hillsdale, NJ: Lawrence Erlbaum Associates, pp. 257–73.

WEINSTEIN, C.E. and MAYER, R.E. (1986) 'The teaching of learning strategies', in WITTROCK, M.C. (ed.) *Handbook of Research on Teaching*, New York: Macmillan Publishing Company, pp. 315–27.

WILLIAMS, A. (1996) *Teaching Physical Education: A Guide for Mentors and Students*, London: David Fulton Publishers.

4   Cognitive Strategies

Ian Luke and Colin A. Hardy

Introduction

It has long been recognized that the cognitive strategies that pupils use when tackling a learning task are a major influence on the quality of the learning outcome (Marton and Saljo, 1976a; Paris and Oka, 1986). 'People rely on cognitive strategies to promote learning, remembering and problem solving' (Paris, 1988, p. 299). Pupils must engage in some form of cognitive strategy to build connections between new ideas, and relate new ideas to prior knowledge (Mayer, 1988; Weinstein and Mayer, 1986). 'Learning and thinking strategies and skills are the tools we use to meet our learning goals' (Weinstein, 1994, p. 259), and would appear to be of most benefit if metacognitive ability is developed concomitantly. Cognitive strategies are beneficial to learning, they can be identified and they can be developed (Kirby and Lawson, 1983; Weinstein and Mayer, 1986). Indeed, cognitive strategy development has provided positive results to pupils of all ages and abilities (Mayo, 1993) regardless of material format and whether strategies are used publicly or privately (Patterson, Dansereau and Newbern, 1992). In support of these claims, cognitive strategy use has been considered crucial to both reading achievement and to the learning of a new language (Chen, 1990; Paris and Oka, 1986). Resnick (1987) suggested that cognitive strategies may not only allow people of limited education to participate in cognitively complex activity systems, but also enhance the capacity of highly educated people well beyond what they could do independently.

In Physical Education, Scantling, McAleese, Tietjen and Strand (1992) successfully encouraged a cognitive strategy, referred to as concept mapping, which helped pupils to fully comprehend and connect ideas and principles presented in lessons. Furthermore, Bouffard and Dunn (1993) claimed that research in the movement domain has demonstrated that, when an appropriate cognitive strategy is shown to pupils and they are requested to use it, motor performance usually improves. This effect has been demonstrated with cognitive strategies that have focused upon labelling (Winter and Thomas, 1981: cited in Bouffard and Dunn, 1993), rehearsal (Weiss, Ebbeck and Rose, 1992; Weiss and Klint, 1987: cited in Bouffard and Dunn, 1993) and organization (Gallagher and Thomas, 1986: cited in Bouffard and Dunn, 1993).

While Luke (1998) also suggested that cognitive strategies would be of benefit to pupils of Physical Education, he indicated some reservation with regard to the simplicity of cognitive strategy development. The variables that interact with cognitive strategies are so vast and complex that there is no simple method from which pupils can fully develop and appreciate them. Wittrock (1988, p. 293) argued that teachers and researchers must move away from attempting to lay cognitive strategies on pupils without appropriate time to develop a full comprehension of them; this argument was also supported by Luke (1998) with respect to Physical Education.

Moreover, McKeachie (1988) implied that while those pupils who achieve high grades differ from those pupils who achieve low grades with regard to their study strategies, their success may not totally be due to these strategies. It is conceivable that the high grade pupils use different cognitive strategies because they already have a good grasp of the material and are able to use more sophisticated cognitive strategies than those of pupils who lack sufficient background and ability. Nevertheless, McKeachie (1988, p. 3) acknowledged that, '. . . the relationship is one in which effective study strategies usually result in greater learning'. Therefore, the nature of pupils' cognitive strategic processing is an important area of consideration for teachers as well as researchers (Christensen and Cooper, 1992).

Cognitive Strategy Definition

There are difficulties in defining cognitive strategy (Crowley and Siegler, 1993; Palmer and Goetz, 1988) as there seem to be concerns for how general and incorporating the term should be (see Bjorkland, 1990). Crowley and Siegler (1993) noted that some definitions argued that cognitive strategies must be conscious, planned processes, whilst other definitions related to any activities that streamlined cognitive performance. Snowman (1986) attempted to clear the problem of strategy definitions by forming a distinction between strategic and tactical ways of learning. A strategy is a sequence of procedures for accomplishing learning (Derry and Murphy, 1986; Schmeck, 1988a; Snowman, 1986) and the specific procedures within this sequence are called tactics (Snowman, 1986). Schmeck (1988a) also suggested that there was a dimension of strategic generality–specificity, whereby the term strategy refers to pupils' general approach or plan during a learning task whereas the term tactics refers to the specific activities of the pupils. Tactics operationalize strategies and, therefore, are the observable activities that imply that certain strategies are being utilized. As such, cognitive strategies signify the collection of mental tactics selected, employed and controlled by an individual in a particular learning situation to facilitate their acquisition of knowledge or skill, and to achieve their desired objectives (Derry and Murphy, 1986; Paris, Lipson and Wixon, 1983). Thus, in Physical Education while analogies, in general, are cognitive strategies that aim to develop a holistic assessment of a learning situation (Miller, 1987; Newton and Newton, 1995; Pask, 1988), specific analogies for a specific learning task, such as the throwing action for a tennis serve, would be technically referred to as tactics.

It has been further claimed that cognitive strategies can be defined as being deliberate, learner-initiated and learner-controlled (Palmer and Goetz, 1988; Paris, Lipson and Wixon, 1983; Winograd and Hare, 1988). Thus, it is implied that cognitive strategies will not be utilized unless a pupil is motivated and deliberately attempts to initiate and control them (Palmer and Goetz, 1988). However, the authors suggest that learning does not always occur consciously and this would seem evident in Physical Education where sports people can often perform actions they cannot explain (Brown, 1987). Therefore, while it is accepted that there is a dimension of strategic generality–specificity with tactics emerging as specific examples of cognitive strategies, from an examination of the origins of various types of cognitive strategies, it can be argued that cognitive strategies are any goal-directed cognitive activities, be they obligatory or non-obligatory, conscious or unconscious, efficient or inefficient (Crowley and Siegler, 1993).

The Connection between Cognitive Style Combinations, Cognitive Strategies and Cognitive Tactics

It has been suggested that both teachers and pupils must acknowledge potential cognitive style combinations in Physical Education (Luke and Hardy, 1996; Mawer, 1995). Cognitive style combinations can be defined as pupils' consistent preferences when representing, organizing and processing information (Riding and Cheema, 1991; Tennant, 1988). There has been considerable confusion over what cognitive style combinations involve, although, following a detailed review of literature, Riding and Cheema (1991) concluded that cognitive style combinations are formed from two fundamental cognitive style dimensions: the holist–analytic and the verbalizer–imager dimensions. These dimensions should be considered as continua with pupils being distributed along them (Riding and Cheema, 1991; Riding and Sadler-Smith, 1992), depending upon the direction and the strength of their tendencies in each dimension.

Holists, as is suggested by the name, tend to organize information into loosely clustered wholes (Douglas and Riding, 1993), whereas analytics prefer to separate information into sections; the cognitive style is, therefore, whether the pupil tends to process information in whole or parts. The verbalizer–imager cognitive style dimension refers to whether the pupil is inclined to represent information verbally or in mental images during thinking (Riding and Ashmore, 1980; Riding, Glass and Douglas, 1993; Riding and Pearson, 1994).

Importantly, the holist–analytic and verbalizer–imager style dimensions are independent of each other (Borg and Riding, 1993; Riding and Douglas, 1993; Riding and Mathias, 1991), implying that a pupil's position along one of the dimensions does not affect the same pupil's position along the other. Thus, pupils may be classified as holist–verbalizers, holist–imagers, analytic–verbalizers or analytic–imagers. Crucially, these cognitive style dimensions will interact with one another in influencing pupils' learning performance (Boulter and Kirby, 1994; Riding and Mathias, 1991), suggesting, therefore, that pupils' cognitive style combinations will influence their learning performance. A reason for the influence and importance of cognitive style combinations upon learning may be that numerous researchers have claimed that pupils' cognitive strategies flow from their cognitive style combinations (Palmer and Goetz, 1988; Riding and Cheema, 1991; Riding and Read, 1996; Rush and Moore, 1991; Witkin, Moore, Goodenough and Cox, 1977). However, while pupils' cognitive style combinations may be relatively stable, pupils' cognitive strategies may be more open to influence (Riding and Read, 1996) especially if efficient metacognitive ability is developed simultaneously (Luke, 1998; McCarthy and Schmeck, 1988). Nevertheless, Pask (1988, p. 85) claimed that 'a style is a disposition to adopt one class of learning strategy' and noted that the 'consistency of the person's strategic preference across tests (and subject matters) is curiously high' (Pask, 1988, p. 97). Schmeck (1988a) similarly suggested that pupils can favour certain cognitive strategies with a bias that seemingly ignores subtle variations in situations and implies the presence and influence of cognitive style combinations. Cognitive style can determine strategy selection more than the contextual demands (Pask, 1988) and the pupils' domain knowledge (Swan, 1993). Therefore, as an example, it would appear that holistic pupils will have a natural tendency to utilize holistic strategies (Kirby, 1988), focusing strongly on contextual features of a task. Interestingly, McCarthy (1990) developed a system known as 4MAT to introduce the idea of cognitive style combinations and their respective cognitive strategies to schools. It would seem that analytic pupils often used planning strategies, with problems being solved by looking at individual sections or parts of the learning tasks with the sequence of these parts being critical. However, the more holistic pupils often based strategies on intuition, beliefs and opinions, and by looking at the whole picture (McCarthy, 1990).

Kirby (1989) referred to the cognitive strategies that immediately emerge from cognitive style combinations as general cognitive strategies. Such general cognitive strategies function like traits and will generalize across domains of performance. Thus, pupils' general cognitive strategies may be categorized under the same headings as cognitive style combinations; that is, holist–verbalizer, holist–imager, analytic–verbalizer and analytic–imager. Perkins and Salomon (1989) suggested that general cognitive strategies act like a gripping device retrieving and wielding more specific cognitive strategies. The implication is that under a general cognitive strategy heading there are various examples of specific cognitive strategies (see Schmeck, 1988b); for example, the mnemonic is a specific cognitive strategy and may be an example of a general analytic–verbalizer cognitive strategy as it involves creating and labelling sections of a whole in a verbal form (Luke and Hardy, 1996). Similarly, Miller (1987) suggested how holistic–imager pupils may frequently use an analogy, which would be a specific cognitive strategy, to relate one area of knowledge to another and to develop a more overall picture. However, it is assumed that cognitive style and general cognitive strategies may not only encourage certain specific cognitive strategies, they will also probably influence how they are used (Kirby, 1989; Pask, 1988). As an example, while holist–imagers may often tend to utilize analogies (Miller, 1987), some pupils in Physical Education may be able to develop their own analogies, such as the throwing action for a tennis serve, while others may require the learning situation to provide the analogies. As those pupils developing their own analogies would seem to be less dependent upon the contextual variables they may have weaker holistic–imager tendencies (Pask, 1988). Thus, although the type of general and specific cognitive strategy may be determined by cognitive

Figure 4.1: An illustration of the continuum from cognitive style combinations to task-specific tactics

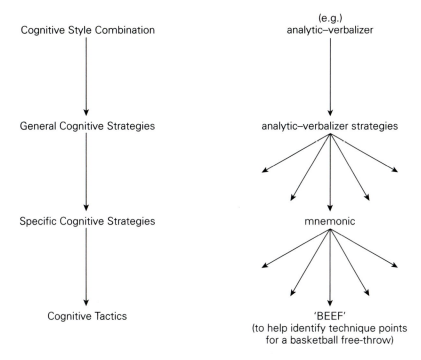

style combinations, there may be variations in the selection and utilization of these cognitive strategies (Pask, 1988).

If specific cognitive strategies are examples of general cognitive strategies, cognitive tactics are examples of specific cognitive strategies within a specific context and for specific tasks. In Physical Education, for example, BEEF (Balance, Elbow up, Extension, Follow through) is a specific example of a mnemonic (a specific cognitive strategy) being used to identify and focus attention on the technique points of a basketball free-throw and, as such, is a cognitive tactic. To illustrate the interaction and connection between cognitive style combinations, general cognitive strategies, specific cognitive strategies and cognitive tactics, Luke (1998) suggested a simple continuum (see Figure 4.1). Spitz (1993) highlighted how specific cognitive strategies are modified for specific content, and he gave the example of a pupil learning to remember numbers by utilizing a mnemonic technique of relating race times to numbers. Thus, there will inevitably be more variability between pupils' tactics compared to their general cognitive strategies, although Schmeck (1988a) noted that when clusters of cognitive tactics were examined there appeared to be some consistency between them. The implication is that cognitive tactics can be clustered together as examples of specific cognitive strategies.

The authors argue that cognitive tactics are sometimes used by pupils without any awareness that they are indeed such tactics. There is little understanding that they were developed from specific cognitive strategies, and that these specific cognitive strategies could be used for other tasks and in other subject areas. Returning to the pupil who utilized the mnemonic technique of relating race times to numbers, Spitz (1993) noted that the same pupil failed to utilize any mnemonic technique for remembering letters. The authors suggest that the pupil failed to appreciate that the initial cognitive tactic had emerged from a type of specific cognitive strategy which could have been modified for the new task. When a pupil utilizes a cognitive tactic without any awareness or appreciation of the connection between that tactic and a specific cognitive strategy, then it is suggested that the pupil is actually utilizing a blind tactic (Luke, 1998).

Interestingly, most attempts at cognitive strategy development through teaching have actually been conducted at the more specific level of cognitive tactics, and worse still, blind tactics. Thus, teaching can often fail to provide sufficient attention as to how or why the cognitive tactics are related to specific cognitive strategies and how or why they can be used to produce an efficient learning outcome (Schmeck, 1988a). Clark and Salomon (1986: cited in Rush and Moore, 1991) have also noted that a lot of research has concentrated on manipulating, or restructuring, instructional tasks, rather than addressing pupils' potential development and utilization of specific cognitive strategies and cognitive tactics. Physical Education is one subject that has strongly followed this pattern (e.g. Brunner and Hill, 1992; Thorpe, Bunker and Almond, 1986). Both of the present authors have witnessed Physical Education lessons whereby a cognitive tactic was taught blindly leaving pupils confused with regard to the purpose of the tactic and with little personal guidance in the use of that tactic. As an example, and returning to the mnemonic BEEF, a teacher had referred to this cognitive tactic during a basketball lesson, but as the pupils were unaware of the development of this cognitive tactic, they struggled to appreciate the benefits of utilizing it. Therefore, they were unable to personally guide their use of this tactic and, as such, their learning had to be questioned. Indeed, pupils were simply shouting 'BEEF' as they threw the basketball and failed to use it to identify and focus attention on the points of the basketball free-throw technique.

However, the efficient development of pupils' cognitive strategies may need to be addressed explicitly as pupils' spontaneous or informal strategies have been both naive and inefficient compared to those developed through explicit guidance in school (Adetula, 1996; Alexander and Judy, 1988; Boulter and Kirby, 1994). Furthermore, the greater the repertoire of cognitive strategies the more successful pupils are likely to be (Watkins and Hattie, 1990), especially if these cognitive strategies can be called upon intuitively or unconsciously (Weinstein, 1994). The argument is not whether pupils should be encouraged in cognitive strategy development but how they should be encouraged. Literature has offered suggestions with regard to the teaching of some specific cognitive strategies, such as analogies (Glynn, 1991; Goswami, 1992: cited in Newton and Newton, 1995), but the development of cognitive strategies and cognitive tactics is complex and not fully understood by either teachers or researchers.

The implication that teachers may need to explicitly consider and develop pupils' cognitive strategies and cognitive tactics does not mean that pupils cannot unconsciously utilize cognitive strategies and cognitive tactics. However, the authors suggest that pupils should be able to consciously modify or evaluate cognitive strategies and cognitive tactics if the learning situation requires them to. Thus, while élite gymnasts may not want or need to overtly think about their cognitive strategies and cognitive tactics for full twisting back somersaults, if the action begins to break down it would be expected for these gymnasts to be able to analyse and adapt their cognitive strategies and cognitive tactics to overcome the problem. Unfortunately, although cognitive strategies can be lengthy, they may also be so rapid in execution that it is almost impossible to recapture, recall or even be aware that one has used a cognitive strategy or tactic (Nisbet and Shucksmith, 1986). However, it was seemingly such conscious awareness of cognitive strategies and cognitive tactics that led Rush and Moore (1991, p. 310) to note that, '... strategies that arise from cognitive styles may be more malleable than the styles themselves', and Witkin, Moore, Goodenough and Cox (1977, p. 27) to claim that there is, '... apparent malleability of learning strategies flowing from cognitive styles'. Pupils may not be able to change their natural preference for a cognitive style combination (Riding and Pearson, 1994), but they may be able to influence their choice of cognitive strategy and cognitive tactic if they understand the type of cognitive strategies that they will tend towards, and other possible cognitive strategies that are available (Riding and Pearson, 1994; Witkin, Moore, Goodenough and Cox, 1977). Notably, it would seem from the discussion in the chapter on pupils' metacognition and learning that such understanding depends strongly upon pupils' development of metacognitive ability.

Thus, it has been suggested that cognitive strategies may be the key to developing a flexible learner who can adapt to the environment without being at the mercy of the limits imposed on them by their cognitive style combination (Paris, 1988; Ramsden, 1988; Witkin, Moore, Goodenough and Cox, 1977). Therefore, it would seem imperative that pupils are encouraged to develop a variety of cognitive strategy types to enhance their potential to learn in a variety of learning situations. Indeed, Roberts and Erdos (1993, p. 265) suggested that the idea of teaching or developing only cognitive strategies that match the cognitive style combination of pupils is of dubious worth as this obviously fails to take into account the different efficiencies of cognitive strategies for different tasks. Furthermore, Pask (1988) argued that both holistic and analytic cognitive strategies are required to achieve complete understanding of a learning situation and Torrance and Rockenstein (1988) suggested creative thinking comes from whole-brain functioning and, therefore, requires a variety of strategy types. Riding and Mathias (1991) argued that when 11-year-olds had a cognitive style combination that offered cognitive strategies to view holistically and to view analytically, namely the holist–verbalizer and the analytic–imager style combinations, learning performance was enhanced. Similarly, it has been noted that difficulty in reading may be due to pupils relying heavily on a single cognitive strategy type rather than using a variety of cognitive strategies in a flexible manner (Kirby, 1988). However, with respect to individual pupils, it has been suggested that not all cognitive strategies will be equal in either their generalizability or their instructability (Nisbet and Shucksmith, 1986; Schmeck, 1988a). That is, the natural cognitive strategies that emerge from a pupil's cognitive style combination may be applied to different tasks in a rather spontaneous, unconscious and consistent manner (Pintrich, 1990), suggesting that these cognitive strategies may be easier to generalize and to guide through instruction. Moreover, Pask (1976) argued that pupils will not relinquish their natural cognitive strategies, even if they cannot successfully execute them, unless very strong advice is provided. Worse still, Miller (1991, p. 235) warned that encouraging a variety of cognitive strategies that could threaten cognitive style combination stability '. . . can be psychologically damaging. Extremely specialised students should be left alone, secure within the confines of their dominant mode.' Clearly, further debate regarding whether teaching should match or mismatch pupils' preferred cognitive style combinations and, therefore, their more natural cognitive strategies, is of the utmost importance.

Should Teaching Match or Mismatch Cognitive Style Combinations and Cognitive Strategies?

It has been implied that pupils who have their cognitive style combinations, and, therefore, their natural cognitive strategies accommodated during a learning situation are more likely to achieve compared to pupils who do not have their cognitive style combinations accommodated (Dunn, Griggs, Olson, Beasley and Gorman, 1995). Carbo (1990) suggested that a match between teaching and pupil cognitive style combination may lead to what Csikszentmilhalyi (1990: cited in Carbo, 1990) referred to as a flow experience, one that is intensely pleasurable. Furthermore, such a match may provide an interpersonal attraction between teacher and pupils whereby each views the other positively (DiStefano, 1970, cited in Witkin, Moore, Goodenough and Cox, 1977), and whereby information is learned more rapidly and retained for longer (Pask, 1976). Thus, it has been argued that teachers should be utilizing a variety of teaching and assessment methods to reach every pupil (Sternberg, 1994), enabling these pupils to further develop and utilize the type of cognitive strategies that they more naturally tend towards as a result of their cognitive style combinations.

However, it is wrong to suggest that pupils will not benefit from teaching that fails to match their tendencies to utilize certain general and specific cognitive strategies (Luke and Hardy, 1996; McCarthy, 1990). Pupils need to be flexible and adapt to a learning situation and they must learn to appreciate that cognitive strategies vary in efficiency depending upon the learning situation. In Physical Education, Mawer (1995) suggested that there may need to be both a match and mismatch between teaching and cognitive style combinations. Similarly Joyce and Weil (1986, p. 440: cited in Mawer, 1995) noted: '. . . to help students grow we need to generate what we currently term "dynamic disequilibrium". Rather than matching teaching approaches to students in such a way as to minimise discomfort, our task is to expose the students to new teaching modalities that will, for some time, be uncomfortable to them.' Moreover, Witkin, Moore, Goodenough and Cox (1977) noted that in some circumstances, a contrast between teaching and pupils' cognitive style combinations and natural cognitive strategies may be more stimulating and may allow pupils to develop their thoughts by learning in a different manner. As a result, pupils may be able to achieve a more complete understanding of a learning situation, balancing the information gained from different cognitive strategies. As an example, pupils who have a holist–imager cognitive style combination may be encouraged to consider the analogy of an uncoiling spring for the free-throw action in basketball; the aim being to develop the pupil's technique of starting the throw from the legs and finishing it with a follow-through of the hand. While the analogy may prove relatively successful there are likely to be a few problems in the pupil's technique due to the limitations of the analogy. That is, the pupil's foot position may be wrong, the ball could be held incorrectly or the elbow of the throwing arm may be too low; the analogy would not specify such points. Thus, the development of a mnemonic such as BEEF (Balance, Elbow up, Extension, Follow-through), although mismatching the pupil's natural type of cognitive strategy, could stimulate the pupil into considering a more analytical perspective of the free-flow technique. As this could provide information that the analogy could not, the pupil may possibly gain a more balanced and complete view of the learning task.

In practice, most Physical Education lessons will include pupils of various cognitive style combinations and, therefore, whether a teacher intends to match or mismatch pupils' cognitive style combinations and natural cognitive strategies, it is extremely likely that the teacher will be matching some pupils and mismatching others. Teachers can only offer variety in approaches and cognitive strategies, and try to present information holistically and analytically (Luke and Hardy, 1996; Riding and Sadler-Smith, 1992) which can be readily represented verbally or visually by pupils (Luke and Hardy, 1996; Riding and Douglas, 1993). However, while the selection of appropriate cognitive strategies for a learning situation is crucial, pupils' learning will also be strongly influenced by the manner in which the cognitive strategies are initiated and controlled.

The Initiation and Control of Cognitive Strategies

If a clear categorization of cognitive strategies is to be developed, it is important to examine how cognitive strategies are initiated and controlled. The initiation and control of a cognitive strategy may arise primarily from pupils' self-instructions and would, therefore, be learner-controlled, or the initiation and control may come from the teacher or an instructional system which would be lesson-controlled. Furthermore, the cognitive strategy may be processed either consciously or unconsciously (Derry and Murphy, 1986; Rigney, 1978). As such, if pupils are attempting to learn a volley in tennis and those pupils utilize the analogy of a punching action in order to aid their learning, then they are not only aware of their strategic action but they have also initiated it. However, if a teacher suggests the use of that analogy, then it is lesson controlled, even though the pupils are aware of the specific cognitive strategy or cognitive tactics being used. Such externally imposed specific cognitive strategies, or more specifically, cognitive tactics, have been found to contribute to achieving in various Physical Education tasks with children (Gallagher and Thomas, 1984: cited in Singer and Chen, 1994) and collegiate athletes (Fenker and Lambiotte, 1987: cited in Singer and Chen, 1994). An assumption in this approach is that it minimizes the time needed for learning (Singer and Chen, 1994). However, a situation can evolve where a specific cognitive strategy, and the cognitive tactics that emerge from that specific cognitive strategy, are learner-controlled but so spontaneous and automatic that there is no conscious awareness of their utilization (Derry and Murphy, 1986; Garner, 1988). Nevertheless, while efficient learning can occur in a state of automaticity, pupils should be able to '. . . switch on to awareness when adaptability is required' (Singer and Chen, 1994, p. 147). The lesson-controlled counterpart of automatic processing would involve the instructional design methodology incorporating controls into a lesson so that the pupils are required or forced to employ particular specific cognitive strategies and cognitive tactics to accomplish learning even though these pupils lack both awareness and control of such specific cognitive strategies and cognitive tactics.

The situation of forcing blind tactics is the most conventional in most schools (Derry and Murphy, 1986; Schmeck, 1988b). Considering 'Teaching Games for Understanding' (Thorpe, Bunker and Almond, 1986), it is apparently based around developing a lesson so that pupils are forced to become aware of problems and are forced to use certain gameplay tactics; for example, the long, thin court forces the gameplay tactics of hitting long and then hitting short. The situation is forcing pupils' discovery of the gameplay tactic rather than guiding their discovery of it (Almond, 1996). Reducing pupils' awareness and control of a specific cognitive strategy or cognitive tactic may be beneficial as pupils trying to learn may see the instructions as demanding something different to what the teacher intended. As an example, Luke (1998) noted how a pupil believed that the teacher had established a tag activity to teach the class about sexism and assess the level of sexism in the class; the tagging and freeing of pupils of the opposite gender would be the critical variable. However, the actual purpose of the activity was simply to warm-up and whether the pupil achieved this or not would have to be questioned. Thus, it is conceivable to structure situations so that some pupils would perform better if they were not trying to learn (Derry and Murphy, 1986; Schmeck, 1988a). However, this situation of forced or hidden blind tactics does little to help pupils cope with requirements for further independent learning of material that is not highly designed (Rigney, 1978). Returning to the 'Teaching Games for Understanding' example, it was noted that although their pupils were able to use the hit long–hit short gameplay tactics on the long, thin court they did not use it on the larger court. The reason offered was that pupils were probably rushed too quickly onto a larger court. While this reason may have some validity, it could be that as the task had lost the task design which initially forced the use of the specified gameplay tactics, the apparent learning of those tactics also disappeared. It may be that the tactics were being drilled in the long, thin court situation, and as Rathmell (1978) argued with respect to mathematics, drill and practice procedures may increase pupils' speed and accuracy of response but these procedures are not sufficient to develop efficient cognitive strategies. Steinberg (1985) supported this view noting that pupils became so proficient at a counting tactic that they could not adopt any other specific cognitive strategies or cognitive tactics to answer addition questions. With respect to Physical Education, the DES document (1991, p. 9) National Curriculum Physical Education Working Group Interim Report stated that 'Children who are required to make few decisions for themselves and who merely respond to instructions are likely to acquire accurate physical skills, but are unlikely to develop judgement, adaptability or independence.' Recent Physical Education research (Luke, 1998) consolidated this opinion as it was noted how pupils seemed to utilize a teacher-directed holist–verbalizer cognitive strategy (i.e. rhythmical counting to help pupils coordinate the movement phases in a discus throw), but were clearly dependent upon the specific cognitive strategy and cognitive tactic being forced upon them to perform as they were completely unaware of it after the lesson. Without any appreciation of the cognitive strategies and the cognitive tactics being utilized, the learning of information and the transfer of information to other tasks and contexts could be limited (Campione, 1987; Luke, 1998).

Interacting Variables with Cognitive Strategy Development and Utilization

The chapter on pupils' metacognition and learning considers the interaction and association between cognitive strategies and metacognitive ability but literature has suggested other variables that may interact with cognitive strategy development. For example, gender may create a slight difference in the choice of cognitive strategies and how they are utilized (Pokay and Blumenfeld, 1990), as may age (Chen, 1990; Palincsar and Brown, 1984; Paris and Oka, 1986), experience (Best, 1990), attention (Wittrock, 1988), ability (Eylon and Linn, 1988; Perkins and Salomon, 1989; Siegler, 1989), typicality and familiarity with the task (Rabinowitz, Freeman and Cohen, 1992) and interest in the task (Hidi, 1990; Reynolds and Shirey, 1988; Watkins, 1982). In addition, and elaborated in the present discussion, are the interactions between pupils' cognitive strategies and their knowledge base, their personal attributes and contextual variables.

Pupils' Knowledge Base

Garner (1990) claimed that knowledge base and cognitive strategies closely interact. Indeed, it is argued that as pupils' knowledge in a domain increases, there will be a change in the selection and utilization of strategies (Alexander and Judy, 1988). Rabinowitz, Freeman and Cohen (1992) noted that the typicality and familiarity of the relevant domain information, when pupils are initially learning a cognitive strategy, will not only enhance the use of that strategy but will also maintain its usage in other situations. Alexander and Judy (1988) suggested that domain knowledge and cognitive strategies have an interdependent relationship as domain knowledge may play a foundation role from which cognitive strategies can be developed, whilst cognitive strategies can contribute to the utilization and acquisition of domain specific knowledge. It is claimed that pupils can distort incoming information to match or fit in with their domain knowledge which clearly influences the development and selection of cognitive strategies (Alexander and Judy, 1988; Eylon and Linn, 1988). Similarly, pupils may be ready to use a cognitive strategy but are prevented by the absence of other non-strategy information in their knowledge base (Garner, 1988); that is, pupils may not be able to use the analogy on bicycle gears to consider heart target zones in health-related exercise if they have never used a bicycle with gears.

Pupils' Personal Attributes

Dean (1977: cited McCarthy and Schmeck, 1988) suggested that there is a significant relationship between self-esteem and the choice of cognitive strategies with high self-esteem pupils using more sophisticated strategies. Furthermore, it appears that pupils who adopt a more intrinsic orientation not only try harder or persist longer, but also recruit more effective cognitive strategies for learning or problem solving (Pintrich, 1990). Perceptions of personal ability, or self-efficacy, can significantly influence whether cognitive strategies are utilized. That is, if pupils think they will fail in a task, even if they did use a cognitive strategy, then they will not bother using it (Garner, 1990; Palmer and Goetz, 1988). It would seem that pupils' motivation can also strongly interact with the development and the use of cognitive strategies. As McCombs (1988, p. 153) claimed, motivation is '. . . a necessary component of strategic behavior and a precursor to strategy use'. It seems that the development of motivation and the development of strategic behaviour may be a two-way process (McCombs, 1988; Pokay and Blumenfeld, 1990). As an example, pupils who are motivated to learn a tumble turn in swimming are more likely than unmotivated pupils to develop cognitive strategies and cognitive tactics, such as the analogy of a forward roll, to help their learning processes. In addition, if pupils appreciate the value of such cognitive strategies and cognitive tactics in aiding their learning of a tumble turn they are more likely to be motivated to learn it.

Contextual Variables

'Context differences impose on or suggest to students different strategies of learning' (Ramsden, 1988, p. 159). The contextual domains that may influence pupils' deployment of cognitive strategies of learning include the way information is taught (Ramsden, 1988), the method of assessment (Doyle, 1983; Ramsden, 1988; Watkins, 1982) and the content and the structure of the curriculum (Casey, 1993; Ramsden, 1988). With respect to the latter, Fennema, Carpenter, Franke, Levi, Jacobs and Empson (1996) noted that pupils can develop their own cognitive strategies and these may be closely integrated with the type of problems and tasks faced. However, when tasks become too predictable, learning and cognitive strategy deployment can become technified (Marton and Saljo, 1976b) and pupils simply develop stock responses, or template-like responses, to specific situations without grasping the underlying principles (Perkins and Simmons, 1988). Casey (1993) argued that the more complex the structure of the problem and task the increased likelihood of a pupil adopting an error prone cognitive strategy.

However, contextual variables operate both directly and indirectly as there may be a difference between what the contextual variables are and what the pupils perceive them to be (Ramsden, 1988; Watkins and Hattie, 1990); for example, whereas the general purpose may be to gain an understanding of the content, pupils may view the purpose as simply trying '. . . to come up with the right answers to the questions' (Marton, 1988, p. 79) and they may do so without any real under-standing of the content at all by utilizing dubious strategies (MacLure and French, 1980). One strategy may be to imitate other pupils' answers, even when the teacher does not offer any positive reinforcement; MacLure and French (1980) noted that there were fifteen calls of 'pliers' and 'clippers' in response to a question which was looking for the answer 'cutters', even though the teacher did not positively respond to any of them. A second strategy may be to retrieve answers that have already been introduced in the discourse (MacLure and French, 1980), almost guessing answers from comments by the teacher earlier in the lesson. Therefore, while in Physical Education it is beneficial to have relevant activities while warming-up and leading to the lesson focus, it cannot be assumed that answers to questions later on in the lesson will be accompanied by understanding, even if the correct answer emerges. To clarify the point, it is conceivable that a teacher in gymnastics could ask the pupils to warm-up for a vaulting lesson by running and practising the vari-ous step-pattern options in gymnastics; one foot to the same foot, one foot to the other foot, one foot to two feet, two feet to one foot and two feet to two feet. Upon the introduction of a springboard into the lesson the teacher may ask the pupils to consider which foot pattern is required in vaulting to utilize the springboard effi-ciently. Pupils using the initial cognitive strategy for answering questions may copy each others' answers; 'one foot to the other foot' 'one foot to two feet', whether or not the answer is incorrect or correct. Pupils utilizing the second cognitive strategy for answering questions may offer the correct answer, 'one foot to two feet', even if they do not understand why, because perhaps the teacher seemed to emphasize that step pattern during an earlier explanation.

Contextual influences on cognitive strategy development and deployment may take on a more sociological, or social interaction, form; for example, the lesson climate can significantly interact with strategy development and use. The pressure of competition, or having goals linked with performance rather than mastery, can affect the choice of cognitive strategy, especially in Physical Education. Indeed, Luke (1998) noted how, during a volleyball lesson that intended to focus upon the dig technique, pupils were only concerned with their competitive performance as opposed to their learning processes because the lesson was purely game-based. Without any lesson focus specifically on the dig technique, the pupils simply wanted to keep the ball in the air irrespective of how it could be achieved. Denscombe (1980) claimed that pupils often exploit how the climate has been developed, copying strategies used by the teacher and focusing on classroom negotiation rather than learning; for example, young male staff may flirt with females, being able to use it to secure cooperation and females may use it as a counter strategy to delay work (Denscombe, 1980). Denscombe argued that pupils may focus cognitive strategy development on gaining control of the teacher–pupil battle and to cope with the demands placed upon them in the lesson situation. However, the focus on these cognitive strategies may strongly influence the efficiency of developing cognitive strategies aimed at understanding and learning. In Physical Education, both Griffin (1984, 1985) and Portman (1995) suggested that task-avoidance and coping strategies utilized by pupils could override pupils' cognitive strategies focused on learning.

Although contextual and sociological variables interact with pupils' development of cognitive strategies, it is assumed that pupils can make calculated decisions and have a degree of cognitive control and not purely be the product of socialization (Brown, Bransford, Ferrarra and Campione, 1983; Hammersley and Turner, 1980; Weinstein and Mayer, 1986).

Conclusions and Reflections

A Summary of Cognitive Strategies

Cognitive strategies are a significant influence on learning efficiency (Weinstein, 1994) in both cognitive and physical tasks (Bouffard and Dunn, 1993). Although there is often confusion about cognitive strategy definitions, it is claimed that they are any goal-directed cognitive activities, be they obligatory or non-obligatory, conscious or unconscious, efficient or inefficient (Crowley and Siegler, 1993). Cognitive strategy selection and deployment appears to be strongly influenced by cognitive style combinations, and may be seen as a continuum from style and the most generalized of cognitive strategies to the most task-specific cognitive tactics (Derry and Murphy, 1986; Nisbet and Shucksmith, 1986). Cognitive strategies may be consciously or unconsciously initiated and may be learner- or lesson-controlled (Derry and Murphy, 1986). However, if a cognitive tactic, emerging from a specific cognitive strategy, is unconsciously initiated and lesson-controlled, it is argued to be a blind tactic. As such, the pupil may struggle to utilize independently the same specific cognitive strategy from which the cognitive tactic emerged for a new learning situation (Rigney, 1978). Finally, there are numerous variables that interact with cognitive strategy selection and deployment and will, therefore, influence whether or not efficient learning takes place. However, it would seem that the development of pupils' metacognitive ability is one of the major influences on whether cognitive strategy development and use will be efficient.

The Focus on Cognitive Strategies

Knoll (1978, p. vii: cited in Nickerson, 1988) referred to a '. . . new vision of teaching' where the teacher not only considers the content and organization of a lesson but also the cognitive strategies required by that content to make learning meaningful, integrated and transferable. Teachers need to balance delicately content goals, cognitive strategies required for achieving those goals, and the experiences the pupils bring to their learning. Thus, teachers must appreciate the origins of cognitive strategies and tactics and utilize a variety of cognitive strategy types in order to both match pupils' natural cognitive strategies and cognitive tactics but also to encourage them to develop a greater variety and a greater repertoire of cognitive strategies for learning (Luke and Hardy, 1996; McCarthy, 1990). Furthermore, by understanding the origins of cognitive strategies and cognitive tactics teachers may have some guidelines for when their initial teaching approaches appear unsuccessful for certain pupils and they need to try something different (Luke and Hardy, 1996). Thus, if pupils' attempts at a tennis serve appear disjointed and lacking flow, teachers may need to focus on a more holistic approach to the action; developing specific cognitive strategies such as analogies or rhythmical counting to help in this approach. Unfortunately, Nisbet and Shucksmith (1986, p. 82) argued that, generally, most teachers have '. . . little notion of the sort of strategies the children would use or need'. However, with reference to Physical Education, Bouffard and Dunn (1993) argued that if pupils can be encouraged to develop and utilize cognitive strategies, they may become more independent learners, which, in turn, may enable teachers to spend more time on the development of technical and aesthetic skills. Furthermore, if cognitive strategies can encourage both physical and cognitive development, it may be that cognitive strategies offer suggestions on how to discourage the task-avoidance and coping behaviours of pupils that have been noted in Physical Education lessons (Griffin, 1984, 1985; Portman, 1995). As Nisbet and Shucksmith (1986) suggested, it is only a short step from pupils failing due to inefficient learning-focused cognitive strategies, to pupils searching for task- or teacher-avoidance strategies that would help them hide their lack of success.

Definition of Terms

- Cognitive style combination
  An individual's consistent preferences in processing (holist–analytic cognitive style dimension) and representing (verbalizer–imager cognitive style dimension) information (Riding and Cheema, 1991; Tennant, 1988).
- Cognitive strategies
  Goal-directed cognitive activities, be they obligatory or non-obligatory, conscious or unconscious, efficient or inefficient (Crowley and Siegler, 1993). Cognitive strategies may be viewed as a continuum from generality to specificity, from cognitive style and the most generalized of cognitive strategies to the most task-specific cognitive tactics (Derry and Murphy, 1986; Nisbet and Shucksmith, 1986).
- Cognitive tactic
  A specific cognitive strategy that has been adapted for a specific task and context.

References

ADETULA, L.O. (1996) 'Effects of counting and thinking strategies in teaching addition and subtraction problems', *Educational Research*, **38**, 2, pp. 183–98.

ALEXANDER, P.A. and JUDY, J.E. (1988) 'The interaction of domain-specific and strategic knowledge in academic performance', *Review of Educational Research*, **58**, 4, pp. 375–404.

ALMOND, L. (1996) Discussion with L. Almond with regard to 'Teaching Games for Understanding'.

BEST, J.B. (1990) 'Knowledge acquisition and strategic action in "mastermind" problems', *Memory and Cognition*, **18**, 1, pp. 54–64.

BJORKLAND, D.F. (ed.) (1990) *Children's Strategies: Contemporary Views of Cognitive Development*, Hillsdale, NJ: Lawrence Erlbaum Associates.

BORG, M.G. and RIDING, R.J. (1993) 'Teacher stress and cognitive style', *British Journal of Educational Psychology*, **63**, pp. 271–86.

BOUFFARD, M. and DUNN, J.G.H. (1993) 'Children's self-regulated learning of movement sequences', *Research Quarterly for Sport and Exercise*, **64**, 4, pp. 393–403.

BOULTER, D.R. and KIRBY, J.R. (1994) 'Identification of strategies used in solving trans-formational geometry problems', *The Journal of Educational Research*, **87**, 5, pp. 298–303.

BROWN, A.L. (1987) 'Metacognition, executive control, self-regulation, and other more mysterious mechanisms', in WEINERT, F.E. and KLUWE, R.H. (eds) *Metacognition, Motivation, and Understanding*, Hillsdale, NJ: Lawrence Erlbaum Associates, pp. 65–116.

BROWN, A.L., BRANSFORD, S.D., FERRARRA, R. and CAMPIONE, J.C. (1983) 'Learning, re-membering and understanding', in FLAVELL, J.H. and MARKMAN, E.M. (eds) *Handbook of Child Psychology*, New York: Wiley, pp. 77–166.

BRUNNER, R. and HILL, D. (1992) 'Using learning styles research in coaching', *Journal of Physical Education, Recreation and Dance*, **63**, pp. 26–8, 61–2.

CAMPIONE, J.C. (1987) 'Metacognitive components of instructional research with problem solvers', in WEINERT, F.E. and KLUWE, R.H. (eds) *Metacognition, Motivation, and Understanding*, Hillsdale, NJ: Lawrence Erlbaum Associates, pp. 117–40.

CARBO, M. (1990) 'Igniting the literacy revolution through reading styles', *Educational Leadership*, **48**, 2, pp. 26–9.

CASEY, P.J. (1993) ' "That man's father is my father's son": The roles of structure, strategy, and working memory in solving convoluted verbal problems', *Memory and Cognition*, **21**, 4, pp. 506–18.

CHEN, H.-C. (1990) 'Lexical processing in a non-native language: Effects of language pro-ficiency and learning strategy', *Memory and Cognition*, **18**, 3, pp. 279–88.

CHRISTENSEN, C.A. and COOPER, T.J. (1992) 'The role of cognitive strategies in the trans-ition from counting to retrieval of basic addition facts', *British Educational Research Journal*, **18**, 1, pp. 37–44.

CROWLEY, K. and SIEGLER, R.S. (1993) 'Flexible strategy use in young children's tic-tac-toe', *Cognitive Science*, **17**, pp. 531–61.

DENSCOMBE, M. (1980) 'Pupil strategies and the open classroom', in WOODS, P. (ed.) *Pupil Strategies: Explorations in the Sociology of the School*, London: Croom Helm, pp. 50–73.

DERRY, S.J. and MURPHY, D.A. (1986) 'Designing systems that train learning ability: From theory to practice', *Review of Educational Research*, **56**, 1, pp. 1–39.

DES (1991) National Curriculum Physical Education Working Group Interim Report, London: HMSO.

DOUGLAS, G. and RIDING, R.J. (1993) 'The effect of pupil cognitive style and position of prose passage title on recall', *Educational Psychology*, **13**, 3, 4, pp. 385–93.

DOYLE, W. (1983) 'Academic work', *Review of Educational Research*, **53**, pp. 159–99.

DUNN, R., GRIGGS, S.A., OLSON, J., BEASLEY, M. and GORMAN, B.S. (1995) 'A meta-analytic validation of the Dunn and Dunn Model of learning-style preferences', *Journal of Education Research*, **88**, 6, pp. 353–62.

EYLON, B.S. and LINN, M.C. (1988) 'Learning and instruction: An examination of four research perspectives in science education', *Review of Educational Research*, **58**, 3, pp. 251–301.

FENNEMA, E., CARPENTER, T.P., FRANKE, M.L., LEVI, L., JACOBS, V.R. and EMPSON, S.B. (1996) 'A longitudinal study of learning to use children's thinking in mathematics instruction', *Journal for Research in Mathematics Education*, **27**, 4, pp. 403–34.

GARNER, R. (1988) 'Verbal-report data on cognitive and metacognitive strategies', in WEINSTEIN, C.E., GOETZ, E.T. and ALEXANDER, P.A. (eds) *Learning and Study Strategies: Issues in Assessment, Instruction, and Evaluation*, San Diego: Academic Press Inc., pp. 63–76.

GARNER, R. (1990) 'When children and adults do not use learning strategies: Toward a theory of settings', *Review of Educational Research*, **60**, 4, pp. 517–29.

GLYNN, S.M. (1991) 'Explaining science concepts', in GLYNN, S., YEANY, R. and BRITTON, B. (eds) *The Psychology of Learning Science*, Hillsdale, NJ: Lawrence Erlbaum Associates.

GRIFFIN, P. (1984) 'Girls' participation patterns in a middle school teams sports unit', *Journal of Teaching in Physical Education*, **4**, 1, pp. 30–8.

GRIFFIN, P.S. (1985) 'Boys' participation styles in a middle school physical education team sports unit', *Journal of Teaching in Physical Education*, **4**, 2, pp. 100–10.

HAMMERSLEY, M. and TURNER, G. (1980) 'Conformist pupils', in WOODS, P. (ed.) *Pupil Strategies: Explorations in the Sociology of the School*, London: Croom Helm, pp. 29–49.

HIDI, S. (1990) 'Interest and its contribution as a mental resource for learning', *Review of Educational Research*, **60**, 4, pp. 549–71.

KIRBY, J.R. (1988) 'Style, strategy, and skill in reading', in SCHMECK, R.R. (ed.) *Learning Strategies and Learning Styles*, New York: Plenum Press, pp. 229–74.

KIRBY, J.R. (1989) 'Generality and specificity in strategy instruction', *Canadian Journal of Special Education*, **5**, 2, pp. 179–86.

KIRBY, J.R. and LAWSON, M.J. (1983) 'Effects of strategy training on progressive matrices performance', *Contemporary Educational Psychology*, **8**, pp. 127–40.

LUKE, I.T. (1998) 'An examination of pupils' metacognitive ability in physical education, Unpublished doctoral thesis: Loughborough University, Leicestershire.

LUKE, I.T. and HARDY, C.A. (1996) 'Differentiation: A consideration of pupils' learning preferences in physical education lessons', *The Bulletin of Physical Education*, **32**, 2, pp. 36–44.

MacLURE, M. and FRENCH, P. (1980) 'Routes to right answers: On pupils' strategies for answering teachers' questions', in WOODS, P. (ed.) *Pupil Strategies: Explorations in the Sociology of the School*, London: Croom Helm, pp. 74–93.

MARTON, F. (1988) 'Describing and improving learning', in SCHMECK, R.R. (ed.) *Learning Strategies and Learning Styles*, New York: Plenum, pp. 53–82.

MARTON, F. and SALJO, R. (1976a) 'On qualitative differences in learning: I-outcome and process', *British Journal of Educational Psychology*, **46**, pp. 4–11.

MARTON, F. and SALJO, F. (1976b) 'Symposium: Learning processes and strategies-I', *British Journal of Educational Psychology*, **46**, pp. 1–3.

MAWER, M. (1995) *The Effective Teaching of Physical Education*, London: Longman.

MAYER, R.E. (1988) 'Learning strategies: An overview', in WEINSTEIN, C.E., GOETZ, E.T. and ALEXANDER, P.A. (eds) *Learning and Study Strategies: Issues in Assessment, Instruction, and Evaluation*, San Diego: Academic Press Inc., pp. 11–22.

MAYO, K.E. (1993) 'Learning strategy instruction: Exploring the potential of metacognition', *Reading Improvement*, **30**, 3, pp. 130–3.

MCCARTHY, B. (1990) 'Using the 4MAT system to bring learning styles to schools', *Educational Leadership*, **48**, 2, pp. 31–7.

MCCARTHY, P. and SCHMECK, R.R. (1988) 'Students' self-concepts and the quality of learning in public schools and universities', in SCHMECK, R.R. (ed.) *Learning Strategies and Learning Styles*, New York: Plenum Press, pp. 131–56.

MCCOMBS, B.L. (1988) 'Motivational skills training: Combining metacognitive, cognitive, and affective learning strategies', in WEINSTEIN, C.E., GOETZ, E.T. and ALEXANDER, P.A. (eds) *Learning and Study Strategies: Issues in Assessment, Instruction, and Evaluation*, San Diego: Academic Press Inc., pp. 141–69.

MCKEACHIE, W.J. (1988) 'The need for study strategy training', in WEINSTEIN, C.E., GOETZ, E.T. and ALEXANDER, P.A. (eds) *Learning and Study Strategies: Issues in Assessment, Instruction, and Evaluation*, San Diego: Academic Press Inc., pp. 3–9.

MILLER, A. (1987) 'Cognitive styles: An integrated model', *Educational Psychology*, 7, 4, pp. 251–68.

MILLER, A. (1991) 'Personality types, learning styles and educational goals', *Educational Psychology*, **11**, 3, 4, pp. 217–37.

NEWTON, D.P. and NEWTON, L.D. (1995) 'Using analogy to help young children understand', *Educational Studies*, **21**, 3, pp. 379–93.

NICKERSON, R.S. (1988) 'On improving thinking through instruction', in ROTHKOPF, E.Z. (ed.) *Review of Research in Education*, Washington, DC: American Educational Research Association, 15, pp. 3–57.

NISBET, J. and SHUCKSMITH, J. (1986) *Learning Strategies*, London: Routledge and Kegan Paul.

PALINCSAR, A.S. and BROWN, A.L. (1984) 'Reciprocal teaching of comprehension-fostering and comprehension-monitoring activities', *Cognition and Instruction*, **1**, 2, pp. 117–75.

PALMER, D.J. and GOETZ, E.T. (1988) 'Selection and use of study strategies: The role of the studier's beliefs about self and strategies', in WEINSTEIN, C.E., GOETZ, E.T. and ALEXANDER, P.A. (eds) *Learning and Study Strategies: Issues in Assessment, Instruction, and Evaluation*, San Diego: Academic Press Inc., pp. 41–61.

PARIS, S.G. (1988) 'Models and metaphors of learning strategies', in WEINSTEIN, C.E., GOETZ, E.T. and ALEXANDER, P.A. (eds) *Learning and Study Strategies: Issues in Assessment, Instruction, and Evaluation*, San Diego: Academic Press Inc., pp. 299–321.

PARIS, S.G., LIPSON, M.Y. and WIXON, K.K. (1983) 'Becoming a strategic reader', *Contemporary Educational Psychology*, **8**, pp. 293–316.

PARIS, S.G. and OKA, E.R. (1986) 'Children's reading strategies, metacognition, and motivation', *Developmental Review*, **6**, pp. 25–56.

PASK, G. (1976) 'Styles and strategies of learning', *British Journal of Educational Psychology*, **46**, pp. 128–48.

PASK, G. (1988) 'Learning strategies, teaching strategies, and conceptual or learning style', in SCHMECK, R.R. (ed.) *Learning Strategies and Learning Styles*, New York: Plenum Press, pp. 83–100.

PATTERSON, M.E., DANSEREAU, D.F. and NEWBERN, D. (1992) 'Effects of communication aids and strategies on cooperative teaching', *Journal of Educational Psychology*, **84**, 4, pp. 453–61.

PERKINS, D.N. and SALOMON, G. (1989) 'Are cognitive skills context-bound?', *Educational Researcher*, **18**, 1, pp. 16–25.

PERKINS, D.N. and SIMMONS, R. (1988) 'Patterns of misunderstanding: An integrative model for science, math, and programming', *Review of Educational Research*, **58**, 3, pp. 303–26.

PINTRICH, P.R. (1990) 'Implications of psychological research on student learning and college teaching for teacher education', in HOUSTON, W.R. (ed.) *Handbook of Research on Teacher Education*, London: Macmillan Publishing Company, pp. 826–53.

POKAY, P. and BLUMENFELD, P.C. (1990) 'Predicting achievement early and late in the semester: The role of motivation and use of learning strategies', *Journal of Educational Psychology*, **82**, 1, pp. 41–50.

PORTMAN, P.A. (1995) 'Coping behaviors of low-skilled students in physical education: Avoid, announce, act out, and accept', *The Physical Educator*, **52**, 1, pp. 29–39.

RABINOWITZ, M., FREEMAN, K. and COHEN, S. (1992) 'Use and maintenance of strategies: The influence of accessibility to knowledge', *Journal of Educational Psychology*, **84**, 2, pp. 211–18.

RAMSDEN, P. (1988) 'Context and strategy: Situational influences on learning', in SCHMECK, R.R. (ed.) *Learning Strategies and Learning Styles*, New York: Plenum Press, pp. 159–84.

RATHMELL, E.C. (1978) 'Using thinking strategies to learn the basic facts', in SUYDAM, M.N. (ed.) *Developing Computational Skills*, Reston, VA: National Council of Teachers of Mathematics, pp. 13–38.

RESNICK, L.B. (1987) 'Learning in school and out', *Educational Researcher*, **16**, 9, pp. 13–20.

REYNOLDS, R.E. and SHIREY, R.E. (1988) 'The role of attention in studying and learning', in WEINSTEIN, C.E., GOETZ, E.T. and ALEXANDER, P.A. (eds) *Learning and Study Strategies: Issues in Assessment, Instruction and Evaluation*, San Diego: Academic Press Inc., pp. 77–100.

RIDING, R.J. and ASHMORE, J. (1980) 'Verbaliser-imager learning style and children's recall of information presented in pictorial versus written form', *Educational Studies*, **6**, 2, pp. 141–5.

RIDING, R. and CHEEMA, I. (1991) 'Cognitive styles: An overview and integration', *Educational Psychology*, **11**, 3, 4, pp. 193–215.

RIDING, R. and DOUGLAS, G. (1993) 'The effect of cognitive style and mode of presentation on learning performance', *British Journal of Educational Psychology*, **63**, pp. 297–307.

RIDING, R.J., GLASS, A. and DOUGLAS, G. (1993) 'Individual differences in thinking: Cognitive and neurophysiological perspectives', *Educational Psychology*, **13**, 3, 4, pp. 267–79.

RIDING, R. and MATHIAS, D. (1991) 'Cognitive styles and preferred learning mode, reading attainment and cognitive ability in 11-year-old children', *Educational Psychology*, **11**, 3, 4, pp. 383–93.

RIDING, R.J. and PEARSON, F. (1994) 'The relationship between cognitive style and intelligence', *Educational Psychology*, **14**, 4, pp. 413–25.

RIDING, R.J. and READ, G. (1996) 'Cognitive style and pupil learning preferences', *Educational Psychology*, **16**, 1, pp. 81–106.

RIDING, R. and SADLER-SMITH, E. (1992) 'Type of instructional material, cognitive style, and learning performance', *Educational Studies*, **18**, 3, pp. 323–39.

RIGNEY, J.W. (1978) 'Learning strategies: A theoretical perspective', in O'NEIL, H.F.J. (ed.) *Learning Strategies*, New York: Academic Press, pp. 165–205.

ROBERTS, M.J. and ERDOS, G. (1993) 'Strategy selection and metacognition', *Educational Psychology*, **13**, 3, 4, pp. 259–66.

RUSH, G.M. and MOORE, D.M. (1991) 'Effects of restructuring training and cognitive style', *Educational Psychology*, **11**, 3, 4, pp. 309–21.

SCANTLING, E., MCALEESE, W., TIETJEN, L. and STRAND, B. (1992) 'Concept mapping: A link to learning', *Strategies*, **6**, 2, pp. 10–12.

SCHMECK, R.R. (1988a) 'Individual differences and learning strategies', in WEINSTEIN, C.E., GOETZ, E.T. and ALEXANDER, P.A. (eds) *Learning and Study Strategies: Issues in Assessment, Instruction, and Evaluation*, San Diego: Academic Press Inc., pp. 171–91.

SCHMECK, R.R. (1988b) 'Strategies and styles of learning: An integration of varied perspectives', in SCHMECK, R.R. (ed.) *Learning Strategies and Learning Styles*, New York: Plenum Press, pp. 317–47.

SIEGLER, R.S. (1989) 'Strategy diversity and cognitive assessment', *Educational Researcher*, **18**, 9, pp. 15–20.

SINGER, R.N. and CHEN, D. (1994) 'A classification scheme for cognitive strategies: Implications for learning and teaching psychomotor skills', *Research Quarterly for Exercise and Sport*, **65**, 2, pp. 143–51.

SNOWMAN, J. (1986) 'Learning tactics and strategies', in PHYE, G.D. and ANDRE, T. (eds) *Cognitive Instructional Psychology: Components of Classroom Learning*, New York: Academic Press.

SPITZ, H.H. (1993) 'The role of the unconscious in thinking and problem solving', *Educational Psychology*, **13**, 3, 4, pp. 229–44.

STEINBERG, R.M. (1985) 'Instruction on derived fact strategies in addition and subtraction', *Journal for Research in Mathematics Education*, **16**, pp. 337–58.

STERNBERG, R.J. (1994) 'Allowing for thinking styles', *Educational Leadership*, **52**, 3, pp. 36–40.

SWAN, K. (1993) 'Domain knowledge, cognitive styles, and problem solving: A qualitative study of student approaches to logo programming', *Journal of Computing in Childhood Education*, **4**, 2, pp. 153–82.

TENNANT, M. (1988) *Psychology and Adult Learning*, London: Routledge.

THORPE, R., BUNKER, D. and ALMOND, L. (1986) *Rethinking Games Teaching*, Loughborough University: Loughborough University Press.

TORRANCE, E.P. and ROCKENSTEIN, Z.L. (1988) 'Styles of thinking and creativity', in SCHMECK, R.R. (ed.) *Learning Strategies and Learning Styles*, New York: Plenum Press, pp. 275–90.

WATKINS, D. (1982) 'Factors influencing the study methods of Australian tertiary students', *Higher Education*, **11**, pp. 369–80.

WATKINS, D. and HATTIE, J. (1990) 'Individual and contextual differences in approaches to learning of Australian secondary school students', *Educational Psychology*, **10**, 4, pp. 333–42.

WEINSTEIN, C.E. (1994) 'Strategic learning/strategic teaching: Flip sides of a coin', in PINTRICH, P.R., BROWN, D.R. and WEINSTEIN, C.E. (eds) *Student Motivation, Cognition, and Learning: Essays in Honour of Wilbert J. McKeachie*, Hillsdale, NJ: Lawrence Erlbaum Associates, pp. 257–73.

WEINSTEIN, C.E. and MAYER, R.E. (1986) 'The teaching of learning strategies', in WITTROCK, M.C. (ed.) *Handbook of Research on Teaching*, New York: Macmillan Publishing Company, pp. 315–27.

WEISS, M.R., EBBECK, V. and ROSE, D.E. (1992) '"Show and tell" in the gymnasium revisited: Developmental differences in modelling and verbal rehearsal of motor skills', *Research Quarterly for Exercise and Sport*, **63**, pp. 292–301.

WINOGRAD, P. and HARE, V.C. (1988) 'Direct instruction of reading comprehension strategies: The nature of teacher explanation', in WEINSTEIN, C.E., GOETZ, E.T. and ALEXANDER, P.A. (eds) *Learning and Study Strategies: Issues in Assessment, Instruction, and Evaluation*, San Diego: Academic Press Inc., pp. 121–39.

WITKIN, H.A., MOORE, C.A., GOODENOUGH, D.R. and COX, P.W. (1977) 'Field-dependent and field-independent cognitive styles and their educational implications', *Review of Educational Research*, **47**, 1, pp. 1–64.

WITTROCK, M.C. (1988) 'A constructive review of research on learning strategies', in WEINSTEIN, C.E., GOETZ, E.T. and ALEXANDER, P.A. (eds) *Learning and Study Strategies: Issues in Assessment, Instruction, and Evaluation*, San Diego: Academic Press Inc., pp. 287–97.

Part 3

The Teaching of Physical Education

5 Teaching Styles and Teaching Approaches in Physical Education: Research Developments

Mick Mawer

Introduction

There has been a great deal of recent interest in teaching models, methods, styles, and strategies. In the UK, government publications have recommended that teachers should employ a range of teaching 'strategies' (Department for Education DfE, 1992, 1995), teaching 'approaches' (Curriculum Council for Wales CCW, 1992), or teaching 'styles', in order to cater for different pupil ages, abilities, needs and attainment levels, and have the flexibility to use a variety of teaching strategies in one lesson (Department of Education and Science DES, 1985).

In order to achieve the various National Curriculum Physical Education (NCPE) objectives that require pupils to develop the ability to 'compare', 'make judgments', 'analyse', 'review', 'adapt', 'refine', 'interpret', 'design', 'find imaginative solutions to challenges', 'devise strategies', 'evaluate' their work, and work cooperatively with others as a member of a team or group (National Curriculum Council NCC, 1992; DfE, 1995), it is suggested that more pupil-centred and less direct teaching approaches would allow pupils to take a more independent and active role in decision making in PE lessons (Whitehead and Capel, 1993; Office for Standards in Education OFSTED, 1995). But, are we confident that the range of recommended teaching approaches are able to achieve their predicted outcomes? In fact, over the last 40 years there has been a degree of scepticism concerning the educational value of different teaching models, methods, strategies and styles.

In 1974 Dunkin and Biddle were critical of the number of ideologies that existed concerning the nature of teaching, most of which had little research support:

> At best such ideologies are unsupported by evidence: at worst they are monstrously in error. The only way we can tell for sure is to subject them to research in which the actual processes of teaching are observed. (p. 29)

Joyce and Weil (1986) endorsed this view:

> There is much quackery abroad in educationland — much selling of models as panaceas with little evidence that they can achieve even limited goals. (p. 490)

They recommended dialogue and research into both the direct instructional and personal and social effects of each model.

At this time Muska Mosston published his 'Spectrum of Teaching Styles' in *Teaching Physical Education* (Mosston, 1966) — a theoretical framework of alternative teaching approaches based on the many decisions that are made within the teaching/learning process, and each 'style' being linked to specific learning outcomes. Also, in the UK, Mauldon and Redfern (1969, 1981) were questioning the more traditional approaches to teaching games, and were advocating an approach to developing games skills within the context of the game. In the early 1980s, Bunker and Thorpe (1983) building upon Mauldon and Redferns' work, developed an 'understanding approach' to teaching games based on the premise that the traditional emphasis on the teaching of the skills of games had led to a general lack of understanding of game principles on the part of many pupils, and particularly those who had difficulty mastering game skills. This 'teaching for understanding' approach to games teaching (TGFU), in which pupils are encouraged to think more about the decisions they make when playing games, is also in keeping with a growing interest in 'constructivist' teaching approaches (Kirk and MacDonald, 1998), and strategies that encourage 'critical thinking' in physical education (McBride, 1991, 1995).

But, in recommending the use of this variety of teaching approaches to achieve NCPE objectives, are we advocating unsubstantiated teaching ideologies, theories or 'philosophical positions', rather than well researched pedagogies? For example, constructivism itself has been viewed as a set of ideological assumptions (Phillips, 1995) and there have been frequent calls for research evidence to support the predicted benefits of TGFU (Chandler and Mitchell, 1990) and other more indirect, inquiry-oriented teaching approaches in physical education (Goldberger and Howarth, 1993). The question is, to what extent has that much needed research begun to materialize, and what has it achieved to date?

The aim of this chapter is to review the following four pedagogical topics that have particularly interested researchers in recent years, and in which there is a growing research base of empirical knowledge of value to practitioners:

- Mosston's Spectrum of Teaching Styles
- Developments in teaching critical thinking skills in PE
- Direct and indirect approaches to teaching games
- Cooperative teaching and learning approaches in PE

However, before proceeding, it is important to clarify the terminology to be used in this chapter, as teaching 'styles', 'strategies' and 'approaches' are often used interchangeably in the literature. As this debate has been conducted elsewhere (Mawer, 1993, 1995), the conclusions of those previous discussions will be applied here. The term 'teaching approach' will be largely preferred because it is used in UK National Curriculum PE (NCPE) documents (CCW, 1992), and in most of the relevant literature. The exception to the rule will be when making reference to Mosston's (1966) work, when his preferred term 'styles' will be used.

Research Related to Mosston's Spectrum of Teaching Styles in Physical Education

In an article summarizing research on teaching physical education up to the early 1970s, Nixon and Locke (1973) considered Mosston's Spectrum of Teaching Styles (Mosston, 1966) as:

> ... the most significant advance in the theory of physical education pedagogy in recent history ... (p. 1227)

As the objective of this review is not to provide a full description of each style in Mosston's Spectrum, the reader is referred to Mosston and Ashworth (1986, 1994) for a more detailed account. However, the brief summary or 'essence' of each style within Mosston's *Reproductive* and *Productive* clusters of styles (see Mosston and Ashworth, 1986, pp. 236–7) shown in Figure 5.1 should inform the reader of what teacher and learner are doing within each style.

Figure 5.1: *Mosston's spectrum of teaching styles*

The Reproductive Cluster of Styles

Style A: Command Style
- The learner responds immediately, precisely and accurately to the stimulus or model provided by the teacher.
- Group teaching would involve a synchronized response.

Style B: Practice Style
- The learner has time to practise the task assigned and demonstrated by the teacher.
- The teacher provides individual and group feedback.

Style C: Reciprocal Style
- Learners work in pairs and take turns to observe and give each other feedback based on performance criteria (provided by the teacher on a criteria task card).
- The teacher provides feedback to observers concerning their role.

Style D: Self-check Style
- Learners use a self-check performance criteria task card provided by the teacher to evaluate their own learning.

Style E: Inclusion Style
- The teacher provides different levels of difficulty for the task.
- Learners decide at which level of difficulty to work at the task.

The Productive Cluster of Styles

Style F: The Guided Discovery or Convergent Problem Solving Style
- The teacher designs a series of questions that leads the learner through a series of small steps to 'discover' the solution to a problem.
- The learner is involved in the convergent process of thinking about a particular conceptual or movement problem.

Style G: The Divergent Problem Solving Style
- The learner is involved in discovering alternative answers to a question or problem set by the teacher to which there may be a number of possible solutions.

Style H: The Individual Programme Learner Design Style
- The learner designs his or her own learning programme, seeking the teacher's help when required.

Based on Mosston, M. and Ashworth, S. (1986) *Teaching Physical Education*, Columbus, OH: Merrill.

Whereas Mosston has always emphasized the *non-versus* notion — that each style can accomplish a certain set of objectives unique to that style — researchers have tended to compare the effects of different styles on learning outcomes. The research to date has therefore tended to either compare teaching styles within the reproductive cluster, or compare reproductive with productive styles.

Reproductive Cluster Research

Is the practice style better than the reciprocal style for skill development, or the reciprocal style better than the practice style for social development? These were the sort of questions asked by researchers examining styles within the reproductive cluster.

Early studies in the 1970s (e.g. Bryant, 1974; Gerney, 1979; Virgilio, 1979) produced inconclusive results because of methodological problems, but more recent research has produced some interesting findings.

Goldberger's first series of studies (Goldberger, Gerney and Chamberlain, 1982; Goldberger, 1983; Goldberger and Gerney, 1986) compared the effects of the practice, reciprocal and inclusion styles on the hockey skill acquisition and social development of elementary school pupils. Goldberger (1992) concluded that although all three styles were effective in terms of motor skill acquisition, it was the practice style that consistently produced the better results, and particularly with low ability pupils. Earlier, Chamberlain (1979) had also noted the superiority of the practice style for skill acquisition. As predicted by Mosston (1966), Goldberger also found that the reciprocal style enhanced social development in that pupils trained to 'help' their partners provided more feedback, praise and encouragement, expressed more empathy, and asked for more feedback than other groups. Results concerning the inclusion style did not support Mosston's predictions, as it was not as effective for exceptional learners, low ability pupils or those from a high or low socio-economic community as anticipated (Goldberger, 1983, 1992). However, Goldberger admits that this aspect of the studies was poorly designed, because pupils had difficulty understanding their inclusion style options (Goldberger, 1995).

Other studies have largely tended to support Goldberger's findings concerning the superiority of the practice style for motor skill acquisition, and the value of the reciprocal style for enhancing social development. For example, Beckett (1990) found the practice style effective for teaching college students a soccer skill, Boyce (1992) found the command and practice styles superior to the inclusion style for skill acquisition and retention in rifle shooting, and studies of the teaching of racketball, volleyball and basketball skills using a 'mastery learning' teaching approach (similar to the practice style) have recorded more effective learning than non-mastery approaches (Blakemore, 1985; Blakemore et al., 1992). Goldberger (Goldberger and Gerney, 1990) went on to compare the traditional practice style with 'station' teaching using elementary school children learning a football punting task. Both practice styles were effective for improving skill performance, but low ability pupils benefited more from the learner-initiated than the teacher-directed rotation.

Regarding investigations of the social benefits of the reciprocal style, Goldberger (1995) cites a lacrosse study by Goldberger, Gerney and Dort, in which the reciprocal group used more social statements a minute and were more skilled at analysing movements and detecting errors than the practice group.

One of the criticisms of earlier spectrum research was that few studies accounted for individual differences in learning. Therefore, some studies focused on which teaching styles were most effective for learners with different aptitudes and abilities, and how different styles influenced self-efficacy. What were referred to as Aptitude Treatment Interactions (ATI) are present '. . . when persons high in some aptitude profit most from one kind of instruction, while persons low in that aptitude profit from another kind of instruction' (Griffey, 1983, p. 265). This occurs when a learner's characteristics (e.g. skill level) and teaching style interact to affect achievement. Teaching style studies examining ATIs include the high school volleyball investigation by Griffey (1983) using the practice and command teaching styles. Results indicated that high ability students and females performed better with the practice style, and low ability students did better with the command style.

In a later ATI study by Harrison et al. (1995) using 58 high school students in two volleyball classes, attempts were made to counter criticisms of some spectrum studies that insufficient instructional time was used to produce the intended outcome (Goldberger, 1992; Piéron, 1995). They used 'rate of improvement' in skill and self-efficacy, rather than skills test results, as measures of learning. Command and practice styles were used with some differentiation by task and progression applied to both styles. Results indicated that low skilled learners did better with the command style for the 'set', and the practice style for the 'spike'. Self-efficacy increased for all subjects regardless of teaching style. The authors considered that low skilled students benefited from the practice style with the spike because of the use of small increments in skill development, and because they could stay at each level for as long as they felt necessary. They felt the command style was better for the set because the students needed the teacher to determine whether they had achieved the criterion level before moving on.

In one of the few studies examining self-check and inclusion styles, Jenkins and Byra (1996), using elementary school pupils, found that the self-check style offered more decision-making opportunities than the practice style as Mosston predicted, and that learners used a greater number of cognitive operations (e.g. comparing, contrasting, evaluating) within the inclusion style.

Productive Cluster Research

There are very few studies that have investigated the productive cluster of the spectrum, and this may be because it is difficult to provide valid and reliable outcome measures (Goldberger, 1995).

The only study examining the guided discovery style was that by Salter and Graham (1985) using an Experimental Teaching Unit with 12 intact elementary school classes being taught a novel golf task once using the command style and once the guided discovery style. Results indicated that cognitive understanding improved significantly for both teaching styles compared with the no-instruction group.

Cleland (1994) compared a direct teaching approach (combination of command and practice styles) with the divergent problem solving style on elementary school childrens' divergent movement ability (DMA), or ability to execute as many movement responses as possible in response to a manipulative ball handling task, obstacle course, and balance/stability bench task. Cleland used thinking and moving creativity measures, and found that the divergent production group significantly improved on the DMA measure, and were superior to both the practice and control group.

In a pilot study reported by Goldberger (1995, 1997), Goldberger, Vedelli and Pitts (1995) used the Purdue Elementary Problem Solving Inventory (PEPSI) as the measure of divergent problem solving ability to compare the practice style with the divergent problem solving style in an elementary school summer gymnastic programme. Preliminary results (Goldberger, 1995, 1997) indicated that the divergent problem solving group had improved on four of the twelve PEPSI factors, including ability to sense the problem, ability to identify key aspects of the problem, ability to redefine the context for new solutions, and ability to judge if more information is needed.

Implications of Spectrum Research

Regardless of his criticism (Goldberger et al., 1982) that many of the earlier inconclusive spectrum studies were limited because of insufficient instructional time, lack of understanding of the spectrum, unreliable dependent measures, lack of control of extraneous variables known to interact with teacher behaviour variables, and that in some cases only one teacher (often the investigator) was used teaching only one intact group per treatment, Goldberger (1995) suggests the following implications of the spectrum research to date:

- the command style has the power to control behaviour;
- the practice style is particularly effective for learning basic motor skills;
- the reciprocal style appears to have positive effects on certain aspects of social development;
- the effects of the self-check and inclusion styles on emotional development is less clear.

Concerning productive cluster research, Goldberger (1995) considers the research to date has tended to support Mosston's predictions, regardless of the problem of defining valid and reliable outcomes. However, Piéron (1995) and Harrison et al. (1995) are more critical, and consider that most research uses elementary school pupils, fails to use intact classes, and is of short duration. Lee (1991), however, highlights one of the problems that has 'dogged' research on teaching and teaching styles — that is the performance versus learning issue, and the 'inability to separate temporary from more permanent learning situations' (p. 376). She considers that the inconclusive results of many of the teaching styles studies that have involved learners in some decision-making responsibility in lessons, might have been due to the lack of a long-term effects measurement.

Although at first sight there appears to be a dearth of studies examining the productive cluster of the spectrum, the two recent areas of research interest about to be discussed have begun to investigate teaching approaches that involve pupils in thinking more critically about what they are learning.

Developments in Teaching Critical Thinking Skills in PE

McBride (1991), in his overview of the literature, defines critical thinking as:

> ... reflective thinking that is used to make reasonable *and* defensible decisions about movement tasks or challenges. (p. 115)

Critical thinking is not simply a set of skills, but a process which involves metacognition — the planning, revision and evaluation of one's own thinking. To effectively teach for critical thinking, Howarth (1997) believes teachers need to be aware of the meaning of metacognition (see Chapter Three for further discussion of metacognition).

For critical thinking to occur McBride (1991) believes that the learner must be placed in a state of cognitive dissonance, disturbance (Festinger, 1957) or mental dissatisfaction, and therefore motivated to inquire and find a solution. This situation then activates the cognitive functions needed for critical thinking, such as comparing, contrasting, drawing inferences and testing hypotheses. Teaching for critical thinking requires teaching approaches that create cognitive dissonance and a state of inquiry, and involves the learner in evaluation, analysis, and diagnosis. The use of questioning, as prompts or cues, assists the learner in the critical thinking process (Schwager and Labate, 1993), with more open-ended or divergent questions considered to be more effective than convergent questions (Miller, 1987).

McBride, Gabbard and Miller (1990) suggest that Mosston's Spectrum of Teaching Styles might be used to inspire critical thinking, particularly more student-centred styles such as guided discovery (Blitzer, 1995).

Both Cleland and Pearse (1995) and McBride (1991) believe that in the initial stages of instruction a more direct approach involving demonstration styles and practice might be used to convey declarative and procedural knowledge of the skills of a sport, and then more student-centred styles, such as reciprocal and problem solving, might be used to enhance the development of critical thinking skills.

Although there are good practical suggestions for teaching critical thinking skills in physical education (Blitzer, 1995; Schwager and Labate, 1993; Tishman and Perkins, 1995; Woods and Book, 1995), research investigating the use of teaching approaches for critical thinking are scarce. Cleland (1994) examined the effect of PE content and teaching style on one component of critical thinking in PE —

divergent movement ability, an amalgam of two aspects of movement creativity in which pupils are encouraged to solve, through movement, a variety of movement problems using various critical thinking strategies (e.g. asking questions, comparing and contrasting solutions). Results indicated that indirect teaching styles, such as divergent production, can lead to greater pupil creativity.

One of the teaching approaches which Schwager and Labate (1993) considered to be particularly effective in encouraging students to think critically, is the TGFU or tactical approach to games education (Thorpe, Bunker and Almond, 1986; Werner, 1989).

Direct and Indirect Approaches to Teaching Games

Direct teaching involves teachers in making most of the decisions concerning the learning environment — selecting content, designing progression, and communicating the task. Mosston's command and practice styles are examples of direct teaching approaches. Indirect approaches such as those in Mosston's productive cluster, offer more opportunity for pupils to make decisions and be more involved in their own learning.

As far as games are concerned, it has generally been assumed that a minimum level of proficiency in the skills of the game is required before one can effectively play the game, and the best way to approach such skill development may be through 'direct instruction' (Rink, 1993). Direct instruction has attracted considerable research support as a model of effective teaching for motor skill development (French et al., 1991; Gustart and Sprigings, 1989; Housner, 1990; Silverman, 1991; Werner and Rink, 1989), whereas attempts to see if simply playing the game would develop motor skills have been unsuccessful (French and Thomas, 1987).

One indirect approach to teaching games has been referred to as the 'tactical' or 'teaching games for understanding' (TGFU) approach (Thorpe, Bunker and Almond, 1986). The authors suggest that pupils may benefit more from being initially taught tactical awareness and game appreciation, rather than by focusing on the teaching of skills, as a means of developing ability to play the game. Because the more traditional approach introduces skills outside the context of the game situation, Thorpe et al. (1986) believe that pupils may not learn the tactical knowledge to be able to make effective decisions in the game. In the TGFU approach, the skills of the game are often 'reduced' or substituted (e.g. throwing for striking), and simplified and modified games introduced, to facilitate understanding of game principles and tactics. Game skills are then taught when the pupils are ready to put a particular game strategy into operation, as with the need to develop force in a clear shot in badminton to enable the player to use the clear offensively.

Rink, French and Tjeerdsma (1996) refer to TGFU as a:

> ... developmental approach to learning and is particularly associated with a developmentalist constructivist orientation to learning and curriculum that emphasises 'experiential learning' and 'discovery learning'. (p. 400)

Constructivist approaches to learning involve the use and transfer of problem solving skills in which the pupils are the prime movers in the learning process, and which enable the learner to see the relationships between content and construct 'cognitive maps' for what has been learned. In this way the content is more meaningful, is learned more easily, and pupil motivation is consequently high. Although research examining such inquiry-oriented approaches is inconclusive, positive outcomes have been reported regarding self-concept and attitude to learning (Gage, 1985; Tamir, 1996).

But, is the tactical, TGFU approach more effective for the learning of games than a skill or technique approach? Until recently, the main criticism of TGFU was that its supporters could only offer philosophical and anecdotal evidence (Doolittle and Girard, 1991; Thorpe et al., 1986; Werner and Almond, 1990) to support their theory, and that more pedagogical research was needed. A number of studies have now been conducted, the majority attempting to compare the effects of the two teaching approaches on the following criteria related to ability to play and enjoy games:

- knowledge
- game playing ability
- skill development
- enjoyment of games

Knowledge

According to Turner and Martinek (1995), one of the advantages of the TGFU approach is that it develops the kind of knowledge needed for effective decision-making in games. By this they mean that a foundation of *declarative knowledge* (factual knowledge of rules, players positions) is necessary for the development of *procedural knowledge* ('what to do'), and therefore, those who are more knowledgeable about a sport, are more likely to make the appropriate decisions in a game situation. This view is supported by studies of basketball and tennis (French and Thomas, 1987; McPherson and Thomas, 1989), hockey (Turner, 1996), soccer (Mitchell, Griffin and Oslin, 1997), volleyball (Griffin, Oslin and Mitchell, 1995) and badminton (French et al., 1996b). All of these studies found that the tactical teaching groups scored significantly higher than other treatment groups concerning tactical knowledge. Only the Lawton (1989) badminton study, and the Turner and Martinek (1992) field hockey study failed to show a significant difference between tactical and technique groups on declarative and procedural knowledge. Although not significant, Turner and Martinek (1996) later evaluated students' ability to match game conditions with appropriate responses in 'if-then' games context scenarios, and found the TGFU group outperforming the techniques group for procedural knowledge. However, they considered that the technique group may have acquired tactical knowledge during games played at the end of technique lessons, or by transfer of tactical knowledge from playing other invasion games. Related to this, McPherson and French (1991) suggest that when instruction is direct and technique-oriented, then skill development occurs, but cognitive components (decision-making and declarative knowledge) also improve concurrently. They also considered that as cognitive aspects of games may be more easily learned than skills, this might explain why their technique group acquired cognitive aspects through game play.

McPherson (1994) also interviewed subjects concerning their thoughts when making game decisions, and found that the tactical group appeared to plan and use more sophisticated tactical responses than the technique group. However, the author also considered that when skill development and strategy appreciation are taught at the same time, an interference or 'attentional capacity' (Kahneman, 1973) effect may occur, in which students appear to have difficulty attending to motor skill development and strategy appreciation at the same time. French et al. (1996b) noted a similar effect with the combination group (skill and tactics) in their badminton study.

Game Playing Ability

Studies that have examined the effects of the two teaching approaches on game playing ability, have used criteria related to control, decision making and execution in the game situation. Earlier research, with limited treatment periods, (Rink, French and Werner, 1991; Turner and Martinek, 1992) found no significant differences between the two approaches. However, Turner and Martinek's later research extended the treatment period to 15 lessons and included a more accurate method of assessing games playing ability. For example, in Turner's (1996) hockey study the TGFU group improved significantly more than the technique group on declarative knowledge, control of the ball, and decision making. In a follow-up hockey study Turner and Martinek (1996) found that the TGFU group were more successful than the technique or control group in terms of control of the hockey ball, making passing, dribbling and shooting decisions, and in passing execution during the game. They believed that ability to control the hockey ball offered more opportunities for decision making. Other studies have been less successful. For example, the soccer study by Mitchell, Oslin and Griffin (1995), using a different instrument to measure game performance, found little improvement in decision making by either TGFU or technique group. However, this study also investigated players 'off the ball' movement (e.g. supporting, marking, covering) as an additional measure of game performance, and found that the tactical group displaying a higher level of game involvement and 'off the ball' movement.

Regarding racket sports, although the French et al. (1996a) three-week badminton study noted no difference between skill, tactical and combination groups in terms of decision making, the longer six-week study (French et al., 1996b) found the tactical and combination groups had improved more in decision making than the skill or control group. Gabrielle and Maxwell (1995) also reported that the game-centred group in their squash study were better at making effective decisions (e.g. shot selection) during the game.

As far as skill execution in the game is concerned, although some studies found no significant differences between tactical and skill groups (Gabrielle and Maxwell, 1995; Griffin et al., 1995; Mitchell et al., 1995; Turner and Martinek, 1992; Turner, 1996), the French et al. (1996a, 1996b) badminton studies did find the skill group outperforming (although not significant) tactical and combination groups. Also, the TGFU group in Turner and Martinek's (1996) hockey study displayed significantly better passing execution during games than the control or technique group, a result which the authors attributed to the combined skill/strategy TGFU instruction they employed. In keeping with the views of McPherson and French (1991), they considered that strategy and skill instruction must be integrated during game play for game execution to improve.

Skill Development

Most studies have found no significant differences between the two teaching approaches in terms of skill development (as measured by skill tests), regardless of the sport being studied. This includes studies of badminton (Lawton, 1989; Rink et al., 1991), soccer (Mitchell et al., 1995, 1997), volleyball (Griffin et al., 1995; Harrison et al., 1998), and field hockey (Turner and Martinek, 1992, 1996; Turner, 1996). However, the Turner and Martinek hockey studies did note an improvement in dribbling skill over time for both treatments, and in their 1996 study the technique group proved to be significantly quicker than the control group on the skill test speed component, and, although not significant, slightly faster than the TGFU group. A similar superior performance for the skill group (although not significant) was noted in the French et al. (1996a, 1996b) badminton studies.

Enjoyment of Games

What do students themselves feel about the TGFU/tactical and skill/technique teaching approaches? Chandler (1996) argues that as the TGFU approach is more student-centred and provides opportunities for task mastery, it therefore facilitates student motivation. But is this the case? Although Tjeerdsma et al. (1996) found no affective advantage for either approach, some students did not like the teacher constantly stopping the game to teach tactics. Turner (1996) and Ronholt and Pieterson (1989) reported that students were more motivated when they used the TGFU approach, and Liu Yuk-kwong and Thorpe (1997) noted that pupils found the cognitive approach more enjoyable. Mitchell, Griffin and Oslin (1997) found no significant motivational differences for the two approaches, but teachers reported a difference in pupil motivation in the tactical class. In Griffin and Oslin's (1997) study of teachers and students perceptions of the tactical approach, students commented that the tactical approach offered a 'deeper meaning to their own game' (p. A79) and did not require them to go through repetitive and redundant skill drills that they already knew.

Implications for Research and Teaching

As an embryonic field of research, there have been criticisms of the studies investigating direct and indirect approaches to teaching games.

According to Rink, French and Tjeerdsma (1996) many earlier inconclusive studies devoted too little time to the instructional intervention to expect any real knowledge and skill development. Consequently, more recent studies employed longer intervention periods.

Some studies have failed to clarify what the teaching approach treatment included, making it difficult to compare results. For example, it is not always clear the extent to which tactical groups are taught skills, skills groups are taught tactics, or whether both treatment groups have the opportunity to play the game without explicit instruction. Although later studies have attempted to provide more detailed information, different treatments still make comparisons difficult.

Rink, French and Tjeerdsma (1996) were also critical of the variables used by a number of studies and the lack of clarity concerning the criteria used to assess decision-making and skill execution.

Therefore, what can be concluded from this brief review of research interest in approaches to teaching games? Which is the superior teaching approach? Rink, French and Graham (1996) feel that the question should not be an either–or question, but that direct and indirect approaches should be viewed on a continuum, and good teachers will use an appropriate approach for the pupil at a particular point in their development of playing and understanding games. Reflecting on the results of their studies, they do consider that the tactical approach to teaching games is not 'the silver bullet its advocates might have hoped', and that a combination of the two approaches might be the 'most logical instructional approach for teaching both tactics and skill' (p. 500). They also consider that although the tactical approach may have its merits, more research with different groups and different sports will help teachers to appreciate *when* it may be more appropriate to teach sports using an indirect or direct approach. Turner and Martinek (1995) also make the point that future research may need to consider the interaction of student learning styles with teaching approach.

But, regardless of these criticisms, the content-specific nature of the research, and the various methodological problems confronting researchers, are there *some* practical suggestions for the teacher of physical education?

In invasion games such as hockey and soccer both Turner and Martinek (1995, 1996) and Mitchell, Griffin and Oslin (1995, 1997) feel that a TGFU/tactical teaching approach is important for the development of the tactical knowledge required for solving the decision-making and skill execution problems that occur in games, and for greater game involvement.

Concerning racket games, both McPherson and French (1991) and Gabrielle and Maxwell (1995) suggest that teaching tactics may lead to pupils making more tactical responses and effective decisions in such games as tennis and squash, and recent evidence suggests that such tactical understanding may transfer to other net games (Oslin and Mitchell, 1998).

On the basis of their literature review and the results of their badminton studies Rink, French and Graham (1996) suggest the following implications for teaching games:

- Based on the badminton studies by French et al. (1996a, 1996b) and the Turner and Martinek (1992, 1996) hockey studies, pupils may need to have minimal control of the object (e.g. ball, shuttle) before they can use tactics, so it may be better to teach skill first.
- As skill and strategy are linked, decision making may be constrained if pupils cannot perform the skills of the game. Therefore, in games such as badminton, the development of force-production skills may need to precede tactics.
- As beginners may have difficulty concentrating on skills and tactics at the same time, the teaching of a block of skills first to provide a basic level of object control may be needed before they can use tactics.
- The indirect teaching of generic tactics within modified or reduced game forms at the primary age may have some value, but as pupils become more skilful, tactics in the form of if-then relationships specific to the sport may then need to be taught more directly. Although research suggests that general tactics can be 'picked up' through playing the game, teachers should teach tactics directly or indirectly whenever appropriate.
- As language facilitates thinking, encouraging pupils to use a specific language for talking about both skill and tactics, whether directly or indirectly (e.g. questioning), may develop pupils expertise in playing games.

But, the main implication of this growing body of literature on the teaching of tactical appreciation in games is the need for curricular time to be devoted to tactical awareness, and skills to have a tactical application and be set in a games context (Siedentop, 1996).

Cooperative Teaching and Learning Approaches

According to the UK NCPE (NCC, 1992), physical education has an important role to play in promoting the development of pupils' personal and social skills through the encouragement of 'an ability to work co-operatively with others by being a member of a team or group' (p. G6). But, what is known about the effectiveness of cooperative teaching approaches?

Cooperative learning is a student-centred 'model' of teaching (Joyce et al., 1997) in which students work together in structured small groups to learn material that is planned and presented by the teacher. Cooperative approaches are designed to develop group interdependence, individual accountability for learning and one's personal contribution to the group task, shared ownership of the outcome, and the social benefits of providing learning support for each other (Sharan, 1990; Slavin, 1983) According to Joyce et al. (1997) research on cooperative learning is 'overwhelmingly positive' (p. 101), and cooperative approaches are effective over a variety of different achievement measures.

Although cooperative approaches have been recommended for games (Orlick, 1978) and primary PE (Lavin, 1989), until recently, there has been little research to support the perceived benefits of this approach in physical education. However, Grineski (1996) reports a number of studies with elementary and disabled children that suggest that a cooperative approach can lead to greater improvement in physical fitness and more positive social interactions than an individual or competitive instructional format. More recently, Grineski (1997) found that a cooperative games intervention programme promoted improved social behaviour in a group of 16 3–4-year-old disabled children. Similarly, Smith et al. (1997) reported that cooperative learning had a positive effect on the social skills and participation of third grade pupils.

Dyson and Harper's (1997) research using a task structure observation system with two sixth grade classes, found that lower class instruction, management, transition, and wait time, more efficient class organization and higher pupil engaged practice time, were the benefits of a cooperative approach. The classteacher also felt that her specific feedback was more effective, and that pupils were more accountable for task completion. Pupils also reported that they had improved their personal skills, and that group discussion of team strategies helped the team to improve.

Strachan and MacCauley (1997) used a cooperative approach with eighth and eleventh grade classes that involved students in reviewing learned material, planning games strategies, and reflection after games. Results revealed that although both groups had low management, transition and wait times, the eleventh grade class (in their fourth year of cooperative instruction) experienced less instruction time, more task engagement time, and more successful responses than the eighth grade class.

The limited research to date therefore suggests that a cooperative teaching approach may have benefits for pupil learning in PE in terms of the development of interpersonal and social skills and greater time on task.

Teaching Approaches in Physical Education:
What Are Teachers Doing?

This short review has provided some idea of the present state of research support concerning a selection of the teaching approaches used in physical education. But, are teachers using the full range of approaches available to them? Except for the earlier investigation by Kane (1976), only two studies have examined the use of different teaching approaches by PE teachers.

Curtner-Smith and Hasty (1997) studied 20 teachers in five schools using videotape analysis to see whether the introduction of NCPE had led to teachers using a wider range of Mosston's teaching styles. Results indicated that there was little change in the styles used pre- and post-NCPE, with 55.94 per cent (pre

NCPE) and 50.35 per cent (post NCPE) use of the practice style, 11.5 per cent and 5.98 per cent the command style, 4.59 per cent and 4.74 per cent the guided discovery style, 4.06 per cent and 3.12 per cent the divergent style, 1.98 per cent and 2.72 per cent the reciprocal style, 1.64 per cent and 1.08 per cent the inclusion style, and 0.00 per cent and 0.73 per cent the self-check style.

Evans, Davies and Penney's (1996) study of teaching after NCPE examined teacher's use of the more teacher-directed 'formal' and student-centred 'informal' (e.g. problem solving) approaches. The authors found that the more formal approaches were used in athletics (81 per cent) and outdoor and adventurous activities (60 per cent), with a tendency towards more informal styles in dance (28 per cent). Dance (53 per cent) and gymnastics (53 per cent) were also more likely to be taught using a mixture of formal and informal approaches than games (44 per cent), with 55 per cent of teachers teaching games with a formal approach. As male teachers were more likely to teach boys using the formal approach, while female teachers preferred the informal approach, the authors suggest that boys may have less opportunity 'to develop the characteristics of spontaneity, creativity, self-discipline and self control', and may become 'educationally disadvantaged' (p. 177).

OFSTED inspectors also noted the use of a restricted range of teaching styles in PE, with learning being mainly teacher-directed and offering little opportunity for pupils to plan and evaluate their work or work independently (Williams, 1997). In a 1997 report by OFSTED (Clay, 1997), it was noted that 'Effective teaching involves pupils both physically and intellectually in their learning; where teaching is weak or narrow in style, pupils are sometimes only passively engaged in the lesson' (p. 6). OFSTED (1995) visualize high quality teaching and learning involving PE teachers using;

> . . . a wide but balanced range of teaching styles — sometimes being firmly didactic when teaching specific skills, sometimes deliberately open-ended in their questioning to encourage pupils to be independent in their decision-making. (p. 4)

According to Evans, Davies and Penney (1996), it was the pupil assessment requirement of NCPE that really exposed PE teachers' lack of knowledge and understanding of the more sophisticated and constructivist teaching approaches that might allow pupils 'independence and opportunities to talk constructively, both to each other and the teacher' (p. 32).

Therefore, there is a developing image of UK PE teachers, and particularly men, using a restricted range of teaching approaches, when many feel that NCPE warrants the use of more productive and constructivist approaches to achieve certain NCPE objectives (Evans, Davies and Penney, 1996; OFSTED, 1995).

Conclusions

The implementation of the UK NCPE, both in terms of curriculum objectives and assessment requirements, appears to require teachers to be aware of the full range of teaching approaches available to them, and understand what each approach may achieve in terms of pupil learning and personal and social development. However, as Evans and Penney (1996) recommend, to improve the quality of teaching and enhance the status of PE, 'We will need to relate teaching to research' (p. 34). But, what can be 'gleaned' from the research evidence to date?

There is certainly a growing body of evidence to suggest that direct teaching approaches, such as the practice style, may be effective for the learning of motor skills; that peer tutor approaches such as the reciprocal teaching style may positively effect aspects of social development; and that cooperative approaches may facilitate interpersonal and social skill development. Unfortunately, many studies supporting these conclusions have been of short duration, and largely used elementary school pupils.

Regardless of the considerable rhetoric and anecdotal support for productive and constructivist approaches, there is still very little empirical evidence to support the predicted benefits of, for example, guided discovery, and problem solving teaching approaches in physical education. However, our research knowledge concerning the value of the tactical approach to teaching games is growing, supporting the need to at least devote curricular time to the teaching of tactical awareness in games, and for skills practices to be set in a game context. To some this is good pedagogy anyway (Fleming, 1994). But, we still know very little about the most effective way to sequence the teaching of skills with the teaching of tactics. There are some suggestions that force-production and minimal control of the object may need to precede the teaching of tactics, but there is also the need for research to consider the complexity of decision making and techniques in certain games (McMorris, 1998).

There is also a paucity of research concerning approaches to differentiation in physical education. UK PE teachers are being constantly criticized for their inability to plan for differentiation (Clay, 1997; OFSTED, 1997) and, although the literature may offer some excellent practical advice for teachers (Williams, 1997), there is little supportive research evidence concerning approaches to differentiation. Regardless of the limited results of studies examining Mosston's inclusion teaching style, there are some suggestions that certain teaching styles may be more appropriate for particular pupil characteristics (Harrison et al., 1995). But, the 'key' variable concerning differentiating through teaching approach may be the pupil's preferred learning style. According to Luke and Hardy (1996), differentiation by teaching approach is problematic if it is assumed that there is a direct link between teaching style and learning outcome, as Mosston and Ashworth (1986) suggest. What Luke and Hardy believe is crucial is how the pupil will interpret the teaching approach being used.

Therefore, more research is needed on teaching approaches in physical education, and one might argue that there is still a degree of 'quackery' abroad in physical educationland. But, just because we don't yet have all the answers, it should not mean that teachers should dismiss the variety of teaching approaches available. As Joyce and Weil (1986) pointed out:

> . . . there is yet so little certain evidence available to us that to wait for a complete picture from research would require us to cease most educational activity for a generation or more. (p. 490)

As much as we need more information about the effectiveness of the teaching approaches we recommend to teachers, we also need to know more about what teachers themselves are thinking and doing. We read anecdotal reports of teachers who have experimented with the more productive and constructivist teaching approaches (British Association of Advisers and Lecturers in Physical Education BAALPE, 1989), but we know very little about what teaching approaches the majority of PE teachers believe in or are using. What teaching approaches *do* they prefer and why? What *is* going on out there?

References

BRITISH ASSOCIATION OF ADVISERS AND LECTURERS IN PHYSICAL EDUCATION (BAALPE) (1989) *Teaching and Learning Strategies in Physical Education*, Leeds: White Line Press.

BECKETT, K. (1990) 'The effects of two teaching styles on college students achievement of selected physical education outcomes', *Journal of Teaching in Physical Education*, **10**, pp. 153–69.

BLAKEMORE, C.L. (1985) 'The effects of mastery learning on the acquisition of psychomotor skills', Unpublished Doctoral Dissertation: Temple University.

BLAKEMORE, C.L., HILTON, H.G., GRESH, J., HARRISON, J.M. and PELLETT, T.L. (1992) 'Comparison of students taught basketball skills using mastery and non-mastery learning methods', *Journal of Teaching in Physical Education*, **12**, pp. 235–47.

BLITZER, L. (1995) 'It's a Gym Class . . . What's There to Think About?', *Journal of Physical Education, Recreation and Dance*, **66**, 6, pp. 44–8.

BOYCE, A. (1992) 'The effects of three styles of teaching on university students motor performance', *Journal of Teaching in Physical Education*, **11**, 1, pp. 389–401.

BRYANT, W. (1974) 'Comparison of the practice and reciprocal styles of teaching', Unpublished Project: Temple University.

BUNKER, D. and THORPE, R. (1983) 'A model for the teaching of games in secondary schools', *Bulletin of Physical Education*, **19**, 1, pp. 5–7.

CHAMBERLAIN, J. (1979) 'The effects of Mosston's practice style and individual programme teacher design on motor skill acquisition and self-concept of fifth grade learners', Unpublished Dissertation: Temple University.

CHANDLER, T. (1996) 'Teaching games for understanding: Reflections and further questions', *Journal of Physical Education, Recreation and Dance*, **67**, 4, pp. 49–55.

CHANDLER, T. and MITCHELL, S. (1990) 'Reflections on models of games education', *Journal of Physical Education, Recreation and Dance*, **61**, 8, pp. 19–21.

CLAY, G. (1997) 'Standards in primary and secondary PE', *British Journal of Physical Education*, **28**, 2, pp. 5–9.

CLELAND, F.E. (1994) 'Young children's divergent movement ability: Study II', *Journal of Teaching in Physical Education*, **13**, 3, pp. 228–41.

CLELAND, F.E. and PEARSE, C. (1995) 'Critical thinking in middle school physical education: Reflections on a yearlong study', *Journal of Physical Education, Recreation and Dance*, **66**, 6, pp. 31–8.

CURRICULUM COUNCIL FOR WALES (CCW) (1992) *Physical Education in the National Curriculum*, Cardiff: CCW.

CURTNER-SMITH, M. and HASTY, D.L. (1997) 'Influence of National Curriculum physical education on teacher's use of teaching styles', *Research Quarterly for Exercise and Sport: Supplement*, **68**, 1, pp. A-75–A-76.

DEPARTMENT FOR EDUCATION (DFE) (1992) *Initial Teacher Training (Secondary Phase)*, Circular 9/92, London: HMSO.

DEPARTMENT FOR EDUCATION (DFE) (1995) *Physical Education in the National Curriculum*, London: HMSO.

DEPARTMENT OF EDUCATION AND SCIENCE (DES) (1985) *Education Observed, 3: Good Teachers*, London: HMSO.

DOOLITTLE, S. and GIRARD, K. (1991) 'A dynamic approach to teaching games in elementary PE', *Journal of Physical Education, Recreation and Dance*, **62**, 4, pp. 57–62.

DUNKIN, M.J. and BIDDLE, B.J. (1974) *The Study of Teaching*, New York: Holt, Rinehart and Winston.

DYSON, B.D. and HARPER, M.L. (1997) 'Co-operative learning in an elementary physical education program', *Research Quarterly for Exercise and Sport: Supplement*, **68**, 1, p. A-68.

EVANS, J. and PENNEY, D. (1996) 'The role of the teacher in physical education: Towards a pedagogy of risk', *British Journal of Physical Education*, **27**, No. 4, pp. 28–36.

EVANS, J., DAVIES, B. and PENNEY, D. (1996) 'Teachers, teaching and the social construction of gender relations', *Sport, Education and Society*, **1**, 2, pp. 165–83.

FESTINGER, L. (1957) *The Theory of Cognitive Dissonance*, Evanstown, IL: Row, Peterson.

FLEMING, S. (1994) 'Understanding "understanding": Making sense of the cognitive approach to the teaching of games', *Physical Education Review*, **17**, 2, pp. 90–6.

FRENCH, K., RINK, J., RIKARD, L., LYNN, S. and WERNER, P. (1991) 'The effect of practice progressions on learning two volleyball skills', *Journal of Teaching in Physical Education*, **10**, pp. 261–74.

FRENCH, K. and THOMAS, J. (1987) 'The relation of knowledge development of children's basketball performance', *Journal of Sport Psychology*, **9**, pp. 15–32.

FRENCH, K., WERNER, P., RINK, J., TAYLOR, K. and HUSSEY, K. (1996a) 'The effects of a 3-week unit of tactical, skill, or combined tactical and skill instruction in badminton performance of ninth-grade students', *Journal of Teaching in Physical Education*, **15**, pp. 418–38.

FRENCH, K., WERNER, P., TAYLOR, K., HUSSEY, K. and JONES, J. (1996b) 'The effects of a 6-week unit of tactical, skill, or combined tactical and skill Instruction on badminton performance of ninth-grade students', *Journal of Teaching in Physical Education*, **15**, pp. 439–63.

GABRIELLE, T. and MAXWELL, T. (1995) 'Direct versus indirect methods of squash instruction', *Research Quarterly for Exercise and Sport: Supplement*, **68**, 1, pp. A-63.

GAGE, N. (1985) *Hard Gains in the Soft Sciences: The Case of Pedagogy*, Bloomington, IN: Phi Delta Kappan.

GERNEY, P.E. (1979) 'The effects of Mosston's practice style and reciprocal style on psychomotor skill acquisition and social development of fifth grade students', Unpublished Dissertation: Temple University.

GOLDBERGER, M. (1983) 'Direct styles of teaching and psychomotor performance', in TEMPLIN, T.J. and OLSON, J. (eds) *Teaching in Physical Education*, Champaign, IL: Human Kinetics, pp. 211–23.

GOLDBERGER, M. (1992) 'The spectrum of teaching styles: A perspective for research on teaching physical education', *Journal of Physical Education, Recreation and Dance*, **63**, 1, pp. 42–6.

GOLDBERGER, M. (1995) 'Research on the spectrum of teaching styles', in LIDOR, R., ELDAR, E. and HARARI, I. (eds) *Windows to the Future: Bridging the Gaps between Disciplines, Curriculum and Instruction*, Proceedings of the 1995 AIESEP World Congress Part 2, Wingate Institute for Physical Education and Sport, Israel, pp. 429–35.

GOLDBERGER, M. (1997) Personal Communication.

GOLDBERGER, M. and GERNEY, P. (1986) 'The effects of direct teaching styles on motor skill acquisition of fifth grade children', *Research Quarterly for Exercise and Sport*, **57**, pp. 215–19.

GOLDBERGER, M. and GERNEY, P. (1990) 'Effects of learner use of practice time on skill acquisition of fifth grade children', *Journal of Teaching in Physical Education*, **10**, pp. 84–95.

GOLDBERGER, M., GERNEY, P. and CHAMBERLAIN, J. (1982) 'The effects of three styles of teaching on the psychomotor performance and social skill development of fifth grade children', *Research Quarterly for Exercise and Sport*, **53**, pp. 116–24.

GOLDBERGER, M. and HOWARTH, K. (1993) 'The National Curriculum in physical education and the spectrum of teaching styles', *British Journal of Physical Education*, **24**, 1, pp. 23–8.

GOLDBERGER, M., VEDELLI, J. and PITTS, C. (1995) 'The effects of the divergent production style of teaching on children's problem solving ability', Paper presented at the Southern District Association AAHPERD Convention, Orlando, FL.

GRIFFEY, D.C. (1983) 'Hunting the elusive ATI: How pupil aptitudes mediate instruction in the gymnasium', in TEMPLIN, T.J. and OLSON, J. (eds) *Teaching in Physical Education*, Champaign, IL: Human Kinetics, pp. 265–76.

GRIFFIN, L. and OSLIN, J. (1997) 'Implementing a tactical approach: Teachers' and students' perspectives', *Research Quarterly for Exercise and Sport: Supplement*, **66**, p. A-79.

GRIFFIN, L., OSLIN, J. and MITCHELL, S.A. (1995) 'An analysis of two instructional approaches to teaching net games', *Research Quarterly for Exercise and Sport: Supplement*, **64**, p. A-64.

GRINESKI, S. (1996) *Cooperative Learning in Physical Education*, Champaign, IL: Human Kinetics.

GRINESKI, S. (1997) 'The effect of co-operative games on the promotion of prosocial behaviours of preschool students', *Research Quarterly for Exercise and Sport: Supplement*, **66**, pp. A-67, A-68.

GUSTART, L. and SPRIGINGS, E. (1989) 'Student learning as a measure of teacher effectiveness', *Journal of Teaching in Physical Education*, **8**, pp. 298–311.

HARRISON, J.M., BLAKEMORE, C.L., RICHARDS, R.P., OLIVER, J., WILKINSON, C. and FELLINGHAM, G.W. (1998) 'The effects of two instructional models — tactical and skill teaching — on skill development, knowledge, self-efficacy, game play, and student's perceptions in volleyball', *Research Quarterly for Exercise and Sport: Supplement*, **67**, pp. A-93, A-94.

HARRISON, J.M., FELLINGHAM, G.W., BUCK, M.M. and PELLETT, T.L. (1995) 'Effects of practice and command styles on rate of change in volleyball performance and self-efficacy of high, medium and low skilled learners', *Journal of Teaching in Physical Education*, **14**, pp. 328–39.

HOUSNER, L. (1990) 'Selecting master teachers: Evidence from process–product research', *Journal of Teaching in Physical Education*, **9**, 3, pp. 201–26.

HOWARTH, K. (1997) 'Teaching thinking skills in physical education', *Research Quarterly for Exercise and Sport*, Supplement 66, pp. A-81–A-82.

JENKINS, J. and BYRA, M. (1996) 'An exploration of theoretical constructs associated with the Spectrum of teaching styles', Paper presented at the AIESEP International Seminar, *Research on Teaching and Research on Teacher Education*, November 21–4, Technical University of Lisbon, Portugal.

JOYCE, B., CALHOUN, E. and HOPKINS, D. (1997) *Models for Learning: Tools for Teaching*, Buckingham: Open University Press.

JOYCE, B. and WEIL, M. (1986) *Models of Teaching*, Englewood Cliffs, NJ: Prentice Hall.

KAHNEMAN, D. (1973) *Attention and Effort*, Englewood Cliffs, NJ: Prentice Hall.

KANE, J. (1976) *Physical Education in Secondary Schools: Schools Council Enquiry*, London: MacMillan.

KIRK, D. and MACDONALD, D. (1998) 'Situated learning in physical education', *Journal of Teaching in Physical Education*, **17**, 3, pp. 376–87.

LAVIN, J. (1989) 'Co-operative learning in the primary physical education context', *British Journal of Physical Education*, **20**, 4, pp. 181–2.

LAWTON, J. (1989) 'A comparison of two teaching methods in games', *Bulletin of Physical Education*, **25**, 1, pp. 35–8.

LEE, A. (1991) 'Research on teaching in physical education: Questions and comments', *Journal of Teaching in Physical Education*, **62**, 4, pp. 374–9.

LIU YUK-KWONG, R. and THORPE, R. (1997) *The Introduction of a Cognitive Approach to Games Teaching in Hong Kong*, Proceedings of AIESEP World Conference on Teaching, Coaching and Fitness Needs in Physical Education, Singapore, pp. 125–30.

LUKE, I. and HARDY, C. (1996) 'Differentiation: A consideration of pupils' learning preferences in Physical Education lessons', *Bulletin of Physical Education*, **32**, 2, pp. 32–44.

MAULDON, E. and REDFERN, H.B. (1969) *Games Teaching: A New Approach for the Primary School*, London: MacDonald and Evans.

MAULDON, E. and REDFERN, H.B. (1981) *Games Teaching: An Approach for the Primary School*, London: MacDonald and Evans.

MAWER, M. (1993) 'Teaching styles, teaching strategies and instructional formats in physical education: Total teaching or ideology?', *British Journal of Physical Education*, **24**, 1, pp. 5–9.

MAWER, M. (1995) *The Effective Teaching of Physical Education*, London: Longman.

McBRIDE, R.E. (1991) 'Critical thinking: An overview with implications for Physical Education', *Journal of Teaching in Physical Education*, **11**, pp. 112–25.

McBRIDE, R.E. (1995) 'Critical thinking in physical education . . . An idea whose time has come', *Journal of Physical Education, Recreation and Dance*, **66**, 6, pp. 21–3.

McBRIDE, R., GABBARD, C. and MILLER, G. (1990) 'Teaching critical thinking skills in the psychomotor domain', *The Clearing House*, **63**, pp. 197–201.

McMORRIS, T. (1998) 'Teaching games for understanding: Its contribution to the knowledge of skill acquisition from a motor learning perspective', *European Journal of Physical Education*, **3**, 1, pp. 65–74.

McPHERSON, S. (1994) 'The development of sport expertise: Mapping the tactical domain', *Quest*, **46**, pp. 223–40.

McPHERSON, S. and FRENCH, K. (1991) 'Changes in cognitive strategy and motor skill in tennis', *Journal of Sport and Exercise Psychology*, **13**, pp. 26–41.

McPHERSON, S. and THOMAS, J. (1989) 'Relation of knowledge and performance in boys tennis: Age and expertise', *Journal of Experimental Child Psychology*, **48**, pp. 190–211.

MILLER, D.M. (1987) 'Energizing the thinking dimension of physical education', *Journal of Physical Education, Recreation and Dance*, **58**, 8, pp. 76–85.

MITCHELL, S.A., GRIFFIN, L. and OSLIN, J. (1997) 'Teaching invasion games: A comparison of two instructional approaches', *Pedagogy in Practice*, **3**, 2, pp. 56–69.

MITCHELL, S.A., OSLIN, J. and GRIFFIN, L. (1995) 'The effects of two instructional approaches on game performance', *Pedagogy in Practice*, **1**, 1, pp. 36–48.

MOSSTON, M. (1966, 1981) *Teaching Physical Education*, Columbus, OH: Merrill.

MOSSTON, M. and ASHWORTH, S. (1986, 1994) *Teaching Physical Education*, Columbus, OH: Merrill.

NATIONAL CURRICULUM COUNCIL (NCC) (1992) *Physical Education Non-statutory Guidance*, York: NCC.

NIXON, J. and LOCKE, L. (1973) 'Research on teaching Physical Education', in TRAVERS, R. (ed.) *Handbook of Research on Teaching*, Chicago: Rand McNally, pp. 1210–42.

OFFICE FOR STANDARDS IN EDUCATION (OFSTED) (1995) *Physical Education and Sport in Schools: A Survey of Good Practice*, London: HMSO.

ORLICK, T. (1978) *The Co-operative Sports and Games Book*, New York: Random House.

OSLIN, J. and MITCHELL, S. (1998) 'An investigation of tactical transfer in net games', *Research Quarterly for Exercise and Sport: Supplement*, **69**, p. A-98.

PHILLIPS, D.C. (1995) 'The good, the bad and the ugly: The many faces of constructivism', *Educational Researcher*, **24**, pp. 5–12.

PIERON, M. (1995) 'Research on the spectrum of teaching styles', in LIDOR, R., ELDAR, E. and HARARI, I. (eds) *Windows to the Future: Bridging the Gaps between Disciplines, Curriculum and Instruction*, Proceedings of the 1995 AIESEP world Congress, Wingate Institute for Physical Education and Sport, Israel, pp. 436–8.

RINK, J. (1993) *Teaching Physical Education for Learning*, St Louis: Mosby.

RINK, J., FRENCH, K.E. and GRAHAM, K.C. (1996) 'Implications for practice and research', *Journal of Teaching in Physical Education*, **15**, pp. 490–508.

RINK, J., FRENCH, K.E. and TJEERDSMA, B.L. (1996) 'Foundations and issues for teaching games and sports', *Journal of Teaching in Physical Education*, **15**, pp. 399–417.

RINK, J., FRENCH, K. and WERNER, P. (1991) 'Tactical awareness as the focus for ninth grade badminton', Paper presented at AIESEP World Congress, Atlanta, Georgia.

RONHOLT, H. and PIETERSON, B. (1989) 'Playing ability and perception: The effect of two instructional strategies in teaching basketball in the tenth grade', Paper presented at the AIESEP International Conference, Jyvaskyla, Finland.

SALTER, W.B. and GRAHAM, G. (1985) 'The effects of three disparate instructional approaches on skill attempts and student learning in an experimental teaching unit', *Journal of Teaching in Physical Education*, **4**, pp. 212–18.

SCHWAGER, S. and LABATE, C. (1993) 'Teaching for critical thinking in physical education', *Journal of Physical Education, Recreation and Dance*, **64**, 5, pp. 24–6.

SHARAN, S. (1990) *Co-operative Learning, Theory and Research*, New York: Praeger.

SIEDENTOP, D. (1996) 'Physical education and education reform: The case of sport education', in SILVERMAN, S.J. and ENNIS, C.D. (eds) *Student Learning in Physical Education: Applying Research to Enhance Instruction*, Champaign, IL: Human Kinetics, pp. 247–68.

SILVERMAN, S. (1991) 'Research on teaching in physical education: Review and commentary', *Research Quarterly for Exercise and Sport*, **62**, pp. 352–64.

SLAVIN, R.E. (1983) *Co-operative Learning*, New York: Longman.

SMITH, B., MARKLEY, R. and GOC KARP, G. (1997) 'The effect of a co-operative learning intervention on the social skill enhancement of a third grade physical education class', *Research Quarterly for Exercise and Sport: Supplement*, **68**, p. A-68.

STRACHAN, K. and MacCAULEY, M. (1997) 'Co-operative learning in a high school Physical Education program', *Research Quarterly for Exercise and Sport: Supplement*, **68**, p. A-69.

TAMIR, P. (1996) 'Discovery learning and teaching', in ANDERSON, L.W. (ed.) *International Encyclopedia of Teaching and Teacher Education*, New York: Pergamon, pp. 149–55.

THORPE, R., BUNKER, D. and ALMOND, L. (1986) *Rethinking Games Teaching*: University of Loughborough.

TISHMAN, S. and PERKINS, D.N. (1995) 'Critical thinking and Physical Education', *Journal of Physical Education, Recreation and Dance*, **66**, 6, pp. 24–30.

TJEERDSMA, B.L., RINK, J.E. and GRAHAM, K.E. (1996) 'Student perceptions, values and beliefs prior to, during, and after badminton instruction', *Journal of Teaching in Physical Education*, **15**, pp. 464–76.

TURNER, A. (1996) 'Teaching for understanding: Myth or reality?', *Journal of Physical Education, Recreation and Dance*, **67**, 4, pp. 46–8.

TURNER, A. and MARTINEK, T. (1992) 'A comparative analysis of two models for teaching games (technique approach and games centred tactical focus approach)', *International Journal of Physical Education*, **24**, 4, pp. 15–31.

TURNER, A. and MARTINEK, T. (1995) 'Teaching for understanding: A model for improving decision-making during game play', *Quest*, **47**, pp. 44–63.

TURNER, A. and MARTINEK, T. (1996) 'An investigation into teaching games for understanding: Effects on skill, knowledge and game play', Unpublished Paper.

VIRGILIO, S. (1979) 'The effects of direct and reciprocal teaching strategies on the cognitive, affective, and psychomotor behaviour of fifth grade pupils in beginning archery', Unpublished doctoral dissertation, Florida State University, Tallahasse.

WERNER, P. (1989) 'Teaching games: A tactical perspective', *Journal of Physical Education, Recreation and Dance*, **60**, 3, pp. 97–101.

WERNER, P. and ALMOND, L. (1990) 'Models of games education', *Journal of Physical Education, Recreation and Dance*, **61**, 4, pp. 23–7.

WERNER, P. and RINK, J. (1989) 'Case studies of teacher effectiveness in physical education', *Journal of Teaching in Physical Education*, **4**, pp. 280–97.

WHITEHEAD, M. and CAPEL, S. (1993) 'Teaching strategies and Physical Education in the National Curriculum', *British Journal of Physical Education*, **24**, 4, pp. 42–6.

WILLIAMS, A. (1997) 'National Curriculum gymnastics at Key Stage 3: Differentiation for planning, performing and evaluating', *British Journal of Physical Education*, **28**, 1, pp. 5–8.

WOODS, A.M. and BOOK, C. (1995) 'Critical thinking in middle school physical education', *Journal of Physical Education, Recreation and Dance*, **66**, 6, pp. 39–43.

6   The Motivation of Pupils in Physical Education

Stuart Biddle

It is obvious to those involved in Physical Education (PE) that it is an environment where motivational issues are highly salient. Some children are strongly motivated towards PE and see it as the highlight of their school day. Indeed, research has long shown that sporting prowess is a major source of social status for children, especially for boys. Motivation to succeed in the PE or sport environment, therefore, is expected to be high for some, if not many, young people. However, PE has also been identified as a source of stress for some children and has even been cited as a major reason for truancy. Clearly such children are 'amotivated' in respect of PE. The arena of PE, therefore, is important for the study of pupil motivation.

What Is Motivation?

Motivation is best defined in terms of five behavioural patterns identified by Maehr and Braskamp (1986). These are direction, persistence, continuing motivation, intensity, and performance. Direction of motivation refers to choice and decision making since any motivated behaviour must be directed toward some goal or object. This is illustrated by the child being motivated towards, say, swimming but not hockey. Persistence is an indicator of motivation through its reflection of effort and 'stickability'. It shows sustained concentration and task involvement. Continuing motivation is similar to persistence but refers to motivation over a longer period of time, usually after taking a break. This is reflected in the child who feels committed to an activity and returns to it on a regular basis.

Intensity of motivation refers to the strength of the motivational drive. Some pupils, for example, cannot wait for their PE lesson and have intense levels of motivation. Finally, performance can indicate motivation although it is not a perfect indicator. We usually seek motivational reasons for performance when other factors, such as ability and environmental conditions, are equal.

Motivation is multidimensional and should be seen as such by teachers. It is a complex aspect of human behaviour that can be studied from different theoretical perspectives. In this chapter, I shall outline three of these perspectives. First, by addressing how pupils react to success and failure I will consider attribution theory. This has enjoyed great popularity over the years in both educational and sport psychology (see Biddle, 1993). I will then consider the domain of achievement motivation from the perspective of achievement goal orientations and motivational climate. This is currently a major topic of interest in our field and has the advantage of a growing body of evidence from PE settings. Finally, I will consider the developing area of intrinsic motivation and pupil autonomy. All sections will be illustrated by research findings from our (see Acknowledgment p. 122) work in British PE contexts, and implications for the role of the teacher will be provided.

How Pupils View Success and Failure

How pupils react to the numerous tasks and challenges in PE will have important consequences for their motivation. Let us consider two examples. John reacts to public failure in PE with the thought 'I am a failure; I'm no good at PE'; he has processed the situation quite differently from Anne who says 'OK, it didn't work this time, but now I will try a different approach'. Both may have experienced the same 'objective failure', but they have processed the likely causes differently. John feels his ability is the main reason whereas Anne sees some possibility of future success by attributing her failure to an inappropriate strategy. The key to trying to rectify the failure, therefore, is the type of attribution given for the failure. Attributions are perceived causes or reasons for actions, either actions of oneself, as in the examples of John and Anne, or of others, such as when teachers give attributions for their pupils' actions. The explanations for such effects will now be considered and are best discussed in terms of confidence and emotions.

Links between Attributions and Confidence

One way of grouping attributions (see Weiner, 1986) is to place them into three main categories. Locus of Causality refers to whether the attribution (e.g. effort) is internal or external to the person. Stability refers to whether the attribution is stable or variable over time. For example, Anne attributed her failure to 'poor strategy', an attribution that could change given another attempt whereas John's attribution of 'lack of ability' is quite a stable attribution and is unlikely to change for his next attempt. The third main dimension for attributions is that of controllability. This refers to whether the attribution is controllable or not. For example, effort can be controlled by the individual but ability or aptitude are considered to be much less controllable.

The key to developing confidence appears to be based on the stability and controllability of the attribution. Figure 6.1 shows a negative confidence cycle in which an attribution for failure that is 'stable' (e.g. lack of ability) perpetuates feelings of incompetence and inadequacy. This is because failure attributed to a stable factor is expected to continue in the future and the individual has little control over changing this factor. On the other hand, Figure 6.2 shows a positive confidence cycle whereby the attribution given for failure is not only unstable but the individual has a good possibility of changing the cause in the future.

Figure 6.1: A negative confidence cycle showing the relationship between attributions and confidence as a function of the attribution made

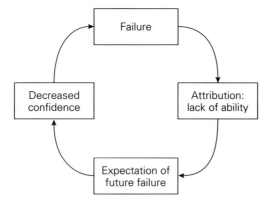

Figure 6.2: A positive confidence cycle showing the relationship between attributions and confidence as a function of the attribution made

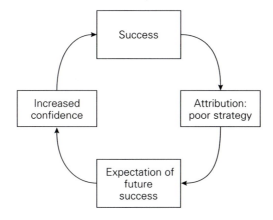

Does this mean that changing pupils' 'bad' attributions for failure can result in enhanced confidence and motivation? Although there is a body of research addressing attribution change programmes in educational and clinical psychology, there is very little in sport and PE contexts. Therefore, we conducted a small study on attribution retraining in a middle school PE context (Sinnott and Biddle, 1998). Fifty-eight boys and girls participated in a 3-person ball-dribbling (bouncing) race along the length of the school hall with their non-dominant hand. The children rated how successful they felt and completed the Causal Dimension Scale II modified for children (CDSII-C; see Vlachopoulos, Biddle, and Fox, 1996, 1997) to assess their attributions along the dimensions of locus of causality, stability, personal control, and external control. Six boys and six girls were then selected and allocated to an attribution retraining (AT) group or a no-training (NO) group based on their perceived success and attribution ratings. The NO group rated themselves as 'quite successful' whereas the AT group saw themselves as 'quite' or 'very' unsuccessful. The six pupils in the AT group were chosen for their maladaptive attributions for failure.

One week after the ball-dribbling test, the children in the AT group were exposed to a 20-min session of attribution retraining where the focus was on the importance of 'strategy' (appropriately defined and explained for this age group). The NO group received a 20-min session with the same investigator but the time was filled with a discussion on sport. Within 24 hours, the two groups were re-tested on the ball dribble task, CDSII-C and perceived success, and also completed the Intrinsic Motivation Inventory (IMI; McAuley, Duncan and Tammen, 1989) modified for the context. During and immediately following the ball dribble, pupils were asked to 'think aloud' about their performance in an effort to elicit 'spontaneous attributions'. These were noted and analysed.

Results showed that the AT group changed markedly from maladaptive to adaptive attributions as well as showing a large increase in their perception of success. The NO group showed little or no change in any variable. The AT group also reported higher intrinsic motivation than the NO group, probably due to the optimistic views of achievement they now held through controllable attributions. This was confirmed by the spontaneous attributions where the AT pupils gave 22 strategy-oriented statements in contrast to only eight from the NO group pupils. In conclusion, changes in attributions appear to affect subsequent motivation and perceptions of control.

Links between Attributions and Emotions

Another way to look at the role of attributions in motivation is through their effects on emotions. Weiner (1986) has proposed a theory of motivation and emotion that accounts for links between attributions and emotional reactions. Weiner and colleagues first studied a range of emotional reactions in educational settings by asking students how they would feel given certain attributions for examination success and failure. From these initial studies (see Weiner, 1986) two categories of emotional responses were proposed. 'Outcome-dependent/attribution-independent' emotions were those associated with the outcome (e.g. success) but were not related to specific attributions. On the other hand, Weiner also found emotions that were strongly related to the nature of the attribution given for the performance; these he labelled 'outcome-independent/attribution-dependent' emotions. Developing this in sport, Vallerand (1987) proposed an 'intuitive-reflective appraisal' model of sport emotion. This suggests that Weiner's outcome-dependent emotions are likely to be generated by immediate appraisal of the outcome (e.g. 'I won therefore I feel good'), and this is the 'intuitive appraisal'. Greater attributional thinking — the 'reflective appraisal' — was proposed for the attribution-dependent emotions.

To test such notions, Vallerand (1987) conducted two studies. In the first, he asked basketball players to rate their intuitive appraisal by giving their general impression of whether they had a 'good or bad game today'. Attributions and emotions were assessed. For those who felt successful, the best predictor of emotion was the intuitive appraisal, but this was augmented by attributions. The results were weaker for those who felt less successful. In his second study, Vallerand (1987) found that controllable and stable attributions were related to self-related emotions for both successful and unsuccessful situations. In conclusion, Vallerand stated:

- the intuitive-reflective model of sport emotion was supported;
- the intuitive appraisal is an important antecedent of self-related emotion in both success and failure situations;
- the intuitive appraisal has a greater impact on emotion than the objective outcome;
- attributional reflective appraisal is also related to emotion but to a lesser extent than the intuitive appraisal.

These conclusions have been supported in our research (Biddle and Hill, 1992a, 1992b; Vlachopoulos et al., 1996, 1997). In a study of 1-v-1 competition on a fencing task in a laboratory, we found that positive self-esteem emotions for winners were predicted by performance satisfaction (a kind of intuitive appraisal), importance of the outcome, and internal attributions (Biddle and Hill, 1992b). In a follow-up study, we also found support for the intuitive-reflective appraisal model with competitive squash players (Biddle and Hill, 1992a). For winners, the intuitive appraisal of performance predicted emotion more than attributions. In addition, we have found that attributions are related to post-exercise emotion in children, but only in a small way after taking account of their achievement goal orientations (Vlachopoulos et al., 1996, 1997).

Weiner's model of attributions and emotions also suggests that qualitatively different emotions result from different attributional appraisals (see Figure 6.3). For example, internal/external attributions might determine the strength of emotional feeling. This was one of the earliest findings in attribution research. Pupils reporting internal attributions tend to have heightened emotional responses compared with when they give external attributions.

In addition, Weiner (1986) proposed that the controllability of the attribution will be related to the generation of social emotions. For example, if a teacher thinks that one of their pupils is missing after-school training simply to see her boyfriend, the teacher will likely report feelings of anger since the 'cause' is controllable by the pupil. Alternatively, these feelings of anger may turn to pity or sympathy if the teacher discovers that the real reason is that the pupil's brother has been injured in a car crash and requires nursing at home. These social emotions — anger, pity, sympathy etc. — are generated towards others as a result of the perceived controllability of the actions (see Weiner, 1995).

Finally, Weiner (1986) proposed that the perceived stability of the attribution will be associated with feelings that are time-related. For example, attributing a failure to lack of ability gives little hope that success can be achieved in the near future. These categories of emotions are shown in Figure. 6.3.

Figure 6.3:   Different emotional reactions are related to the types of attributions made

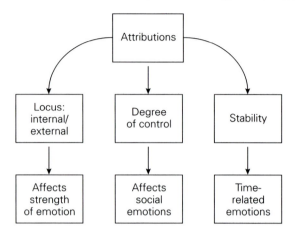

Attributions Given by Teachers

An underdeveloped area of study is that of the attributions, motivation and emotions generated as a result of how teachers make attributions for the actions of their pupils. However, we do have a theoretical base for the study of this phenomenon. In the 1970s, social psychologists discussed the 'actor-observer' issue in attributions whereby it was thought that 'actors' (those who acted out the behaviour — in our case the pupil) will use situational attributions for their behaviour more than 'observers' (in our case the teacher). Observers are thought to make more dispositional attributions for the behaviour of the pupil. This 'divergence' of view could be a source of attributional conflict between the teacher and pupil. Of course, attributional thinking between teacher and pupil can also be compatible and positive.

Here is an example of attributions given by a track and field coach in referring to Elizabeth, the athlete he is coaching. The comments in italics could be construed as attributional in nature and open to qualitative analysis (see Biddle and Hanrahan, 1998). Possible attributional dimensions are given in square brackets.

> the last two months she's done really well. *I think she's begun to feel the benefit of the speedwork we've been doing* [internal; unstable; controllable?] . . . ; her high jump has reached a plateau — *it's her layout* [internal; stable?] . . . ; shot put has been a good event for Elizabeth — *she's got quite a good throwing arm and a fair amount of speed.* [internal; stable; controllable?]

It would appear that a great deal can be learned in sport psychology by studying the interactions between teacher and pupil or coach and athlete from an attributional point of view.

Figure 6.4:   Preferences expressed by teachers for pupils who vary on outcome, effort, and ability

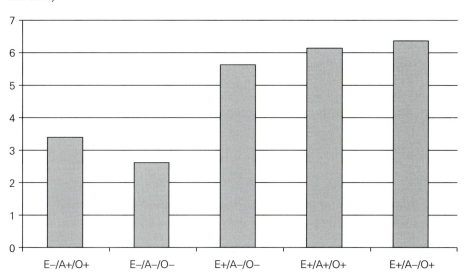

Note: data key: E: effort; A: ability; O: outcome; +: positive (or high); –: negative (or low)

A similar view is to look at the reactions of teachers to pupils based on how they view the reasons for the behaviour of the pupils. For example, we conducted a study with three samples of teachers to test these effects (Biddle and Goudas, 1997). The three groups were Primary pre-service students who did not opt for a specialized programme in PE (n = 90), a group of Primary students who did opt to specialize in PE (n = 16), and secondary PE teachers (n = 91). Five hypothetical pupils were presented to them on a questionnaire and the teachers were asked to rate their degree of preference for working with each pupil. Ratings were made on 7-point scales ranging from 1 (prefer not to work with the pupil) to 7 (strongly prefer to work with the pupil). The pupils were differentiated by their outcome (successful or unsuccessful), effort (high or low), and ability (high or low). Results, averaged across the three groups, are shown in Figure 6.4 and reveal a strong preference for all teachers to favour pupils who try hard. This can be explained by effort being a 'virtuous' quality in our society as well as effort being a factor controllable by the pupil. Ability and outcome are less favoured by teachers as indicators of 'virtue'.

Attributions: Implications for the Teacher

So far, I have outlined some research findings that suggest that the motivational and emotional reactions of pupils may be related to the type of attribution given for their performance. The role of the teacher, therefore, might involve the following:

- being a 'listener' in the first instance. The emotions generated by the pupil are 'real' and result from the way the pupil thinks about the situation.

> There is no 'right' or 'wrong' view at this stage — only the perception of the individual;
>
> • the teacher needs to develop good 'listening skills' so that they attempt to empathize and understand the feelings of the pupil;
>
> • after further discussion, the teacher may wish to attempt to change the attributions the pupil is reporting if these are thought to be generating negative emotions or a lack of motivation. This will require some under-standing of attribution change procedures, as illustrated in the study by Sinnott and Biddle (1998). In particular, attributions for failure that suggest stability or lack of control should be changed to those that give hope and confidence for future success.

How Pupils Define Success

So far, I have discussed how pupils might react to success and failure and how this can impact on motivation and emotion. However, a great deal of research has accumulated in recent years to show that pupils do not all define success in the same way. Motivational researchers refer to this as 'achievement goal perspectives' or 'goal orientations'.

Sport and exercise psychologists have readily adopted the achievement goal orientations approach for the study of motivation, and quite often with children and youth (Duda, 1993; Roberts, 1992). The achievement goals most often studied are 'task' and 'ego' goals. Nicholls (1989) has argued that different conceptions of ability in achievement contexts are embedded in these goals. Task-involved indi-viduals view 'success' or 'ability' being demonstrated through mastery attempts. Those who are ego-involved, however, view ability as limiting the effects of effort on performance. This perspective is labelled 'ability as capacity'. Nicholls (1989), therefore, refers to task-involved individuals as holding a 'less differentiated' con-ception of ability (effort-based), where those ego-involved hold a 'more differenti-ated' view (ability and effort). Being task-involved means that perceptions of success and ability are made in terms of self-referenced criteria, such as task mastery, learning, and skill development. Ego-involved perceptions of success and ability are based on externally and normative-referenced criteria, such as outperforming others.

Nicholls (1989) has argued that task or ego goal involvement in specific situ-ations may reflect more dispositional orientations. Consequently, sport and exercise psychologists have assessed task and ego goal orientations as potential antecedents of cognitions, emotions and behaviour, hence they are important constructs in the study of motivation in PE contexts.

The motivational properties of goal orientations for young people in sport and PE can be studied from several different perspectives. Goals have been shown to correlate with beliefs about the causes of success and ability, intrinsic motivation, and emotion. There is also some evidence pointing to an association between goals and behaviour.

Goals and Beliefs

The study of the links between goal orientations and beliefs about the causes of success is fundamental to the understanding of motivated achievement behaviour in PE. Research in classroom and PE/sport contexts has shown that task and ego goal orientations are differentially correlated with beliefs about the causes of success. For example, Duda, Fox, Biddle and Armstrong (1992) found for 10–11-year-old boys and girls that a task orientation was strongly correlated with the belief that success in sport is due to motivation/effort but unrelated to the belief that ability causes success in sport. Conversely, ego orientation was strongly correlated with ability beliefs but correlated with motivation/effort rather weakly. These findings have been replicated on many occasions (see Duda, 1993).

While ability and effort beliefs are important and highly salient in PE contexts, research has suggested that beliefs concerning ability are multidimensional. For example, Dweck and colleagues have discussed conceptions of ability in terms of beliefs about the nature of intelligence (Dweck and Leggett, 1988; Elliott and Dweck, 1988). They distinguished between intelligence that is thought to be relatively fixed and intelligence that is thought to be changeable. Children believing in a more fixed notion of intelligence (an 'entity theory' of intelligence) were found to be more likely to adopt an ego-oriented achievement goal. Conversely, children believing that intelligence is changeable (an 'incremental theory' of intelligence) were more likely to adopt a task goal.

Using a 3-item 'Sport Incremental Ability Scale', we tested whether beliefs concerning the fixed or incremental nature of sport ability were related to achievement goal orientations in 11–12-year-old children (Sarrazin et al., 1996). We assessed goals using the Task and Ego Orientation in Sport Questionnaire (TEOSQ) as well as asking the children to choose their preferred goal in the same way as Dweck and Leggett (1988) had done. We found that children choosing a task goal were more likely to be represented in the incremental beliefs group. This provided support for the propositions of Dweck and Leggett and showed that such notions could be extended into the domain of sport.

The conception of sport ability, however, is likely to be broader than that suggested by either Dweck or Nicholls. Consequently, we went back to the views of Fleishman (1964) in the motor behaviour literature. Fleishman distinguished between abilities and skills in his 'scientific' conception of motor performance factors. He distinguished abilities from skills in relation to their determinants (inheritance/learning), specificity (specific/general), and malleability (stable/changeable). He saw skills as evolving from learning and being specific to a task or group of tasks. Abilities were viewed as quite stable, sometimes genetically determined, rather general, and they limit the effect of learning on performance.

As well as Fleishman's scientific view, one can identify a 'lay view' of sport ability as expressed by parents, journalists or sport spectators. Such notions include beliefs that sport ability is a gift ('God-given') or is natural.

Using both scientific and lay conceptions, Sarrazin et al. (1996) developed a questionnaire to assess such beliefs and tested it with over 300 French adolescents.

It was labelled the Conception of the Nature of Athletic Ability Questionnaire and it assessed beliefs in the following properties of sport ability:

- learning: sport ability is the product of learning
- incremental: sport ability can change
- specific ability: sport ability is specific to certain sports or types of sports
- general ability: sport ability generalizes across many sports
- stable ability: sport ability is stable across time
- gift-induced: sport ability is a 'gift', i.e. 'God-given'.

Correlations were in the predicted directions with task orientation being associated with beliefs that sport ability is incremental, the product of learning, and unstable. Beliefs that sport ability is a gift and general were associated with an ego goal orientation.

Nicholls (1989) has pointed out that task and ego goal orientations are largely orthogonal. This means that children may report high scores for both task and ego, or low scores on both factors, or some combination of this. To tackle task and ego goals separately, therefore, may not represent the true picture and therefore it is important to analyse goal profiles where possible (Fox, Goudas, Biddle, Duda and Armstrong, 1994). Most studies in this area have used a mean or median split to create the following four groups: high task and high ego (hi/hi), high task and low ego (hi-T/lo-E), high ego and low task (hi-E/lo-T), low task and low ego (lo/lo).

In terms of beliefs concerning sport success, we (Biddle, Akande, Vlachopoulos and Fox, 1996) found no differences between the four goal groups concerning ability beliefs, but those in the hi-T/lo-E group were significantly stronger in their effort beliefs than those in the hi-E/lo-T group. Also, hi-T/lo-E scored higher in effort beliefs than the lo/lo group. Sarrazin et al. (1996) found that the highest scores on the incremental and learning scales were reported by those in the hi/hi and hi-T/lo-E groups, whereas the lowest score for gift beliefs were reported by those in the hi-T/lo-E group.

It is clear, therefore, that a task orientation is associated with the belief that effort is a main determinant of success in PE and sport for children. Effort is often believed to be controllable by the individual. Believing that trying hard will bring some success is a reflection of the 'I can!' feeling so often desired by teachers or coaches. This is consistent with the results of Biddle and Goudas (1997) reported earlier on the preferences teachers had for pupils who showed effort.

The approach we adopted in assessing the nature of sport ability beliefs (Sarrazin et al., 1996) leads to a more differentiated view of how pupils might think about sport ability and how these beliefs may impact on motivation. Consistent with the correlations between a task orientation and effort beliefs, we found that a task goal was associated with more controllable aspects of 'ability', such as sport ability being incremental and developed through learning. Central to motivational enhancement, therefore, is the controllable and self-determined nature of sport ability. Believing that sport ability can change is correlated with a task goal and seems more motivationally adaptive.

Goals and Intrinsic Motivation

When goal orientations have been studied in respect of their relationships with motivational indices, one popular index has involved the assessment of intrinsic motivation using the IMI (McAuley et al., 1989). We studied achievement goals and 'intrinsic interest' of children in three PE classes, specifically boys in football, girls in netball, as well as both boys and girls in gymnastics (Goudas, Biddle and Fox, 1994b). It was found that a task orientation was directly related to intrinsic interest for the football/netball lessons whereas the relationship between ego orientation and intrinsic interest was moderated by perceptions of competence. For gymnastics lessons, only a task orientation was related to intrinsic interest. These findings were supported by our study of Romanian children (Dorobantu and Biddle, 1997), confirming cross-cultural validity.

In addition to studying generalized perceptions of intrinsic motivation we (Goudas, Biddle and Fox, 1994a) assessed 255 adolescents performing an aerobic shuttle endurance run 'test' in normal PE lessons. Prior to the test the students completed the TEOSQ and immediately after the run they completed the IMI with reference to their current motivational state. Results were analysed according to the four goal groups specified earlier. In addition, the sample was split into two based on their objective running performance.

Results showed that for the less objectively successful runners, IMI enjoyment scores were higher for those in the hi-T/lo-E group in comparison to the lo/lo and hi-E/lo-T groups. Similarly, hi-T/lo-E children had higher IMI effort scores than those classified as hi-E/lo-T. These results suggest that a high task orientation, even for those performing below the group average, preserved some form of intrinsic motivation.

Goals and Behaviour

It is surprising that so few studies have investigated behavioural correlates of goals. We still know little about how goals may affect behaviours such as choice or persistence. One application of goal orientations we adopted was to study whether goals predicted voluntary participation in school PE (Spray and Biddle, 1997). Since PE classes are compulsory until the age of 16 years, we sampled students in the 16–18-year-old age group. These students could choose to take PE as part of a wider programme of study options in a sixth form college. The results showed clearly that participation is higher for those students with a high task orientation, either singly or in combination with a high ego orientation (see Figure 6.5).

Similar participation differences were found in our study of 11–12-year-old children (Fox et al., 1994). We assessed, through self-report, their frequency of voluntary participation in sport both in and out of school. Results revealed a graded relationship; sport involvement was higher for those high in task orientation and for those high in perceived competence. Low sport involvement was clear for those in the lo/lo group, especially when they reported low perceived competence. This group may be particularly vulnerable to low motivation.

Figure 6.5: *Percentage of each goal group represented as participants (PART) or non-participants (NON-PART) in voluntary PE for 16–18-year-olds*

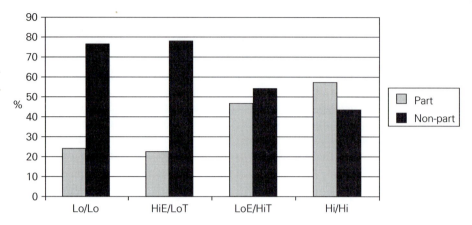

We have also conducted two experiments with 12–15-year-old French school pupils to see if goal orientations and perceived competence were predictive of motivation to learn a sport task (Cury, Biddle, Sarrazin and Famose, 1997). In our first study, we selected 57 male students on the basis of their goal orientation and perceived competence profiles. Specifically, the following four groups were created:

a)   high ego, low task, low perceived competence (PC);
b)   high ego, low task, high PC;
c)   low ego, high task, low PC;
d)   low ego, high task, high PC.

The study involved the boys taking part in a timed attempt at a basketball dribbling task around an obstacle course. The test was performed alone and was preceded by a period of training and practice. Since the main purpose of the experiment was to test for the amount of investment in practice shown by the boys, the PE teacher (experimenter) left the gymnasium for five minutes with a suitable excuse for his absence but leaving the instructions that the boys could practise if they wished. During this period the boys were observed unobtrusively and the time spent practising was recorded. After five minutes the experimenter returned and continued with the basketball test. The amount of time spent practising the task during the experimenter's absence was significantly less for those boys who were ego-oriented with low perceived competence compared to the other three groups.

In a second study, we used similar methods to investigate the investment made in learning the same basketball task, but this time after failure. A different group of male French school students, aged 13–15 years of age, were selected on the basis of the same groupings as used in the first study. Again, the boys high in ego orientation with low perceived competence invested much less time in practice than others. Overall, therefore, the results of the two experiments confirm the difficulties ego-oriented pupils may have in adhering to practice when given the free choice to do so. However, it is important to note that it is not ego orientation *per se* that is the problem, but it is ego orientation *when accompanied by low perceived competence*. This is wholly consistent with theoretical predictions from goal orientations theory (Nicholls, 1989).

Implications for the Teacher

Much of what I have said about goal orientations centres on the individual pupil. So what might be the role of the teacher in such contexts?

- the teacher might need to understand more fully the goals of pupils; probe the pupil's goal orientations ('what is important to you?'; 'how do you define success?');
- find out why they like to participate and what they hope to achieve from PE and sport;
- modify excessively high ego goals if they are accompanied by low task goals;
- the teacher is in a position to create an environment in which a task orientation is developed and encouraged. This relates to my next section — that of the PE class climate or environment;
- teachers need to promote the belief that 'ability' is changeable through learning and trying;
- using feedback based on personal rather than normative feedback is recommended.

Motivational Climate of PE Lessons

From the data presented, achievement goal orientations form an important and powerful influence on motivation. However, individual differences are sometimes difficult to influence directly and, as Treasure and Roberts (1995) have argued, 'a growing body of literature exists to suggest that the teacher plays an active role in the construction of children's perceptions of the motivational climate and, consequently, the quality of children's motivation' (p. 480). Some researchers, therefore, have emphasized the importance of the achievement environment, or climate.

Two main climates have been identified and follow the work of Ames in school classrooms (see Ames, 1992; Ames and Archer, 1988; Treasure and Roberts, 1995). A 'mastery' (task) climate is perceived by class or team members when they are directed towards self-improvement, the teacher/coach emphasizes learning and personal progress, effort is rewarded, mistakes are seen as part of learning, and choice is allowed. On the other hand, a 'performance' (ego) climate is one that encourages inter-individual comparison, where mistakes are punished, and high normative ability is rewarded (see Ames, 1992; Biddle et al., 1995; Papaioannou, 1995). Although the general dimensions of mastery and performance climate have been used satisfactorily in PE research (Biddle et al., 1995; Dorobantu and Biddle,

1997; Goudas and Biddle, 1994; Papaioannou, 1994), factors underlying these dimensions are less clear (Ntoumanis and Biddle, in press).

We have calculated effect sizes for a small number of physical activity climate studies to indicate the strength of relationships between motivational climate and selected cognitive and affective variables (Ntoumanis and Biddle, in press). Although the studies were not restricted to children, they indicate the strength of links between climate and associated psychological outcomes likely to influence motivation.

From a quantitative synthesis of 14 studies with a total sample size of almost 4,500, the correlation between mastery climate and positive motivational outcomes (e.g. satisfaction, positive attitudes towards lessons, intrinsic motivation) was 0.71, indicating a large effect. By contrast, performance climate correlated in a small-to-moderate way and in a negative direction with positive outcomes (ES = −0.30). Negative outcomes were also assessed and these comprised factors such as worry and the emphasis on normative ability. The effect for mastery climate on negative outcomes was small-to-moderate and negative (ES = −0.26), and for performance climate on these outcomes was moderate and positive (ES = 0.46). These results indicate the importance of a mastery climate in promoting positive psychological outcomes in physical activity.

Given the similar theoretical basis of achievement goals and motivational climate, an important question is whether goal orientations or climate affect motivation the most. We asked 700 French adolescent girls about their PE class climate, achievement goals, perceived competence, and intrinsic interest in PE (Cury et al., 1996). Results showed, as expected, that perceived competence is a strong predictor of interest in PE. However, in addition, interest was predicted by a mastery climate rather than directly by a task orientation. A performance climate was negatively associated with interest. We concluded from this study that in situations where compulsory involvement is required, such as PE lessons, the situational cues are likely to be more important than when people volunteer to take part.

Few studies have manipulated constructs associated with climate to test the efficacy of interventions in PE. Therefore, we sought to investigate whether manipulating teaching styles in line with climate dimensions would result in differential motivational effects (Goudas, Biddle, Fox and Underwood, 1995).

A small intact class of young adolescent girls was taught track and field for ten weeks in their normal PE lessons. An experienced university lecturer, well versed in teaching styles, was the class teacher and alternated lessons according to two teaching styles:

- direct style: most of the decisions were made by the teacher; the type of task, duration of practice and degree of difficulty were determined by the teacher. This style was chosen to approximate the creation of a climate low in mastery orientation.
- differentiated style: the teacher gave the children choices; varied activities were provided, degree of difficulty and pace of practice/learning were decided by the child. This style was chosen to approximate the creation of a climate high in mastery orientation.

At the end of each lesson, measures were taken of intrinsic motivation, task and work avoidance goal involvement (in the lesson), and intention to participate in future lessons. Results showed more positive effects for lessons taught by the differentiated style, suggesting an influence for mastery climate. Specifically, after the differentiated style lessons, the children reported higher intrinsic motivation and task involvement scores than after direct style lessons. Motivation for track and field was therefore enhanced through this teaching approach.

Implications for the Teacher

Teachers have known for a long time that the creation of the 'right atmosphere' in their classes is an important prerequisite for motivation and positive experiences. Research on motivational climate suggests that this can best be achieved through the creation of a mastery climate. Therefore the PE teacher might want to consider the TARGET model outlined by Ames (1992):

- T = task: make tasks challenging and diverse
- A = authority: give the pupils choice and leadership roles
- R = recognition: give recognition to pupils privately and based on individual progress
- G = grouping: promote cooperation, learning, and peer interaction
- E = evaluation: base evaluation on task mastery and individual progress
- T = time: adjust time requirements to individual capabilities.

Motivating through Pupil Autonomy

Intrinsic and extrinsic motivation are well known constructs in psychology and are thought to be central to any discussion on motivation. Teachers often refer to their desire to instil 'motivation' (usually meaning intrinsic motivation) in their pupils. Deci and Ryan (1985) proposed that three key psychological needs are related to intrinsically motivated behaviour. These are the needs for competence, autonomy, and relatedness. Competence refers to strivings to control outcomes and to experience mastery. Autonomy is related to self-determination and reflects the need to feel actions emanating from the self. Finally, relatedness refers to strivings to relate to, and care for, others; to feel that others can relate to oneself; 'to feel a satisfying and coherent involvement with the social world more generally' (Deci and Ryan, 1991, p. 345).

Sport psychologists are familiar with the basic tenets of 'Cognitive Evaluation Theory' (CET), itself a 'mini-theory' within 'Self-Determination Theory' (Deci and Ryan, 1985). CET states that rewards are best understood in terms of their impact on control and motivation by looking at the functions rewards may have. If the reward provides information about the individual's competence then it is quite likely that intrinsic motivation can be enhanced with appropriate rewards (information function of rewards). If the rewards are seen to be controlling behaviour (i.e. the goal is to obtain the reward), then withdrawal of the reward is likely to lead to subsequent deterioration in intrinsic motivation (controlling function of rewards).

It is important to note that informational events are those that are perceived to convey feedback about one's competence *within the context of autonomy*. Events where positive feedback occurs under pressure may be less powerful in influencing intrinsic motivation. Choice and positive feedback are perceived as informational, while rewards, deadlines and surveillance tend to be controlling. Negative feedback is seen to undermine motivation and is therefore referred to as 'amotivating'.

CET involves the processing by the pupil of information concerning reward structures. Extending this perspective, and including the psychological needs for competence, autonomy and relatedness, Deci and Ryan (1985, 1991) have proposed their 'Self-Determination Theory' (SDT) approach to motivation. This is relatively new to PE and sport research but may provide further insight into the understanding and enhancing of motivation in PE.

The nature of motivated behaviour, according to Deci and Ryan, is based on striving to satisfy the three basic needs of competence, autonomy and relatedness. This, they say, leads to a process of 'internalization' — 'taking in' behaviours not initially intrinsically motivating. Deci and Ryan (1985) have linked the internalization concept to that of extrinsic and intrinsic motivation. In contrast to earlier formulations in which these two motivational types were regarded as mutually exclusive, they proposed that they form a continuum where different types of extrinsically regulated behaviour can be located. Deci and Ryan (1991) refer to the continuum as one representing 'the degree to which the regulation of a nonintrinsically motivated behavior has been internalized' (p. 254).

The main types of extrinsic motivation are external, introjected, and identified regulation. External regulation might be illustrated by someone saying 'OK, I'll go to the PE class if I really must.' This is an example of where behaviour is controlled by rewards and threats, such as in the case of coercion of children in school.

Introjected regulation might be when one says 'I feel guilty if I don't go to practice tonight.' This is more internal in the sense that the individual internalizes the reasons for acting, but is not truly self-determined. The individual is acting out of avoidance of negative feelings, such as guilt, or to seek approval from others for their performance or behaviour. The term introjection refers to someone 'taking in' a value but, at the same time, not really identifying with it; it is not accepted as one's own and so is illustrated by feelings of 'ought' rather than 'want'.

Identified regulation might be illustrated by someone who says 'I must go to PE to get fitter'. This is further towards the self-determined end of the motivation continuum where action is motivated by an appreciation of the outcomes of participation, such as skill or fitness improvement. Although this is a more internalized perspective, and is moderately correlated with future intentions, it is still focused on a product or outcome. In physical activity it can be the most strongly endorsed reason for exercising (Chatzisarantis and Biddle, 1998) and has been identified by Whitehead (1993) as the 'threshold of autonomy'. It is behaviour acted out of choice where the behaviour is highly valued and important to the individual. It is illustrated by feelings of 'want' rather than 'ought'. The values associated with the behaviour are now accepted.

In contrast to these forms of external behavioural regulation, intrinsic motivation is shown when the individual participates for fun and for the activity itself. Clearly moving towards intrinsically motivated forms of behavioural regulation are advised for higher levels of intention and sustained motivation in PE since they are likely to involve stronger feelings of personal investment and autonomy.

In a study of 11–15-year-olds in England, we assessed intentions to participate in leisure-time exercise in terms of both 'autonomous' and 'controlling' forms (Chatzisarantis, Biddle and Meek, 1997). Specifically, we asked the children to rate the degree to which they intended to exercise because they 'have to' (controlling) or because they 'want to' (autonomous). Results showed that intentions predict physical activity when they are autonomous rather than controlling, lending support to a self-determination theory perspective.

Implications for the Teacher

Self-determination theory suggests that motivation is enhanced if more internalized reasons are given for behaviour. This is consistent with the arguments presented for attribution, achievement goal, and motivational climate approaches. The key implications for practice, therefore, are:

- seek to satisfy pupil needs for competence, autonomy and relatedness;
- understand why pupils participate and try to move them further towards the intrinsic end of the motivation continuum;
- create an autonomy-supporting environment by providing a meaningful rationale for activities, acknowledging the perspective of others (i.e. teaching seeing the point of view of the pupil), and conveying an element of choice rather than control (Deci, Eghrari, Patrick and Leone, 1994).

However, creating an autonomy-supporting environment is not easy in the current educational climate, as recognized some time ago by Deci and Ryan (1985, p. 269):

> Most educators agree that having children gain conceptual understanding, having them learn to learn, having them take responsibility for their own learning, are preferred goals for education. Yet the educators' task of achieving these goals is not easy, for they too are under pressure from the government and from parents and they live and work in a society that is accustomed to controlling and pressuring people toward performing up to standards and conforming to societal norms.

Deci and Ryan (1985) refer to the pressures on teachers from 'above' (administrators, parents, government) and 'below' (children) that affect their own autonomy and motivation. A self-determination theory perspective, therefore, may prove a fruitful one for both the study of pupil *and* teacher motivation.

Summary and Conclusions

Understanding the motivation of pupils in PE is complex but necessary if motivational enhancement is one of our goals. I have proposed three approaches to further this understanding. The following points, therefore, can be made in conclusion:

- attributions made by pupils are related to their confidence and emotional reactions;
- changing maladaptive attributions is possible and desirable;
- attributions of teachers for pupils' behaviour show they favour effort over ability and outcome;
- motivation will be enhanced if pupils have a high task goal orientation, either singly or in combination with a high ego goal;
- the climate promoted by the teacher should be oriented towards mastery rather than normative performance;
- motivation is enhanced through feelings of competence and autonomy rather than coercion and control;
- teachers can create autonomy-supporting environments;
- one theme to run through these conclusions is that pupil motivation is likely to be enhanced through the development of feelings of control and autonomy or, in lay terms, feelings of 'I can!' and 'I want to!'.

Acknowledgment

I am grateful to my friend and former colleague Ken Fox and our excellent research students who have contributed so much to our research programme on motivation, including some of that cited here. The contribution of the 'Greek Mafia' — Marios Goudas, Symos Vlachopoulos, Nikos Chatzisarantis, Antonis Hatzigeorgiadis, Manos Georgiadis and Nikos Ntoumanis — as well as that of Chris Spray, Sue Bock, Edward Chow, Chris Sellars, and Monica Dorobantu, and the 'French connection' — François Cury, Marc Durand, Jean Pierre Famose, and Philippe Sarrazin — has been outstanding and all have helped in their different ways. Working with all of them has been a true mastery experience!

References

AMES, C. (1992) 'Achievement goals, motivational climate and motivational processes', in ROBERTS, G.C. (ed.) *Motivation in Sport and Exercise*, Champaign, IL: Human Kinetics, pp. 161–76.

AMES, C. and ARCHER, J. (1988) 'Achievement goals in the classroom: Students' learning strategies and motivation processes', *Journal of Educational Psychology*, **80**, pp. 260–7.

BIDDLE, S.J.H. (1993) 'Attribution research and sport psychology', in SINGER, R.N., MURPHEY, M. and TENNANT, L.K. (eds) *Handbook of Research on Sport Psychology*, New York: Macmillan, pp. 437–64.

BIDDLE, S.J.H., AKANDE, A., VLACHOPOULOS, S. and FOX, K.R. (1996) 'Towards an under-standing of children's motivation for physical activity: Achievement goal orientations, beliefs about sport success, and sport emotion in Zimbabwean children', *Psychology and Health*, **12**, pp. 49–55.

BIDDLE, S., CURY, F., GOUDAS, M., SARRAZIN, P., FAMOSE, J-P. and DURAND, M. (1995) 'Development of scales to measure perceived physical education class climate: A cross-national project', *British Journal of Educational Psychology*, **65**, pp. 341–58.

BIDDLE, S.J.H. and GOUDAS, M. (1997) 'Effort is virtuous: Teacher preferences of pupil effort, ability and grading in physical education', *Educational Research*, **39**, pp. 350–5.

BIDDLE, S.J.H. and HANRAHAN, S.J. (1998) 'Attributions and attributional style', in DUDA, J.L. (ed.) *Advances in Sport and Exercise Psychology Measurement*, Morgantown, WV: Fitness Information Technology, pp. 3–19.

BIDDLE, S.J.H. and HILL, A.B. (1992a) 'Attributions for objective outcome and subjective appraisal of performance: Their relationship with emotional reactions in sport', *British Journal of Social Psychology*, **31**, pp. 215–26.

BIDDLE, S.J.H. and HILL, A.B. (1992b) 'Relationships between attributions and emotions in a laboratory-based sporting contest', *Journal of Sports Sciences*, **10**, pp. 65–75.

CHATZISARANTIS, N. and BIDDLE, S.J.H. (1998) 'Functional significance of psychological variables that are included in the theory of planned behaviour: A self-determination theory approach to the study of attitudes, subjective norms, perceptions of control and intentions', *European Journal of Social Psychology*, **28**, pp. 303–22.

CHATZISARANTIS, N., BIDDLE, S.J.H. and MEEK, G.A. (1997) 'A self-determination theory approach to the study of intentions and the intention-behaviour relationship in chil-dren's physical activity', *British Journal of Health Psychology*, **2**, pp. 342–60.

CURY, F., BIDDLE, S., FAMOSE, J-P., GOUDAS, M., SARRAZIN, P. and DURAND, M. (1996) 'Personal and situational factors influencing intrinsic interest of adolescent girls in school physical education: A structural equation modelling analysis', *Educational Psy-chology*, **16**, pp. 305–15.

CURY, F., BIDDLE, S., SARRAZIN, P. and FAMOSE, J-P. (1997) 'Achievement goals and perceived ability predict investment in learning a sport task', *British Journal of Educa-tional Psychology*, **67**, pp. 293–309.

DECI, E.L. and RYAN, R.M. (1985) *Intrinsic Motivation and Self-determination in Human Behavior*, New York: Plenum.

DECI, E.L. and RYAN, R.M. (1991) 'A motivational approach to self: Integration in person-ality', in DIENSTBIER, R. (ed.) *Nebraska Symposium on Motivation 1990*, Lincoln, NE: University of Nebraska Press, pp. 237–88.

DECI, E.L., EGHRARI, H., PATRICK, B.C. and LEONE, D.R. (1994) 'Facilitating internalization: The self-determination theory perspective', *Journal of Personality*, **62**, pp. 119–42.

DOROBANTU, M. and BIDDLE, S.J.H. (1997) 'The influence of situational and individual goals on the intrinsic motivation of Romanian adolescents towards physical education', *European Yearbook of Sport Psychology*, **1**, pp. 148–65.

DUDA, J.L. (1993) 'Goals: A social-cognitive approach to the study of achievement motiva-tion in sport', in SINGER, R.N., MURPHEY, M. and TENNANT, L.K. (eds) *Handbook of Research on Sport Psychology*, New York: Macmillan, pp. 421–36.

DUDA, J.L., FOX, K.R., BIDDLE, S.J.H. and ARMSTRONG, N. (1992) 'Children's achievement goals and beliefs about success in sport', *British Journal of Educational Psychology*, **62**, pp. 313–23.

DWECK, C.S. and LEGGETT, E.L. (1988) 'A social-cognitive approach to motivation and personality', *Psychological Review*, **95**, pp. 256–73.

ELLIOTT, E.S. and DWECK, C.S. (1988) 'Goals: An approach to motivation and achievement', *Journal of Personality and Social Psychology*, **54**, pp. 5–12.

FLEISHMAN, E.A. (1964) *Structure and Measurement of Physical Fitness*, Englewood Cliffs, NJ: Prentice-Hall.

FOX, K., GOUDAS, M., BIDDLE, S., DUDA, J. and ARMSTRONG, N. (1994) 'Children's task and ego goal profiles in sport', *British Journal of Educational Psychology*, **64**, pp. 253–61.

GOUDAS, M. and BIDDLE, S.J.H. (1994) 'Perceived motivational climate and intrinsic motivation in school physical education classes', *European Journal of Psychology of Education*, **9**, pp. 241–50.

GOUDAS, M., BIDDLE, S. and FOX, K. (1994a) 'Achievement goal orientations and intrinsic motivation in physical fitness testing with children', *Pediatric Exercise Science*, **6**, pp. 159–67.

GOUDAS, M., BIDDLE, S. and FOX, K. (1994b) 'Perceived locus of causality, goal orientations, and perceived competence in school physical education classes', *British Journal of Educational Psychology*, **64**, pp. 453–63.

GOUDAS, M., BIDDLE, S., FOX, K. and UNDERWOOD, M. (1995) 'It ain't what you do, it's the way that you do it! Teaching style affects children's motivation in track and field lessons', *The Sport Psychologist*, **9**, pp. 254–64.

MAEHR, M.L. and BRASKAMP, L.A. (1986) *The Motivation Factor: A Theory of Personal Investment*, Lexington, MA: Lexington Books.

MCAULEY, E., DUNCAN, T. and TAMMEN, V. (1989) 'Psychometric properties of the Intrinsic Motivation Inventory in a competitive sport setting: A confirmatory factor analysis', *Research Quarterly for Exercise and Sport*, **60**, pp. 48–58.

NICHOLLS, J.G. (1989) *The Competitive Ethos and Democratic Education*, Cambridge, MA: Harvard University Press.

NTOUMANIS, N. and BIDDLE, S. (in press) 'A review of motivational climate in physical activity', *Journal of Sports Sciences*.

PAPAIOANNOU, A. (1994) 'The development of a questionnaire to measure achievement orientations in physical education', *Research Quarterly for Exercise and Sport*, **65**, pp. 11–20.

PAPAIOANNOU, A. (1995) 'Motivation and goal perspectives in children's physical education', in BIDDLE, S.J.H. (ed.) *European Perspectives in Exercise and Sport Psychology*, Champaign, IL: Human Kinetics, pp. 245–69.

ROBERTS, G.C. (1992) 'Motivation in sport and exercise: Conceptual constraints and convergence', in ROBERTS, G.C. (ed.) *Motivation in Sport and Exercise*, Champaign, IL: Human Kinetics, pp. 3–29.

SARRAZIN, P., BIDDLE, S., FAMOSE, J-P., CURY, F., FOX, K. and DURAND, M. (1996) 'Goal orientations and conceptions of the nature of sport ability in children: A social cognitive approach', *British Journal of Social Psychology*, **35**, pp. 399–414.

SINNOTT, K. and BIDDLE, S. (1998) 'Changes in attributions, perceptions of success and intrinsic motivation after attribution retraining in children's sport', *International Journal of Adolescence and Youth*, **7**, pp. 137–44.

SPRAY, C.M. and BIDDLE, S.J.H. (1997) 'Achievement goal orientations and participation in physical education among male and female sixth form students', *European Physical Education Review*, **3**, pp. 83–90.

TREASURE, D. and ROBERTS, G.C. (1995) 'Applications of achievement goal theory to physical education: Implications for enhancing motivation', *Quest*, **47**, pp. 475–89.

VALLERAND, R.J. (1987) 'Antecedents of self-related affect in sport: Preliminary evidence on the intuitive–reflective appraisal model', *Journal of Sport Psychology*, **9**, pp. 161–82.

VLACHOPOULOS, S., BIDDLE, S. and FOX, K. (1996) 'A social-cognitive investigation into the mechanisms of affect generation in children's physical activity', *Journal of Sport and Exercise Psychology*, **18**, pp. 174–93.

VLACHOPOULOS, S., BIDDLE, S. and FOX, K. (1997) 'Determinants of emotion in children's physical activity: A test of goal perspectives and attribution theories', *Pediatric Exercise Science*, **9**, pp. 65–79.

WEINER, B. (1986) *An Attributional Theory of Motivation and Emotion*, New York: Springer-Verlag.

WEINER, B. (1995) *Judgments of Responsibility: A Foundation for a Theory of Social Conduct*, New York: The Guilford Press.

WHITEHEAD, J.R. (1993) 'Physical activity and intrinsic motivation', *President's Council on Physical Fitness and Sports Physical Activity and Fitness Research Digest*, **1**, 2, pp. 1–8.

7   Student Misbehaviours and Teachers' Responses in Physical Education Lessons

Colin A. Hardy

Introduction

It is suggested that student misbehaviour is any action that a teacher perceives as disruptive to classroom order and which competes with or threatens the academic proceedings at a particular moment (Bellon, Bellon, and Blank, 1992). Excessive and unnecessary talking and clowning and out-of-seat behaviour are most common in classroom settings (Cangelosi, 1993), although misbehaviour can range from mild verbal misbehaviour to physically aggressive acts such as fighting. In addition, it has been noted that teachers are having to respond more frequently to students' use of narcotics, alcohol and weapons (Bellon et al., 1992). However, severely disruptive incidents related to such latter factors are usually located in corridors, lunch areas and outside school buildings and not in classrooms, and, fortunately, are the rarer types of behaviour in most schools (Doyle, 1986).

Dreikers, Grunwald and Pepper (1982) suggest that students misbehave in order to meet such basic needs as seeking attention, seeking power, seeking revenge and seeking isolation, whereas Burden (1995) focuses on the biophysical variables that affect behaviour (e.g. attention deficit disorder), the physical environment of the home, school and community (e.g. parental supervision and types of discipline) and the psycho-social environment (e.g. values, motivation, preferences and conditioning history). In addition, Sylwester (1971) identified the teacher behaviours of inadequate preparation, differential treatment of students (e.g. favourites), verbal abuse and unfair responses (as perceived by students) to misbehaviour as contributing to the problem.

Research also suggests that males appear to be more of a problem than females (Houghton, Wheldall and Merrett, 1988) in that '. . . boys, in comparison to girls, have been observed to receive more frequent and intense disciplinary contacts from teachers, more disapproval and more disciplinary referrals to school counsellors and administrators' (p. 573). Oswald (1995) reinforced this point when he noted, in his study of 'difficult-to-manage' students, that they were predominantly male, although Lawrence, Steed and Young (1984) did point out that females were likely to be involved in more serious problems just as frequently as males even though they were less likely to be involved in misbehaviour problems overall. Furthermore, it was noted by the latter authors that the afternoon lessons are likely to produce misbehaviour incidents, as teachers become tired and less tolerant and students find it difficult to maintain attention as the day progresses.

As teacher interventions draw attention to disruptive behaviours that may have already slowed down the pace of lessons, it is important that interventions occur early, are brief and do not invite retorts from the target groups in order not to further interrupt the lesson flow. However, as an intervention is a complex judgment made about an act, an actor and the circumstances of a particular moment in time (Doyle, 1986), it is important that there is a consistency in the processes of making those judgments. In other words, teachers must be able to make reliable judgments, based on the evidence available, about the probable consequences of students' actions in different situations and the impact of their interventions.

Physical Education Investigations

In physical education a number of authors have focused on types of intervention strategy (French, Silliman and Henderson, 1990; Graham, 1992; Rink, 1993; Wurzer and McKenzie, 1987) although there is a dearth of research evidence on pupil misbehaviour, control and discipline in physical education lessons. Thus, if physical education pre-service teachers are to learn how to control their classes, they must try and unravel the many complex and personal reasons why students misbehave. For this to happen researchers must examine such topics as:

1 the occurrence of student misbehaviour and teachers' responses to the types of misbehaviour;
2 the relevance of gender and time of day to student misbehaviour;
3 the manner of teachers' responses;
4 the reasons for the particular misbehaviours and responses.

Occurrence of Student Misbehaviour and Teachers' Responses and the Types of Misbehaviour

(a) In an investigation of 39 physical education lessons involving 12 different activities, Hardy (1992) reported that the majority of the misbehaviour incidents occurred during class instruction (58.19 per cent) with a further quarter of the incidents (25 per cent) taking place once students had been sent off to carry out a set task; incidents during group and individual instruction only accounted for 13.79 per cent and 3.02 per cent respectively.

Initially, misbehaviour incidents usually involved either one student (43.16 per cent) or a group (41.88 per cent) with the class as a whole being less involved at this stage (14.96 per cent). Although the initial misbehaviour incidents mainly involved individuals or groups, other students were soon affected by the episode; for example, 27.78 per cent of the individual and group incidents ultimately affected the whole class.

The incidents, once teachers became aware of the problem, lasted mainly for 15 seconds and less (60.68 per cent) with 20.94 per cent of the incidents lasting from 16–30 seconds, 8.55 per cent of incidents from 31–45 seconds and 9.83 per cent over 45 seconds.

Comment

Teachers tend to be more sensitive to, and react more quickly to, student mis-behaviours during class instruction as an interruption during an explanation or de-monstration often results in a public reaction and disruption of other students (Emmer, 1987). The emphasis placed by physical education teachers on reacting to student misbehaviours during class instruction perhaps indicates the importance that teachers place on this situation in developing standards of behaviour. For example, expected student behaviours include listening attentively when teachers or students are talk-ing, raising the hand to gain attention and answering when acknowledged.

The importance of good preparation and presentation is reinforced by the fact that one quarter of the misbehaviour incidents took place after the students had been sent off to carry out set tasks. If the tasks are not appropriate, off-task behavi-our may soon take place, and, if the instructions are not presented clearly, disrup-tion may take place irrespective of the appropriateness or inappropriateness of the task. In addition, teachers must maintain the flow of the lesson by moving from class instruction to set tasks smoothly, and avoid interrupting the students once they have been sent off (i.e. 'just one more point').

Whether one or a group of students misbehave it can usually lead to other students behaving in a similar way or a disruption of those involved in the learning activity. The results of the present study indicate that, although the initial incidents mainly involved individuals or groups of students, many more students were dis-rupted at a group and class level. Whereas 43.16 per cent of the incidents involved one student, only 26.5 per cent of those incidents were contained to the misbehav-ing student. This 'ripple' effect is a situation teachers try to avoid by dealing with the initial incident as quickly as possible and in a way that causes little interruption to the flow of a lesson. The teachers in the present study were obviously aware of the problem as four-fifths of the incidents were dealt with in 30 seconds or less once the incident had been noticed, and in 90 per cent of the cases the student continued in the class.

(b) With regard to the types of student misbehaviour (Hardy, 1993) the main type was 'not paying attention during teacher's instructions' (49.15 per cent) with the students in that category disrupting the teachers' lessons verbally (63.48 per cent), physically (18.26 per cent) and by playing with equipment (18.26 per cent). For example:

Verbal:	Student talks to another student while teacher attempts to ex-plain warm-up.
Physical:	One girl was fidgeting whilst the teacher gave out instructions.
Playing with equipment:	Boy rolled ball along the floor while the teacher was talking.

'Not carrying out the teacher's instructions' (22.22 per cent), 'disrupting others' (13.25 per cent), 'refusing to take part in the lesson' (9.40 per cent), 'not carrying out the policy procedure' (3.85 per cent) and 'wishing to be centre of attraction' (2.14 per cent) were less frequent incidents, but they were often more challenging to the teacher's authority. For example:

Not carrying out the teacher's instructions:	Students messing about on equipment and not doing the exercises properly.
Disrupting others:	Student was pulling somebody under the water.
Refusing to take part in the lesson:	One mixed group wouldn't work on the task in dance. The girls wouldn't work with the boys.
Not carrying out the policy procedures:	A student still wearing a watch in the gymnastics lesson.
Wishing to be the centre of attraction:	One student was pulling faces at the teacher and making the class laugh.

Teachers' reactions to student misbehaviours were mainly verbal (72.65 per cent) with non-verbal (10.26 per cent), verbal and non-verbal (9.40 per cent) and ignored (7.69 per cent) being used less frequently. For example:

Verbal:	Told them to stop messing around and get up and on with the game.
Non-verbal:	Teacher clicked his fingers and pointed at them.
Verbal and non-verbal:	Told them to be quiet — directed at class as a whole but looked at a particular group of girls.
Ignored:	While the teacher demonstrated two children talked. The incident only lasted a couple of seconds and it was ignored by the teacher.

The focus of the teacher's reactions tended to be on the behaviour (78.24 per cent) rather than on the student (21.76 per cent). When the focus was on the behaviour teachers placed more emphasis on their dislike of the behaviour (62.13 per cent) than what was to be done (37.87 per cent), and when the focus was on the student the main emphasis was on making the student feel guilty or foolish (68.09 per cent) rather than showing little concern for the student as a person (31.91 per cent). For example:

Emphasizes dislike of the behaviour:	The teacher told the boys that he disapproved of such behaviour and that he didn't want to see it at the school.
Emphasizes what is to be done (a reminder):	Quietly went over to the child and put him back on task.
Makes the student feel guilty or foolish:	Called to the students to come back. Asked them to repeat what the teacher had said. They hadn't listened!

Withdraws respect showing little concern for student:	Student was told to go and stand facing the wall for the rest of the lesson (18 minutes).

Student misbehaviours were dealt with by the physical education teachers mainly in public (86.57 per cent) and only occasionally in private (13.43 per cent), and they tended to carry out their reprimands in a controlled and firm way (81.48 per cent) rather than in an emotional and threatening manner (18.52 per cent). For example:

Public:	Reprimanded for talking by the teacher in front of the whole group. References made to time-wasting.
Private:	He was taken aside and told that he was expected to come in quietly and sensibly.
Controlled/firm:	Stayed quiet and looked at the class until all the students were quiet — held silence for a few seconds. Told the students that was more like it and then started the race.
Emotional/ threatening:	The teacher was screaming, 'Manners!' He then yelled at the boys to stop fighting over the use of a particular rugby grid.

Comment

In dealing with student misbehaviours teachers mainly reacted in a firm and controlled way with brief comments focused upon the student behaviours. For example, 'Sit still — no one goes until all the equipment is put away' was directed at a group of students who were trying to leave the gymnasium. Non-verbal and verbal with non-verbal reactions, such as eye contact and 'be quiet' followed by a hand clap respectively, were used on occasions, and there were times when teachers felt that the appropriate reaction was to ignore the misbehaviour. The teachers' reactions to student misbehaviours supported findings reported by Reynolds (1992) that competent teachers ignore minor distractions and deal with potential disruptions by using eye contact, movement through the class or by short comments to the disruptive student.

The reprimands that attack the students and make them feel guilty or foolish may help them to conform to social standards, but too much guilt can have detrimental effects on how the students feel about themselves (Goldenson, 1984). The even more negative response of withdrawing respect for the students and showing little concern for them as people could result in the students developing a negative attitude towards the teacher, the class, the school and, in some cases, learning in general (Henderson and French, 1990). By withdrawing their respect for students, teachers must be careful that they do not categorize them as low-expectancy students and start to expect less of them in performance terms (Brophy and Good, 1970).

Although it is suggested that competent teachers talk with students in private to minimize confrontation (Brophy, 1987), the physical education teachers dealt with the majority of the incidents in public. However, their immediate and controlled reactions to incidents, their succinctness in dealing with them and their well-established reputations (Smith and Geoffrey, 1968) prevented any escalation of the problem. It is possible that, because of the nature of physical education classes with their large spaces, noise, variety of equipment, risks and challenges of the activities and the opportunities for students to talk and cooperate, immediate public reaction is the most effective way of dealing with misbehaviour incidents.

Relevance of Gender and Time of Day to Student Misbehaviour

In an examination of student misbehaviour in 119 physical education lessons according to gender and the time of day, Hardy, Hardy and Thorpe (1994) reported a difference in the frequency of incidents between girls and boys but no difference in the frequency between morning and afternoon sessions. With the former point, males committed more misbehaviour incidents than females in secondary school mixed-sex physical education lessons ($p < 0.01$), but incidents involving one student were mainly experienced by teachers of the same sex ($p < 0.01$).

Comment

Previous research in comparing male and female misbehaviour in classrooms has noted that males have tended to misbehave more than females (Bank, 1987). In physical education, Tinning (1987) suggested that teachers expect males to be more aggressive and boisterous than females, and Lopez (1995) concluded that it is basically males who make loud disruptions and demand to be centre stage while females take a passive role, fearing embarrassment if they are spotlighted.

The explanation for the relationship between the sex of the misbehaving students and the sex of the teacher is not clear but, if female physical education teachers still stress the good behaviour of females, it is possible that they quickly bring to task any female student stepping outside certain expected standards. However, as female teachers may be expecting more aggressive and boisterous behaviour from males they may be ignoring behaviour that they are less likely to tolerate from females. As it has been suggested that female teachers are more tolerant of misbehaviour (Good, Sikes and Brophy, 1972), the tolerance may be related to their expectations of how male and female students should behave. An explanation for male teachers reprimanding more single males than females may be that male students are pressurized by peers to take centre stage and to behave as 'class clowns' (Bank, 1987, p. 573), and that male teachers respond quickly and frequently to avoid incidents developing and having their authority challenged. In addition, it may be that individual male students change their behaviours when taken by female teachers.

More general research on classroom misbehaviour noted that nearly half of daily incidents occurred in the shorter afternoon period (Lawrence, Steed and Young, 1984) but the evidence from the present study indicated that there is no significant difference in the frequency of student misbehaviour incidents between morning and afternoon lessons in mixed-sex physical education lessons. The explanation for this may be that physical education takes students out of the classroom environment and into another type of setting, and that this change raises the students' motivational levels.

In addition, teachers may be modifying activities to the moods of students by ensuring that closely fought competitive games in a restricted space are not timetabled late in the afternoon when students are tired and have less control over their responses to opponents' misdemeanours.

Manner of Teachers' Responses

Although pre-service and inexperienced teachers may be provided with guidelines on how to deal with student misbehaviour, the manner of teachers' responses and their communication patterns are crucial elements in the application of reprimands. In a study of data collected by 56 pre-service teachers on the responses of 56 experienced teachers' (five years experience or more) responses to student misbehaviour, Hardy and Hardy (1995) examined the teachers' tone of the reprimand, the accompanying body language, the length and structure of the communication, the choice of vocabulary and the term of address. Based on this analysis, six teacher approaches were identified and these were defined as authoritarian, business-like, humorous, reasoning, reproachful and sarcastic (Table 7.1). The examples that follow have been selected for the generally consistent approach of the teacher, but it must be noted that there are others where teachers change their approaches throughout a lesson.

In the following paragraphs examples are given of how individual teachers responded to misbehaviour incidents in a specific lesson.

In the authoritarian approach (example 1), the teacher is showing who is in charge and apportioning blame to the student for any problem. The voice is loud and stern, eye contact is used and the teacher may shout across the physical education setting. Reprimands can be in the form of exclamations or hectoring questions and the students are not addressed by name at all but, instead, are called 'you'. All this suggests an accusatory and threatening atmosphere, heightened by the use of 'if' (laying down a condition) and 'I warned you all'.

Table 7.1: Teacher approaches to student misbehaviour

Approach	Definition
Authoritarian	Teacher shows who is in charge and apportions blame to the students for any problems.
Business-like	Teacher intent on maintaining lesson flow and wasting as little time as possible on distractions.
Humorous	Teacher exerts control in a light-hearted and teasing manner whilst maintaining good, informal working relationships with the students.
Reasoning	Teacher suggests that everyone is a member of the same community and should understand and take responsibility for their actions.
Reproachful	Teacher is saddened by lack of student commitment to the task and feels that students have let themselves and the teachers down.
Sarcastic	Teacher attempts to humiliate and isolate the offender in front of the class.

Example 1: Authoritarian approach

Class: year 7 Teacher: female Activity: gymnastics

Incident	Teacher's response
• Boy talks to friend during teacher's lesson introduction.	• The teacher made eye contact and in a loud, stern voice says, 'You again, just as last week!'
• The general noise level rises during warm-up.	• Teacher says, 'If you are making this much noise you can't be concentrating. Listen to your feet — quietly.'
• One group doesn't react immediately to instruction to rest.	• 'If you can't act sensibly you will have to sit out and watch.'
• One girl is incorrectly performing on a piece of apparatus.	• 'Weren't you listening earlier? . . . Then you know the safety procedure don't you?'
• One boy acts irresponsibly on the wall bars.	• Teacher shouts across hall, 'I warned you all earlier . . . right, off you go and get changed . . . I'm not having you in the lesson.'

With the business-like approach (example 2), the teacher is intent on maintaining lesson flow and wasting as little time as possible on distractions. All the communications are in the form of short, sharp instructions of no more than eight words, and the language lacks any sort of colour or individuality. The tone of voice is calm, firm and even, the students are referred to by their Christian names and 'please' and 'thank you' are used. An air of politeness is thus maintained but with a slight edge that suggests hidden strength.

Example 2: Business-like approach

Class: year 8 Teacher: female Activity: swimming

Incident	Teacher's response
• Most of the class were sitting on the side of the pool with legs in the water. This led to noise, so the teacher could not be heard properly.	• 'Stop fidgeting in the water' was said calmly, then teacher added names of individual offenders — 'Luke', 'Daniel'.
• Boy was talking and splashing at pool wall.	• 'Out of the water please, Guy' — said in firm, even voice.
• Two boys were 'fighting' during the swimming of widths.	• Spoke to boys as they came up to side, 'None of that behaviour, thank you.'
• Half the class, sitting on the side waiting for instructions, were chatting.	• 'Be quiet on the side of the pool.'

Incident	**Teacher's response**
• Several children moved before the signal was given to swim a length.	• Teacher gestured for them to go back and said, 'Wait for it!'

The humorous approach (example 3) is where the teacher adopts a light-hearted and teasing manner whilst maintaining a good working relationship. In the particular example illustrated the teacher assumes a mock 'hard-man' persona as the words actually spoken could appear to be hard but they are said in a friendly tone and with a smile. The teacher uses demotic language such as 'berks' and 'gob' and make a reference to popular culture. Such remarks could be seen as the teacher putting himself on a level with the students by using their language rather than the language of authority.

Example 3:   Humorous approach

Class: year 8   Teacher: male   Activity: volleyball

Incident	**Teacher's response**
• Girl wearing street clothes says, 'Mr G, I've forgotten my PE kit.'	• 'I am not Mr G, I have never been Mr G and I never will be Mr G (Said in friendly tone). I can see you've forgotten your kit. Today you can wear that, next lesson your proper kit. OK?'
• Girl whispering during class instruction.	• 'And now those immortal words, when I open my gob you shut yours' — said with a smile.
• The group was put in a game situation and one boy persisted in hitting the ball into the ceiling.	• The teacher mocked him and said, 'Did you have three weetabix this morning or something?'
• Two boys were not doing the practice properly.	• 'Two berks here haven't been listening.'
• One boy was pushing and kicking another against a crash mat while the rest of class put away equipment.	• The teacher called 'Oi' to get their attention, approached him and pretended to cuff him from a distance.

The teacher who uses the reasoning approach (example 4) is trying to suggest that everyone is a member of the same community, and that one should understand and take responsibility for one's actions. By using 'we' the teacher includes himself in that community and so underlines the idea of sharing a problem. Of all the approaches, this one has the longest and most complex communications. Sentences often have several main clauses or a main clause with subordinate clauses, and the use of linking words such as 'so' and 'or' suggest outcomes and options. The students are not simply told to obey but are invited to consider their behaviour in a mature way. The tone is generally calm and confiding and the student may be taken to one side and dealt with privately.

Example 4:   Reasoning approach
Class: year 8   Teacher: male   Activity: volleyball

Incident	Teacher's response
• Boy lying down on floor.	• 'Sit up please, Stewart' — said calmly by teacher.
• Less able student missed the ball — others had a go at him — less able student ran off to changing room.	• Teacher left student who had run off and spoke to others, 'Look we're not all good at everything. Some of you might find Maths hard and some of you are not very experienced at sport, so you need to give them a chance . . . I'm going to get Mark back now, so be patient with him next time.'
• One boy swore as he had messed up a shot and the whole class heard.	• Teacher stopped whole class and pointed to the boy and said, 'That kind of language is not appropriate in this lesson — or anywhere else in school.'
• Boy kicked volleyball.	• Teacher took the boy aside and explained the dangers of kicking a ball — 'You might break a window or knock a piece of apparatus over or you might hit someone in the face or on another part of the body — so no kicking balls.'
• Students talking when teacher told everyone to stop and sit down.	• Teacher said, 'We're wasting valuable time here.'
• A group were arguing over who won the point in a game. Teacher indicated they should calm down and student asked teacher who won.	• Teacher said, 'That's the sort of thing you've got to sort out for yourselves without squabbling — you're grown up now.'
• Students were talking when teacher told everyone to stop and sit down.	• 'We can either spend the last five minutes shouting at each other or we can play some volleyball.'

In the reproachful response (example 5), the teacher is often saddened by the lack of student commitment to the task. The frequent use of 'I' and the ironic use of such terms as 'excuse me' convey the impression that the students are frustrating the needs of the teacher. The tone, however, is calm and polite, and the language is deliberately understated (e.g. '. . . getting a little angry'; '. . . not very happy'), and this implies a deliberate restraint and hints at the possibility of stronger measures being imposed.

Example 5:   Reproachful approach
Class: year 8   Teacher: female   Activity: dance

Incident	Teacher's response
• A group of boys reading a piece of paper while teacher is instructing the class.	• 'Excuse me, I'm talking' — spoken calmly.
• Class not carrying out set task of practising their dance.	• 'I'm getting a little angry — I can't see much good work going on.' The teacher spoke calmly but strongly (not really angry).
• A group of girls was fidgeting while teacher was instructing the class.	• 'Girls, there's no need to get so excited' — spoken calmly.
• A group of girls was giggling during the task.	• 'I hope that giggling is about the work and you know what you're doing' — serious tone and pointing.
• Girl was chewing gum.	• 'Can you empty your mouth please.' Spoken in calm but strict tone.
• A group of boys was not carrying out the task i.e. to polish their dance — they were pushing each other.	• 'I'm not very happy about what's going on there' — said calmly and seriously.
• A girl whispered to a friend during class discussion.	• 'Excuse me' — said quickly and carried on with discussion.

In the sarcastic approach (example 6), the intention is largely to humiliate and isolate the offender. The tone is frequently unpleasant, being aggressive or biting, and may be reinforced by strong body language. The remarks are very personal and strongly concentrate the offender in a spotlight of attention, a situation that most adolescents find very uncomfortable.

Example 6:   Sarcastic approach
Class: year 8   Teacher: male   Activity: basketball

Incident	Teacher's response
• Student did not stop bouncing basketball when told to.	• Teacher said, 'Are you deaf son? Everyone else seems to understand me. Why can't you?' — aggressive and very public.
• Student talking while teacher was talking.	• 'Come on then, share it with the rest of us. It's obviously important if you're talking while I am' — humiliatingly.
• One girl was not doing what she was supposed to be doing.	• 'Get on with it Carole — you're wasting your time but more importantly, my time' — calmly, wagging finger.

Incident	Teacher's response
• Student fiddling with basket-ball when supposed to be listening.	• 'Pass it here . . . you haven't got the brains to listen and bounce a ball son' — sarcastically.
• Student talking while teacher was talking.	• 'John, do your chatting up outside my lesson — I need your full concentration.' Calmly — making eye contact and keeping it after he had finished speaking.

Comment

The language used by experienced physical education teachers in reprimanding students may reflect their own personalities and the context in which the misbehaviour incidents occur. Whether students conform or not is another matter, as is whether the message they receive is the same as that intended by the teacher. For example, if the content and the relationship levels of the communication conflict then disruption could continue (Wubbels, Creton and Holvast, 1989); an angry, emotional communication may be regarded as an authoritative move by the teacher (i.e. content of the message) whereas the students may view the interaction as a sign of the teacher losing control (i.e. relationship level). Therefore, control is not just about learning recommended techniques, it is understanding how to communicate clearly a message in a particular context so that there is no confusion about what is intended.

Reasons for the Particular Misbehaviours and Responses

With all the studies cited so far, the focus has been on data describing the misbehaviour incident and the perceptions of teachers to that event. However, an element of a survey of discipline in Scotland (Munn and Johnstone, 1991), involving primary and secondary schools, focused on 800 students writing about their teachers' classroom practices, rules, rule-breaking and sanctions. The students saw effective teachers as those who made the work interesting, explained and helped, avoided making students look or feel foolish, used sanctions when misbehaviour occurred and could use humour to defuse a situation. Such information is crucial to the 'student misbehaviour' debate as students' views give another dimension to the issue and may help to explain the cause of incidents and give some direction on the use of teacher responses.

With the student dimension in mind, the present study (Hardy, 1996) focused on one randomly selected incident from each of 64 physical education lessons taken by different teachers. Working in pairs, 64 pre-service teachers in 32 different schools systematically recorded all student misbehaviour incidents in two physical education lessons and then examined one of the incidents by:

• asking the teachers why they had responded in particular ways to what they regarded as student misbehaviour;

• asking the student or students involved in the selected incident to explain why they misbehaved or why they were regarded as misbehaving.

With reference to the students' explanations, permission was given by teachers prior to the lessons starting and they also agreed to the students' explanations remaining confidential to the interviewers. On two occasions, teachers refused to give permission as they felt it undermined their authority.

In the 64 physical education lessons there were 528 student misbehaviour incidents ranging from 3 to 13 incidents per lesson. Of the 64 lessons, 35 were taught by male teachers and 29 by females. The classes were mainly mixed-sex (n = 35) with male classes accounting for a further 21 and female classes for only 8. Of the misbehaviour incidents, nearly two-thirds of the incidents were committed by males or groups of males. In the randomly selected incidents 49 of the incidents involved males and groups of males, 12 involved females and groups of females and 3 incidents involved a mixture of male and female students.

In giving reasons for reacting to particular student misbehaviours, teachers focused on such student characteristics as being disruptive, attention-seeking, physically aggressive, verbally aggressive, lazy and lacking in concentration. With regard to student non-adherence, teachers focused on not listening to instructions, not carrying out set tasks and not following school rules and procedures. Occasionally teachers did report that giving unclear instructions was a reason for student misbehaviour. The rationale for addressing these incidents fell into the three categories of establishing authority, ensuring a safe environment and maintaining a positive learning climate. In making their interventions, whether in public or private, the perceived level of disruption within a particular context was central to their responses.

Students' reasons for behaving in ways designated as misbehaviour by teachers seldom agreed with those of teachers. Such teacher behaviours as giving unclear instructions and targeting student behaviours unfairly and peer conflict were frequently reported, although students also admitted to their own misbehaviours because they were having fun or they were being inattentive. The nature of the activity was another category of reasons reported by the students and they included dislike of, or boredom with, the practice or activity, their interpretation of the practice or activity and inability to perform the practice or activity.

The following examples of misbehaviour incidents illustrate the various types of reasons (Table 7.2) given by teachers and students for acting as they did.

Example 1:
Teacher's reason: students' characteristics — disruptive
Student's reason: nature of the physical activity — dislike of the activity
During a year 8 dance lesson 'S' would ignore the teacher's instructions to sit down and listen to the music, and would either click his fingers or shout and talk to a neighbour. The teacher found this misbehaviour frustrating and, very sharply, she verbally reprimanded the student in public and excluded him from the rest of the lesson. The teacher explained that 'S's behaviour is an ongoing problem as it happens every week in this particular lesson. She felt that 'S' (and his friends)

Table 7.2:   Views of teachers and students in explaining the reasons for student misbehaviour in physical education lessons

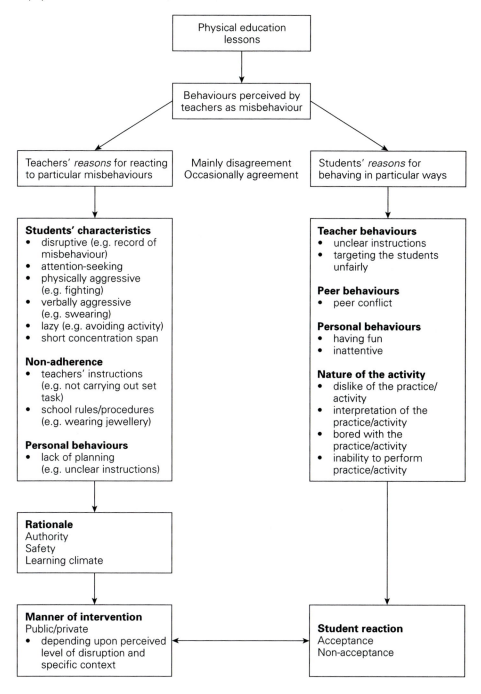

needed to be squashed because of their 'previous form'. It appears that a letter had already been sent to S's form tutor and to the year head concerning his misbehaviour in dance. 'S', in explaining his behaviour, said, 'I find the lesson boring — dance is boring and poofy — only girls do dance.' However, he did admit that some of the dances from other countries were interesting (e.g. Ireland, China), but said that he was not keen on expressive dance. He was a little upset at being excluded from the rest of this particular lesson as he was unable to participate in the fight scene of 'West Side Story'.

Although the teacher had become frustrated by 'S's behaviour over a number of lessons, S's admission that there were aspects of dance that he liked suggests that he did not perceive dance as a completely unacceptable activity. However, the problem for the teacher is how far she is willing to compromise her dance programme to cater for the 'likes' and 'dislikes' of one male student and his friends.

Example 2:
Teacher's reason: students' characteristics — attention-seeking
Student's reason: peer behaviours — peer conflict

During a year 9 soccer lesson for female students, one female continually talked and started kicking the ball into another group of students. This particular misbehaviour not only annoyed the teacher but also the group of students. The teacher took the student to one side and gave her a school detention and threatened to send a letter to her parents. The teacher explained that the student was a 'renowned attention-seeker' and that a public reprimand would only raise her status in front of the rest of the class. It appeared that the student was continually disrupting students in other lessons and that the final threat of informing her parents was the only form of admonishment that appeared to work. The student's explanation was that another student had been arguing with her and that she kicked the ball against this person's legs because the latter had said something that had upset her. She was quite blasé about being told off although she was concerned about her parents being informed because of the reaction of her father. In addition, she did note that she found the lessons boring and that she 'hated football'.

The teacher's expectations of the student were obviously fulfilled, and the question is whether this is just a Physical Education problem or a school one. Undoubtedly the teacher is able to deal with misbehaviour in the short-term, although the antagonism shown by the student to lessons and peers is perhaps indicative of a much wider problem that goes beyond the remit of any one teacher.

Example 3:
Teacher's reason: students' characteristics — physically aggressive
Student's reason: nature of physical activity — interpretation of the practice/activity

During a mixed-sex unihoc lesson a year 9 male student slapped his stick across the back of an opponent's legs when going for the ball. It appears that the student had been warned repeatedly for waving his stick around in an uncontrolled way. The teacher's response was to take the student to one side and then to exclude him from the activity. The teacher explained that the student was very aggressive and that he had to be constantly warned when playing such contact activities. In this particular activity the teacher felt that, if he had not removed him from the game 'to calm down', someone would have got seriously hurt. However, the teacher did feel that the student 'got carried away', and that many of his actions were not intentional. In his explanation, the student did not seem to be aware of the safety problem. He knew that he had made contact with someone's legs but he felt that 'fighting for the puck' was part of the game.

With this particular incident, the teacher had to calm down the student in case of an accident occurring, although future teacher strategies would have to focus on the behaviours expected within the rules of the game. Such a case is not unusual in contact sports and it is a problem all Physical Education teachers have to focus upon through the school years.

Example 4:
Teacher's reason: students' characteristics — verbally aggressive
Student's reason: teacher behaviours — targeting the student unfairly
In a mixed-sex year 8 rugby lesson, a male student swore at another student whilst the teacher was giving class instructions. The student was told publicly by the teacher to get changed and to report back to him in his school uniform. The teacher said that he did not tolerate swearing in his lessons and that, as the student hadn't apologized, he would also be kept in for a lunch-time detention. The student felt that he had been unfairly dealt with as another male student had pushed his head in the mud. Although he admitted swearing, he felt he had been provoked and targeted unfairly by the teacher and said that he would do the same thing again in similar circumstances.

Undoubtedly, the teacher had failed to notice the initial incident and the student's immediate response was not only to react aggressively to the other student but also to the teacher by not apologizing. In this particular case the teacher was correct to adhere to a basic discipline policy, although targeting a behaviour without considering the context does raise the question of fairness in the eyes of students.

Example 5:
Teacher's reason: students' characteristics — lazy
Student's reason: nature of the activity — bored with the practice/activity
In a year 7 soccer lesson, a male student was lying down on the ground when he was supposed to be playing a small-sided game. The teacher shouted at the student in a stern voice to get up and get on with the activity. The explanation for the authoritative rebuke by the teacher was that he felt that the student had ability but was lazy. He continued that, if he had felt that the student was weak and was lacking in confidence, he would have dealt with him in a more private and encouraging manner. The student's explanation was that he had got bored with the practice because nobody would pass to him and he had got tired running around and not receiving the ball. He was unhappy about being told off as he felt that the practice hadn't worked for him.

The teacher's response would not have been unexpected, although the student's explanation might suggest that there were grounds for his discontented attitude. However, this is a situation that requires the student to work harder and the teacher to ensure that practice conditions allow for involvement.

Example 6:

Teacher's reason: students' characteristics — short concentration span
Student's reason: nature of the activity — bored with the practice/activity

During a year 9 badminton lesson, a male student sat down in the middle of the court and rested. The teacher's explanation was that the student lacked concentration and often became bored and stopped participating in activities. Furthermore, the teacher felt that his actions often had a ripple effect and disrupted others. The student's explanation was that he wanted to play the game because 'doing hits with his partner was boring' and 'we did the same last week'.

The teacher was aware in the present incident that the student needed continual motivation, and that giving incentives such as 'I told him we would soon be playing the game' tended to work. However, the student's lack of understanding of how the game might be learned is perhaps a teaching problem that may have to be addressed.

Example 7:

Teacher's reason: non-adherence — to teacher's instructions
Student's reason: personal behaviours — having fun

In a mixed-sex year 7 swimming lesson, 'M' persisted in staying in the water after being told to leave the pool and to change. The teacher spoke to the student sternly and pointed to the changing room door. The teacher had noted that 'M' had been rather talkative throughout the lesson and he felt that his final non-verbal communication to the student was a clear and firm indication of what he expected the student to do. The student said that he enjoyed swimming and that he knew that he should have stopped talking and got out of the pool.

Such a situation is a common one but, as safety is an issue in the pool and such disobedience can undermine the teacher's authority, the strictness of the communication could have been expected.

Example 8:

Teacher's reason: non-adherence — to rules/procedures
Student's reason: teacher behaviours — targeting the student unfairly

Prior to a year 7 mixed-sex athletics lesson starting, the teacher told a female student to tie her shoe laces up. The teacher explained that a female student had had an accident in a previous lesson because of loose laces and had damaged an ankle. Although the student had been told the reason for tying up her shoe laces, she maintained that loose laces were fashionable and that she should be allowed to tuck her laces inside her shoes. In this sense she felt that she had been targeted unfairly by the teacher on several occasions for the way she dressed.

With such situations, no teacher is going to allow an unsafe practice to continue in a physical education lesson, and the teacher's explanation to the student for adhering to the procedure is a common practice. However, the conflict between safety and fashion will not go away, and it is one that teachers may have to continually contend with and hope that safety and fashion may not always be a mis-match.

Example 9:
Teachers' reason: non-adherence — teachers' instructions
Student's reason: nature of physical activity — inability to perform practice/activity
In a year 8 mixed-sex gymnastics lesson, a group of male students were performing movements other than what was being asked of them. The teacher very quietly went over to the group of students and calmly placed them back on task. The students' explanation was that they would never be able to perform a cartwheel, and that they had become bored with their apparent lack of success.

Although the teacher must have felt that their attempts were worthwhile, the students did not share this perception of success. Unfortunately, blaming failure on lack of ability often leads to giving up, and, in such cases, teachers may have to look more closely at their methods of presentation and practices.

Example 10:
Teacher's reason: personal behaviours — lack of planning
Student's reason: teacher behaviours — unclear instructions
On one occasion during a year 9 basketball lesson, when a group of students put on a set of bibs of the wrong colour, the teacher admitted that his instructions could have been clearer. Although the students agreed that the instruction could have been clearer, they felt that they should have listened more attentively.

The relationship between the teacher and the students was very positive and there was no hard feeling between either party. Accepting that all teachers can make mistakes, the excellent rapport between the teacher and the students ensured a favourable outcome. Furthermore, this incident highlights the importance of a classroom climate that allows mistakes to be made without confrontation or recrimination.

Comment

In general, teachers dealt with the misbehaviour incidents quickly and succinctly, seldom allowing the incident to escalate. The rationale given by teachers to explain their reactions to student misbehaviours highlights their concern for a controlled, safe and positive learning environment. Although the students' reasons for misbehaving seldom agree with the reasons given by teachers for the same incident, the long-term effectiveness of disciplinary procedures will depend upon teachers helping students to understand the rationale behind their reactions, but, at the same time, accepting that some of the conditions that give rise to student misbehaviours may be their own fault. In one sense it is unlikely that the two parties will ever be completely reconciled, but understanding students' perceptions of certain behaviours will help teachers to arrive at decisions in a more reflective way. Furthermore, as student cooperation is essential for order in a classroom, explaining to students the rationale behind a decision is a necessity. However, for all this to happen a trust must be built up between teachers and students and this can only be achieved by teachers being consistent and fair in their responses to all students' behaviours.

The complexity of any one misbehaviour incident highlights the problem for teacher educators in helping pre-service teachers develop strategies for control and discipline. To use a technique with little knowledge of the students and without fully understanding the events and conditions that may have influenced a behaviour ignores the subtleness required of teachers in a complex situation. Pre-service teachers must learn about effective teachers' strategies, they must watch and get these teachers to explain their responses and they themselves must be observed practising techniques and examining their use with their mentors. Pre-service teachers must study control and discipline in PE settings rather than just learning competencies in the techniques.

Other investigations

In physical education, Piéron (1994) noted the dearth of studies related to student misbehaviour. His own research (Piéron and Emonts, 1988; Piéron and Brito, 1990) examined the misbehaviour event with particular reference to the persons involved in misbehaviour incidents and the reactions of teachers to those situations. It was concluded that the frequency of misbehaviour (i.e. an average of nine incidents per class) was high enough to put any teaching and learning objectives at risk, that boys were the main source of trouble to teachers in mixed-sex classes, that some physical activities are at the origin of many student misbehaviours and that teachers should use more structured non-verbal responses to deal with misbehaviour in order to avoid the spreading of incidents to on-task students. With regard to teachers' reaction to student misbehaviours Piéron and Brito noted the variety of verbal and non-verbal techniques used by teachers, although nearly one half of the incidents observed were not identified by the teachers.

In an examination of misbehaviour incidents as perceived by pre-service teachers (Gadaan, Marzouk, Brunelle and Goyette, 1993), it was reported that the pre-service teachers targeted pupils talking and being noisy during instruction, and pupils modifying the task, stopping the activity and being disobedient during the practice. Brunelle, Brunelle, Lamy and Paré (1996) noted that one half of registered misbehaviour experienced by pre-service teachers could have disturbed teaching activities, and that just over one-tenth of all misbehaviours showed a high level of violence. Fernández-Balboa (1991) also focused upon pre-service teachers and he reported that the latter felt that the causes of misbehaviour were predominantly student-related (e.g. boredom, lack of interest towards physical education, personal characteristics of students), and that they believed that there was very little that they could do to prevent misbehaviours happening. In fact, it was suggested that the pre-service teachers thought very little about what might have caused misbehaviour or how they could have avoided it.

Comment

It has been suggested that Physical Education teachers do not perceive major problems in their classes (Houghton, Wheldall and Merrett, 1988), and that many of the misbehaviour incidents are not of a severe nature (O'Sullivan and Dyson, 1994). However, the frequency of misbehaviour incidents in physical education classes can still disrupt lesson flow, and such influences as gender and the activity may need to be investigated more thoroughly. In addition, the fact that many incidents are not identified by experienced teachers indicates the complexity and 'hidden' nature of many classroom events, and the use of a variety of techniques to deal with misbehaviour perhaps reflects the uniqueness of each incident. If the problem is to be more fully understood by teacher educators, not only do they need the views of pre-service teachers on the topic, but they will need data on what actually happens in their classes.

Conclusions and Recommendations

Data collected on student misbehaviour in physical education classes give some pointers as to when misbehaviour occurs, experienced teachers' responses to misbehaviour and the complexity of the misbehaviour event. For example, class instruction can be a problem area for teachers, the public reprimand of one or two students can interrupt the lesson flow and teachers' and students' perceptions of the misbehaviour event indicate a hidden conflict. However, the effectiveness of any teacher reprimand will not only depend upon the sensitivity of the teacher's response to a particular set of events but to the position adopted by both the teacher and the student. The teacher who adopts an authoritarian position will react differently to the teacher who adopts a counselling one, and the interaction will be affected in different ways depending upon whether the students adopts either a compliant or resistant position. Therefore, the application of control and discipline strategies without such understanding may result in short-term control, but it may leave a situation that is smouldering and ready to explode at any time.

If teacher educators are to help pre-service teachers learn how to develop effective control and discipline strategies and experienced teachers are to examine their practices, more evidence is needed in the following areas:

- How do experienced physical education teachers react to different individuals within any one class?
- How do experienced teachers react to different age-groups?
- Why do some physical education teachers have more student misbehaviour problems than others?

- Does the frequency and type of student misbehaviour differ between single-sex and mixed-sex classes?
- Are the more severe student misbehaviour incidents the result of immediate events or are they results of long-term conflicts?
- How do pre-service and inexperienced physical education teachers respond to student misbehaviour?
- What are the most effective ways of helping pre-service and inexperienced physical education teachers to learn control and discipline strategies?

Such an examination of student misbehaviour in physical education classes cannot do justice to the very complex topic of control and discipline in schools. However, it can provide evidence for teacher reflection and a platform from which to develop further research.

References

BANK, B.J. (1987) 'Students' sex', in DUNKIN, M.J. (ed.) *The International Encyclopaedia of Teaching and Teacher Education*, Oxford: Pergamon Press, pp. 571–4.

BELLON, J.J., BELLON, E.C. and BLANK, M.A. (1992) *Teaching from a Research Knowledge Base*, New York: Macmillan.

BROPHY, J.E. (1987) 'Educating teachers about managing classrooms and students' (Occasional Paper No. 115), E. Lansing, MI, Michigan State University: Institute for Research on Teaching.

BROPHY, J.E. and GOOD, T.L. (1970) 'Teachers' communication of differential expectations for children's classroom performance: Some behavioural data', *Journal of Educational Psychology*, **61**, pp. 365–74.

BRUNELLE, J.-P., BRUNELLE, J., LAMY, S. and PARÉ, C. (1996) 'Disciplinary incidents experienced by physical education student teachers', in *Abstracts, International Seminar, Research on Teaching and Research on Teacher Education*, Lisbon, Technical University of Lisbon, November 21–24, p. 76.

BURDEN, P.R. (1995) *Classroom Management and Discipline: Methods to Facilitate Cooperation and Instruction*, New York: Longman.

CANGELOSI, J.S. (1993) *Classroom Management Strategies: Gaining and Maintaining Students' Cooperation*, New York: Longman.

DOYLE, W. (1986) 'Classroom organisation and management', in WITTROCK, M.C. (ed.) *Handbook of Research on Teaching* (3rd ed.), New York: Macmillan, pp. 392–431.

DREIKERS, R., GRUNWALD, B. and PEPPER, F. (1982) *Maintaining Sanity in the Classroom: Classroom Management Techniques* (3rd ed.), New York: Harper and Row.

EMMER, E.T. (1987) 'Classroom management', in DUNKIN, M.J. (ed.) *The International Encyclopaedia of Teaching and Teacher Education*, Oxford: Pergamon Press, pp. 437–46.

FERNÁNDEZ-BALBOA, J.-M. (1991) 'Beliefs, interactive thoughts and actions of physical education student teachers regarding student misbehaviours', *Journal of Teaching in Physical Education*, **11**, 1, pp. 59–78.

FRENCH, R., SILLIMAN, L. and HENDERSON, H. (1990) 'Too much time in time out!', *Strategies*, January, pp. 5–7.

GADAAN, M., MARZOUK, A., BRUNELLE, J. and GOYETTE, R. (1993) 'Etude des incidents disciplinaires qui interpellent le plus des stagiaires en éducation physique au secondaire selon les divers moments de la séance', Poster presented at the AIESEP International Seminar, The Training of Teachers in Reflective Practice of Physical Education, held in Trois-Rivières, Québec, CDN, July 1993.

GOLDENSON, R.M. (1984) *Longman Dictionary of Psychology of Psychiatry*, New York: Longman.

GOOD, T.L., SIKES, J.N. and BROPHY, J.E. (1972) 'Effects of teacher sex and student sex and student achievement on classroom interaction', *Technical Report No. 61*, Centre for Research in Social Behaviour, University of Missouri at Columbia, Missouri.

GRAHAM, G. (1992) *Teaching Children Physical Education: Becoming a Master Teacher*, Champaign, IL: Human Kinetics.

HARDY, C.A. (1992) 'Student misbehaviour during physical education lessons', *The Bulletin of Physical Education*, **28**, 2, pp. 59–67.

HARDY, C.A. (1993) 'A content analysis study of types of student misbehaviour and teacher reaction in physical education classes', Paper presented at the International Conference, Teacher Education: From Practice to Theory, June 27–July 1, Tel-Aviv, Israel.

HARDY, C.A. (1996) 'Student misbehaviour and teacher response in physical education lessons', Paper presented at the International Seminar, Research on Teaching and Research on Teacher Education, November 21–24, Technical University of Lisbon, Portugal.

HARDY, C.A. and HARDY, J.O. (1995) 'The language physical education teachers use in reprimanding students', Paper presented at the International Conference, Windows to the Future, Bridging the Gaps between Disciplines, Curriculum and Instruction, June 26–30, Wingate Institute, Israel.

HARDY, C.A., HARDY, C.E. and THORPE, R.D. (1994) 'Student misbehaviour in secondary school mixed-sex physical education lessons', *British Journal of Physical Education*, **25**, 4, Research Supplement, pp. 7–11.

HENDERSON, H.L. and FRENCH, R. (1990) 'How to use verbal reprimands in a positive manner', *Physical Educator*, **47**, 4, pp. 193–6.

HOUGHTON, S., WHELDALL, K. and MERRETT, F. (1988) 'Classroom behaviour problems which secondary school teachers say they find most troublesome', *British Educational Research Journal*, **14**, 3, pp. 297–312.

LAWRENCE, J., STEED, D. and YOUNG, P. (1984) *Disruptive Children: Disruptive Schools*, New York: Croom Helm Nichols Publishing Company.

LOPEZ, S.M. (1985) 'An innovation in mixed gender P.E. — with special reference to whether this form of grouping can undermine gender stereotypical attitudes towards P.E.', Unpublished Master's dissertation, University of Southampton.

MUNN, P. and JOHNSTONE, M. (1991) 'A research project on discipline in primary and secondary schools', funded by the Scottish Office Education Department.

O'SULLIVAN, M. and DYSON, B. (1994) *Journal of Teaching in Physical Education*, **13**, 4, pp. 361–74.

OSWALD, M. (1995) 'Difficult-to-manage students: A survey of children who fail to respond to student discipline strategies in government schools', *Educational Studies*, **21**, 2, pp. 265–76.

PIÉRON, M. (1994) *Sport Pedagogy: Highlights on Research on Teaching/Teacher Preparation*, Liège, University of Liège.

PIÉRON, M. and BRITO, M. (1990) 'Analyse d'incidents d'indiscipline survenant dans des classes de l'enseignment préparatoire (10–12 ans)', in RURAN, J., HERNANDEZ, J.L. and

Ruiz, L.M. (eds) *Humanismo y Nuevas Tecnologias en la Educación Física y el Deporte*, Madrid, Instituto Nacional de Educación Física, pp. 113–17.

Piéron, M. and Emonts, M. (1988) 'Analyse des problèmes de discipline dans des classes d'éducation physique', *Revue de l'Education Physique*, **28**, 1, pp. 33–40.

Reynolds, A. (1992) 'What is competent beginning teaching? A review of the literature', *Review of Educational Research*, **62**, 1, pp. 1–35.

Rink, J.E. (1993) *Teaching Physical Education for Learning* (2nd ed.), St Louis, MO: Mosby.

Smith, L.M. and Geoffrey, W. (1968) *The Complexities of an Urban Classroom*, New York: Holt, Rinehart and Winston.

Sylwester, R. (1971) *The Elementary Teacher and Student Misbehaviour*, West Nyack, NY: Parker.

Tinning, R. (1987) *Improving Teaching in Physical Education*, Victoria: Deakin University Press.

Wubbels, T., Creton, H.A. and Holvast, A. (1989) 'Undesirable classroom situation: A systems communication perspective', in *Teaching and Teacher Education Newsletter*, Spring, 1, 2 (American Educational Research Association).

Wurzer, D. and McKenzie, T. (1987) 'Constructive alternatives to punishment', *Strategies*, September–October, pp. 6–9.

8   Instruction from a Learning Perspective

Judith E. Rink

The term instruction is usually meant to describe a process that is used to bring a learner to intended learning. Several key notions characterize instruction. First, the purpose of instruction is learning, and second, this learning is intended by the teacher. Students may learn much that is not intended, both as part of the instructional process as well as apart from the instructional process. What distinguishes instruction is the teacher's intended learning: the design of learning experiences for a particular intent. Two theoretical and research bases provide a framework for instruction: what we know about learning and what we know about teaching for learning. Too often these perspectives operate in isolation of each other.

The purpose of this chapter is to review what we know about teaching from a learning perspective. The focus will be the learning of motor skills as applied to physical education content. The chapter begins with a brief discussion of learner needs and learning theory. The last section reviews the critical variables often established as principles of quality instruction from the perspective of learning. The intent is to provide a discussion of important instructional issues that is grounded in both learning theory and practice.

Meeting Student Needs As a Learner

Instruction, regardless of its roots must meet particular learner needs. The task provided to the learner must be individually appropriate; the learner must have a clear idea of what he or she is expected to do and be motivated to engage at a high level with the task; the learner must have sufficient opportunity to learn the task; and, the learner must receive information on their performance (Rink, 1998). These learner needs for instruction are said to be generic to the content to be learned and the situation.

Appropriate Task

The idea of the learning task is used here to describe what the learner is expected to do substantively. In physical education the learning task is usually, but not always, a movement task: the learner is expected to respond motorically. Tasks are not appropriate in physical education when students are not able to approach success in executing a motor response, whether that motor response is created, selected, or, is a match to what the teacher demonstrated. Tasks are appropriate when learners have the prerequisite abilities and skills to make the learning process successful.

Learner prerequisites may involve physical abilities such as those described under organismic restraints in dynamical systems (Magill, 1993; Newell, 1986). The ability to execute a motor response may be limited by fitness components (e.g. muscular strength and endurance, cardio-vascular endurance, flexibility) as well as motor ability constraints such as reaction time, visual acuity, and multi-limb coordination. For example, students who do not have the abdominal and arm strength to do a hip circle on the bar could practise a very long time at that skill and still not be successful.

Task appropriateness is also affected by the acquisition of skills and abilities thought to be prerequisites for a more difficult skill. Of particular concern is the ability to execute an open motor skill in simpler conditions before the learner is expected to use the skill in complex conditions (Rink, French, Werner, Lynn and Mays, 1992). An example of an ability being a prerequisite would be the ability to do a lay up shot without defenders before a player is asked to do a lay up in a game. This idea will be discussed later in the chapter as part of the idea of content development. Decisions relative to how much to reduce a skill or how much to break it down are often made by the teacher who must balance issues of student success with ideas of 'meaningful wholes'. What constitutes a meaningful whole is a major issue in learning theory and the practice of teaching.

Motivational/Attentional Disposition to the Task

Student motivation to learn (degree of attraction the learner has toward doing something) has always been considered an essential aspect of learning regardless of the espoused learning theory guiding instruction. When students are motivated to learn they are likely to be more extensively involved in the learning process and actively processing what they are doing. A high level of student engagement is an essential ingredient of all learning theories and therefore a strong part of any instructional recommendation. Different instructional orientations involve the student in different ways, and therefore have different potentials for active processing. Student motivation and attentional disposition to the task is effected by a variety of contextual factors including student prior experience and the learning environment.

Clear Idea of the Task

In order for learning to occur, the student must have a clear idea of the task they are being asked to do (Kennedy, Cruickshank, Bush and Meyers, 1978; Werner and Rink, 1988). The motor task explanations and demonstrations common to direct instruction are examples of attempts at teacher clarity. However, the notion of task clarity is not the same as the idea of giving the learner precise and explicit directions and descriptions of what to do and how to do it. Instructional strategies that attempt to transfer responsibility for learning to the learner, engage the learner in higher order processes, or establish environments that elicit responses also have a responsibility to be clear. Instruction should not be a search for what the teacher wants a student to do, but rather students should be able to articulate task expectations, regardless of the nature of that task.

Opportunity to Learn

The opportunity students have to learn a skill is the biggest single factor that will predict how much a student learns (Brophy and Good, 1986; Metzler, 1989; Silverman, 1990). If you are not engaged with a particular content you cannot learn that content. Therefore, a major characteristic of good instruction is that learners are provided time to learn. The refinement of motor skills is ultimately dependent on good practice.

Information on Performance

Learners need information on their performance. This information can come in a variety of forms, at different times and from a variety of sources. Information can relate to the effectiveness of a learner's movement (e.g. Did the ball go into the basket?) or the process characteristics of the movement (e.g. Did the learner square up before taking the shot?). Learning theorists often refer to these characteristics as knowledge of results and knowledge of performance respectively (Magill, 1994b). Different approaches to skill learning have attempted to enhance learning by manipulating the form, source, and time at which the learner receives information on performance.

Grounding Instructional Theory in Learning Theory

Different approaches to instruction attempt to meet learner needs in different ways. Although there is always a danger in setting up dichotomies, different approaches to instruction are often characterized as either direct or indirect instructional processes. Direct instruction usually means that the teaching is explicit. The teacher breaks down skills and organizes instruction in a step by step manner, and gives specific directions on how to do whatever is expected of the learner. Direct instruction is usually highly monitored by the teacher and is most often explicit (Rosenshine, 1987). Indirect instruction usually implies that the learning outcomes are not as specifically described or prescribed by the teacher. The goals of indirect instruction are usually more holistic in nature and implicit rather than explicit in their delivery. Indirect instruction strategies usually are most often intended to involve the learner in the process of creating rather than duplicating the response identified and communicated by the teacher (Peterson, 1979). Each of these orientations to instruction are grounded either directly or indirectly in learning theory.

Although it is not always the case, efforts to identify appropriate instructional methods and strategies would seem to need grounding in efforts to understand how students learn what content under what conditions. The assumption is that in order to help students learn we need to understand how learning occurs in school settings. No single comprehensive learning theory exists that would explain learning or the lack of it in all situations. Behaviourist, information processing, cognitive strategy, and social learning models of learning have had the most influence on approaches to teaching physical education and motor skills. More recently the concept of dynamical systems has been offered, not as a model explaining learning, but a model explaining the factors contributing to the selection of a motor response (Magill, 1993; Newell, 1986). Dynamical systems is included here because of its singular importance to the discussion of learning motor skills. Each of these theories will be identified only briefly and then discussed in terms of their implications for instructional practice. No attempt is made to do justice to the ideas inherent in these theories. The reader is encouraged to consult more extensive references if needed.

Behaviourist models of learning emphasize the importance of the external environment in shaping behaviour. Teachers are encouraged to reward and positively reinforce appropriate behaviour and gradually shape behaviour to clearly define appropriate performance. Step by step success oriented models of instruction have their roots in behavioural psychology (Bandura, 1969). Many learning experiences in schools are conducted using a behaviourist orientation to learning.

An information processing orientation to learning has sought to study internal cognitive processes of learners (Starkes and Allard, 1993). Information processing is concerned with the manner in which individuals select, use, store, and interpret information. From a teaching perspective a major contribution of information processing has been the emphasis placed on the nature and delivery of information to the learner.

Cognitive theorists have been concerned with the holistic nature of learning and the strategies people use to solve problems, create, and learn (Anderson, Reder and Simon, 1996; Grehaigne and Godbout, 1995). Constructivism and notions of situated learning are current popular philosophical orientations to the teaching–learning process that would be identified with cognitive theories of learning (Kirk and MacDonald, 1998). Constructivist orientations emphasize that learning is an active process on the part of a learner who interacts with both a meaningful task and the learning environment to literally organize experiences and construct personal meaning. Constructivist theories focus more on the nature of the content presented to the learner, the environment, and the role of the learner. Larger chunks of content and efforts to involve the learner at higher levels of processing characterize the pedagogy of the constructivists.

Social learning theorists emphasize the effectiveness and importance of learning in a social context with others (Salomon and Perkins, 1998; Vygotsky, 1978). Social learning theorists contend that groups of learners construct knowledge through an interactive process. Constructing knowledge is different from acquiring knowledge. Knowledge acquisition assumes that knowledge is out there to be acquired by the learner in a summative fashion. Social learning theorists assume that what is constructed in a social interaction process is far different not only in terms of process but in terms of substance.

Although not a learning theory, recent work in motor behaviour has focused on dynamical systems as an explanation for the manner in which an individual responds motorically to their environment. Dynamical systems suggests that patterns of motor coordination are not the result of prescriptions for action but rather the interaction of organismic (e.g. physical strength), environmental (e.g. size of the equipment) and task constraints (e.g. what the learner thinks are the parameters of the task) (Magill, 1998; Newell, 1986). A motor response is not a selection but rather the result of constraining the system in particular ways. A motor response given by an individual is a response based on the interaction of all three constraints. Given this assumption, the teacher in the instructional process must consider and can manipulate task factors in all three types of constraints to facilitate appropriate motor responses.

It should be clear to the reader that direct instructional strategies find their roots in more behavioural and information processing explanations for learning and more indirect strategies find their roots in learning theories more associated with describing cognitive strategies and social learning. These different perspectives on learning form the basis for much of the dialogue on teaching and tend to come into and out of favour with the socio-political climate of a time. Several key differences divide the learning theories described in the previous section.

Identifying Instructional Issues

What is at issue between direct and indirect approaches to teaching, and the learning theories they attach themselves to, is: the nature of cognitive processing essential for learning; the appropriate size of the 'chunk' of content presented to the learner; the amount of information the learner needs on that chunk of content; and, the learning environment that best facilitates this process. In one form or another it is these issues that tend to be the focus of professional discourse on how best to instruct.

All approaches to instruction recognize the need for high levels of learner involvement with the content. There is less consensus on issues related to the level of cognitive processing essential for learning and whether or not cognitive processing has to be at a conscious level. Constructivists would advocate a high cognitive level of engagement sometimes referred to as higher order thinking (Anderson, Reder and Simon, 1996), while the behaviourists are not as concerned with the level of processing as they are with the nature of the response of the learner. The behaviourist is concerned with getting the learner to produce an appropriate response and reinforcing that response. The process the learner uses to produce that response may not be critical.

While constructivists and behaviourists do not address the issue of conscious level of processing, the issue is imbedded in the pedagogy of the constructivist and the behaviourist. The synonyms for the terms direct (explicit) and indirect (implicit) instruction are the terms used by the psychology literature to indicate conscious and unconscious processing respectively. The dynamical systems literature coming out of motor control clearly eludes to the idea that the learner does not have to process what they are doing at a conscious level in order to make an appropriate motor response to a task. The 'system' will always choose an appropriate response based on the constraints (Newell, 1986). Magill in a recent presentation (1998) explored the notion that learners can acquire knowledge about how to perform motor skills without being able to verbalize that knowledge. Knowledge in the context of this work means environmental critical cues necessary to perform primarily open skills. Psychologists refer to knowledge gained through unconscious processing as implicit knowledge rather than explicit knowledge. Magill also suggests that while it is not important for learners to be able to verbalize that knowledge it is important that learners visually focus on the environmental cues. Learners need time to acquire essential knowledge about the environment through active processing of environmental cues. How much knowledge learners need about motor responses is beginning to be of interest to motor behaviour researchers (Wulf and Weigelt, 1997).

Constructivists have advocated that a larger and more meaningful 'chunk' of content be presented to learners as opposed to breaking down content into less than 'wholes' characteristic of more behaviourist orientations to instruction (Anderson et al., 1996; Kirk and MacDonald, 1998). Constructivist orientations to instruction also advocate that the learner be permitted to find their own way through tasks to promote higher levels of cognitive processing, rather than being given explicit detailed information on how the task is to be accomplished. The pedagogy of the behaviourist is concerned with creating small step by step increments of content to create success oriented learning.

Related to both the type of processing and the level of processing are issues of student motivation, particularly as student motivation relates to levels of student engagement and processing. Recent educational literature has given a lot of attention to notions of student motivation (Pintrich, Marx and Boyle, 1993; Wigfield, Eccles and Rodriguez, 1998). If student engagement is crucial to learning, then how to increase student engagement is critical. Of particular concern are issues related to choosing teaching strategies and creating environmental conditions that facilitate student motivation, which should lead to higher levels of student engagement and therefore higher levels of student processing. As Wigfield et al. (1998) suggest, the literature on motivation has been problematic. Most studies have not addressed motivation as a multi-dimensional concept that has both content specific as well as generalizable aspects. In school settings both academic goals and social goals of the learner interact to influence learning and are linked to notions of an appropriate learning environment.

Most learning theories have assumed that learning is a private experience: groups do not learn, individuals do. Social contructivists would say that all learning is social, as meaning is socially constructed (Salomon and Perkins, 1998; Vygotsky, 1978). From the learner perspective, individual self perceptions, goals and the social learning environment all mediate student choices, performance and effort, and therefore student learning. Sorting out the specific role created by the learning environment has been most difficult. When translated into practice, the learning environments created by the social learning theorists rest heavily on pedagogy that involves the learner in social ways with others (peer teaching, cooperative learning, creating learning communities etc.).

What is significant about the more recent emphasis on constructivism and social learning is the recognition that teaching and learning does not always have to be explicit and is not always an independent experience. While there is sufficient documentation to support explicit teaching and explicit learning there is now also the beginning of support for teaching and learning that rests heavily on implicit strategies.

Meeting Learner Needs through Effective Pedagogy

The predominant approach to identifying effective pedagogy has been to study what teachers do who produce the most learning. While this direct approach is limited in some respects, particularly in theory building, it has been successful in identifying critical instructional characteristics related to student learning. What follows is a discussion of these instructional characteristics. The intent is to look at the ideas from both a learning theory perspective and learner need perspective in terms of the major issues previously identified.

Providing Opportunity to Respond

Since the beginning teacher studies of the 1970s, time with the content has been identified as an essential component of effective instruction (Brophy and Good, 1986; Metzler, 1989; Rosenshine, 1987). Put quite simply, students who spend more time with the content learn more. Over the years this notion of time with the content has been somewhat refined. What initially started out as a concept of teacher allocated time has been refined to include ideas of success, appropriate content, and high levels of student engagement with the content. Students who are engaged with some success, with content appropriate to their developmental level, and in a manner that produces a high level of processing will learn more (Ashy, Lee and Landin, 1988; Magill, 1993; Silverman, 1990; Solmon and Lee, 1997).

Most of the research base on opportunity to respond has been done with the concept of academic learning time (ALT), which emerged from the beginning teacher effectiveness research (Peterson, 1979). Key to the notion of academic learning time both in the classroom and in physical education (ALT-PE) is the amount of time the student is engaged with the content at a high level of success. Academic learning time is not only an indicator of time the student is engaged with the content in general. In order to be related to learning the student has to be engaged successfully at an appropriate level. In the classroom research this indicator was defined very specifically to the content that was taught. In physical education a more generic sense of appropriateness and success defines the constructs of the instrument used to measure ALT-PE (Metzler, 1979). The more generic definitions used in the physical education instrument allow the instrument to be used across content within physical education.

The relationship between ALT-PE and student learning in physical education is a positive one but perhaps not as strong as what might have been expected (Silverman, Divillier and Rammirez, 1991). There are several potential alternative explanations for the failure of ALT-PE to demonstrate a very high relationship with learning. The most obvious is the notion that the definitions used in the instrumentation are generic to physical education rather than specific to particular kinds of content within physical education (e.g. gymnastics handstand). Generic definitions would cause some error in 'counting' or not 'counting' time engaged as motor appropriate time. A good example of this is the player who in a game infrequently touches the ball and yet would be considered motor engaged. A less obvious explanation for the lack of the expected relationship of learning with ALT-PE might be related to the actual relationship between what the student is practising and what is being measured as an indicator for learning. A student can be highly engaged with a task, but, if that task is not related to the learning objective being measured, or is but one step in a series of steps that leads to learning of complex skills, then motor appropriate time for just that one task would be insufficient to produce learning. In other words, the nature of development of skill over time is also a key element. A third alternative is that motor engaged time, the way it has been defined, is just not as critical to learning as we have thought.

Students for whom a skill or task is inappropriate do not achieve a high enough level of success for learning to occur. The personal research of the author over three studies clearly demonstrates the futility of practice for learners for whom the task is inappropriate because they do not have the prerequisite abilities (French, Rink, Rickard, Mays, Lynn and Werner, 1991; Rink, French, Werner, Lynn and Mays, 1992). However, the notion of appropriate success level is also an idea related to academic learning time that deserves a second look. The idea of high levels of success recommended by classroom literature is obviously a problem for motor skills that are eye hand and eye foot complex skills (e.g. golf drives, basketball free throws, tennis serves etc.). Even professional players cannot achieve recommended levels of success in some of the skills part of our programmes.

From a motor learning perspective, there is some suggestion that learners more successful in acquisition stages may not be the most successful when actual learning is measured (when time has elapsed after practice) (Sidaway, Fairweather, Powell and Hall, 1992; Schmidt, Young, Swinnen and Shapiro, 1989). Motor learning researchers refer to this as the difference between the acquisition phase and the retention phase (Magill, 1993). This research would indicate that the very highest levels of success in practice, particularly those achieved with a high dependence on knowledge of results, may not be the ultimate goal of instruction. Motor learning theorists suggest that high levels of processing may be more important than high levels of initial success.

The level of student processing is an issue that is not as easily measured as success is measured. Some more recent work on the use of learner strategies would seem to indicate that the level of cognitive involvement in learning motor skills may be a function of the skill level of the learner (Solmon and Lee, 1997). A process that facilitates a high level of cognitive processing for one student may elicit a very low level of processing for another student for a variety of reasons other than just skill level. This idea holds suspect the notion that you can predict the level of cognitive activity of the learner in a task with any accuracy, a view that is consistent with the idea that with practice we reduce the cognitive level at which we handle a task. The individual nature of learner processing is an idea that is also consistent with the notion that the student is the mediator of instruction (Solmon and Lee, 1997). Not attaching learner processing too strongly to a pedagogical strategy is important. From a teaching strategy, higher order thinking may not be occurring just because a teacher has selected a process that has the potential for higher order thinking. Likewise, some students may process what they are doing at a high level in spite of an instructional strategy that may not seem to encourage a high level of processing. More important than the pedagogical strategy is the level of student engagement.

By any measure, knowing how much time the student is engaged at an appropriate level with the content is an important dimension of effective teaching. Exactly what this level of success needs to be may be different for different skills and may not be as high as what was previously hypothesized. Designing learning experiences to promote challenge and processing without putting the learning task out of reach of the learner would seem to be the challenge. Notice that the phrase 'out of reach' has been substituted for the phrase 'lack of success'. What is less clear to researchers and what is most important to teachers is to recognize what takes place in an instructional environment that creates either high or low levels of appropriate task engagement. What do teachers do to create high ALT-PE motor engaged time that is appropriate for a diverse student group and promotes high levels of student success and processing.

Communication Skills

The communication skills of the teacher are essential aspects of effectiveness. Communication skills of teaching usually involve issues related to teacher clarity, the use of verbal cues and demonstration in presenting information, and concerns related to the type of information the learner needs, how much information the learner needs and when information is needed by the learner (Brophy and Good, 1986; Gould and Roberts, 1982).

The results of the initial research on teacher clarity done in the classroom focused on the importance of the ability of the teacher to carefully select the information needed by the learner, organize that information, and communicate that information to the learner. Ideas such as clarity, step by step progressions, specific and concrete procedures and checking for understanding were identified early as having a relationship to effective teaching (Kennedy, Cruickshank, Bush and Meyers, 1978; Rink, 1994; Rosenshine and Stevens, 1986). There is no reason to assume that these characteristics of teacher clarity are not still important components of all effective instruction.

Before we pursue any discussion of how teachers can best communicate how to do motor tasks, we must first acknowledge that how to do a motor task does not always have to be communicated. As dynamical systems and newer research on implicit learning (Magill, 1998) has suggested, and some constructivist orientations to teaching have utilized, a learner will organize a response to a task based on the organismic, task, and environmental constraints of the task. A study done by Sweeting and Rink (1998) contrasted the effects of kindergarten and second graders learning a long jump either directly or through an environmentally designed task approach. The environmental design put students in a variety of situations where they had to complete the task using the standing long jump skill with no teacher information on how to do the skill. The environmentally designed task clearly increased initial performance, particularly for younger and less skilled students but lost its effect with time and increasing skill. A second study that attempted to sort out how much information a learner needs on how to perform was done in the context of volleyball progressions (Rink et al., 1992). One group was given helpful information during practice of how to best perform and another was not. For most initial tasks in the progression the success levels during practice were similar. For a later stage of the progression the group that did not receive information from the teacher on how to make an adjustment to a task that had increased in complexity was not successful. This lack of success was maintained through later stages in the progression.

Advocates of a 'games for understanding' approach to developing games players suggest that students should not be taught how to execute motor skills prior to needing them in the context of game play (Almond, 1986; Chandler and Mitchell, 1991). In a sense, games for understanding is another approach that down plays giving information to learners on how to execute skills. The results of this research is mixed (Rink, 1996). However, the real issue for all of these orientations is not if, but when, the learner should receive information on how to execute a motor skill. Does the learner need specific information on how to execute a motor response — not always — but clearly sometimes. Is not giving learners information on how to do a skill non-teaching and trial and error learning, or, is the teaching just different. If beginners do not need explicit information do learners who are refining skills profit from explicit teaching? Learning requires processing, regardless of whether information is given by the teacher. Knowing how to get learners processing what they are doing enough to 'generate' appropriate motor responses and knowing when to intervene with more specific help and different tasks that elicit more advanced responses may be the art of teaching.

If the teacher is to provide the learner with information on how to do a skill, the presentation skills of the teacher are important components of effective teaching. In the development of skill the teacher is going to have to have the ability to clearly communicate the essential aspects of performance. The use of demonstration and the selection of learning cues are essential aspects of communicating to learners how to execute a motor skill (Landin, 1994; Lee, Swinnen and Serrien, 1995; Magill, 1994a; McCullagh, Stiehl and Weiss, 1990). Sometimes these cues may be explicit cues on performance and sometimes these cues may be environmental cues necessary for implicit knowledge about how to perform.

The notion of demonstrating (modeling) is another aspect of communication that has maintained strong support in the research done in a variety of fields including classroom research, research in social learning, motor learning research, as well as the pedagogy research that has been done in physical education (Martens, Burwitz and Zuckerman, 1976; McCullagh et al., 1990). Most of this research assumes that the teacher is attempting to communicate to learners how a skill is to be performed with the expectation that the learners will be attempting to closely approximate the demonstration. Teaching strategies that have been more direct teaching have assumed that if the learner can verbalize what they are doing or should be doing then learning is enhanced (Kwak, 1993). Young and beginning learners are most likely to pick up implicit cues from a demonstration without being able to verbalize what they are doing.

Most research has assumed that the demonstration should be accurate, and in the case of new and complex skills should be performed more than once (Landin, 1994; McCullagh et al., 1990; Rink, 1998). More recent research has questioned that assumption and has suggested that a 'learning' demonstrator, meaning a student who is also learning the skill who may not be proficient at the skill, might be equally as effective as an accurate demonstrator (Solmon and Lee, 1996). The support for this idea is again related to the notion that 'learner' demonstrators may facilitate the learner processing more information. The parameters of this idea have yet to be explored. It is possible that learners who have a clear cognitive understanding of the intent of the skill can function with an inaccurate model. Learners who have little cognitive understanding of what they are trying to do are unlikely to be helped by watching someone perform a skill poorly.

The use of verbal cues has been identified as one way in which teachers can give students a clear cognitive understanding of what they are trying to do (Landin, 1994). There is some support for the use of verbal cues and for encouraging students to verbally rehearse how they are going to do motor skills as part of task presentations (Kwak, 1993). Teachers can increase the likelihood of student success with a movement response by carefully selecting the cues they use to describe how a skill is done and by sequencing (ordering) the cues for the learner to facilitate student rehearsal of the skill (McCullagh et al., 1990). The issue is of course whether this initial acquisition success elicited with teacher cues supports or hinders learner processing critical to retention. When students are asked to verbally rehearse, either through self-talk or outloud methods, it is more likely to focus their attention on what is important and to increase the likelihood that they will process what they are doing, than if students are asked to just practise. More recent research on the use of strategies by beginning learners would tend to support the importance of providing learners who are at beginning stages in learning skills with strategies for learning (Solmon and Lee, 1997).

Most of the research that has been done with task presentation and communication skills of the teacher has been done in the context of direct instruction. The teacher's intent is that the learner replicate the response the teacher demonstrates and communicates. In this context task presentation skills are part of the task presentation and communication skills of the teacher. Although it may not always be the intent of the teacher for students to replicate a motor response, indirect teaching is no excuse for a lack of communication between the teacher and the student. Students should know what they are trying to do in a learning experience.

The research base on indirect teaching, particularly in physical education, is not extensive (Rink, 1996). This does not mean that we cannot postulate what clarity might mean in indirect teaching. Generally speaking the teacher using more indirect methods intends to transfer responsibility for learning to the student, and more commonly to engage the student in the learning process in different ways. Teachers who are effective communicators would communicate to learners exactly what the student's responsibility is in the learning process and what process they intend the student to engage in. Teachers who are good communicators in indirect teaching would make sure students understand exactly what they are supposed to be doing before they send them off to do it. Often this means demonstrating examples of appropriate responses and structuring task presentations to guide students through initial steps before sending students off to engage in a more complex learning process.

Selecting and Developing the Content in the Instructional Process

The selection of the learning task is perhaps the single most critical decision that the teacher has to face. Unless the content is appropriate and unless it has a clear relationship to the learning goal it matters little how it is delivered. Content development is the process teachers use to bring the learner from one level of ability with the content to another level of ability (Rink, 1998). Two major issues constitute decisions relative to content development. The first involves the nature of the task and the starting point for instruction, and, the second the process used to move the student from an initial level with the content to a more advanced level.

What constitutes a 'meaningful chunk' of content was identified earlier as a critical issue for learning theorists. Current learning theory is concerned that the content the learner is asked to work with has 'meaning' in and of itself and is not just a fragmented part of something else (Anderson, Reder and Simon, 1996; Kirk and MacDonald, 1998). Likewise, motor learning theorists have vigorously suggested that it is the whole skill that should be practised when possible and not the individual parts (Magill, 1998). In addition, skills should be practised in the context in which they are going to be used. Both research groups would support the idea that students are not likely to use what they have learned in meaningful contexts if learning is fragmented and out of context.

In the context of physical education is a meaningful whole the individual skills of a sport, the game, or something in between? What constitutes a meaningful whole? At a more micro level the issue for sport skill instruction becomes an issue of whole part whole learning: should the teacher break down individual skills? Ample evidence exists to support the idea that unless safety is an issue, practice of the whole should precede any attempt to temporarily fragment the skill and practice part of a skill. At a more macro level the notion of progressions also involves reducing the complexity of the context in which skills are learned and practised. No one is suggesting that the learning of motor skills occur in a game. As a matter of fact, research done on skill improvement over time would suggest that players do not improve their individual motor skills by playing the game (French and Thomas, 1987; Parker and O'Sullivan, 1983). Research also supports the idea that reducing skills and learning tasks is essential when students are not successful. In some of the studies done by the author, students who practised a final skill task in a volleyball study (receiving a pass from one direction and sending it to another direction) were not as ultimately successful as those students who practised with a progression that initially reduced the complexity and then gradually increased it (French et al., 1991; Rink et al., 1992).

As stated earlier the selection of an appropriate task will largely be based on the teacher's ability to balance the need for meaning and the need for success. While many behavioural models of step by step instruction may have overemphasized the need for immediate success and become mindless and meaningless exercises for many students, learning theories which are overly concerned with meaning for the learner may choose too large a chunk of content for learner success. Designing learning experiences to promote challenge and processing without putting the learning task out of reach of the learner would seem to be the challenge.

Another factor involved in teacher decisions about the development of content is related to the nature of the practice. Motor skill learning has often been associated with 'drill like' practice. While there may be merit in developing some level of consistency in performance at particular stages of learning, for most situations repetition of the same movement discourages high levels of processing, and in the case of open motor skills reduces the variability of practice essential to prepare the learner to use a skill in a more complex context. For beginners who do not have any consistency there might be enough 'variability' repeating the same skill to encourage processing and some consistency. The higher skilled player who can perform consistently may need to practise particular skills in complex environments, including unpredictable environments that require decision making. The beginning learner who is highly involved in processing may need to gain some consistency of response through repetition in less complex environments before high levels of decision making are required.

The process the teacher uses in instruction to manipulate the level of difficulty to establish progressions, refine learner performance, and apply and assess what the student has learned has been referred to as content development (Rink, 1998). Teachers do this through a series of different kinds of tasks (extending, refining, applying) during the instructional process. There is not a great deal of research on content development. Several studies have documented the role of refining and extending tasks in learning (French et al., 1991; Masser, 1985, 1993; Rink et al., 1992). Good refining tasks have a prescriptive focus and can focus the learner on what is important to improve performance. It is likely that refining tasks increase learner processing of what they are doing and create accountability for good performance. As stated earlier, extension tasks establish progressions that are important for the development of complex skills and the use of complex skills in more difficult contexts. Like all instructional skills, the content development of the teacher is part of an interactive process. The teacher's decision of what to do next is based on what the students do.

Guidance and Teacher Feedback

Teacher feedback has come in and out of favour as a critical variable in the instructional process. Classroom work with effective tutors has demonstrated the value of a learner receiving information on their performance, encouragement, situationally specific guidance, eliciting responses from students etc., as supportive evidence of the fidelity of meeting learner individual needs (Lepper, 1988). Originally introduced from motor learning theory, the relationship between teacher feedback and student learning in pedagogy research in physical education has not been strong. There are several potential reasons for this lack of anticipated relationship. First, it is most difficult to find relationships with learning for single teacher behaviours, particularly those that are more critically individually applied and content specific. Second, it is also unlikely that a single teacher in a large group instructional setting can meet individual needs for feedback, even if feedback did have a high relationship to student learning in a one on one situation. Third, teacher feedback may not be the essential ingredient of learning it was once thought to be.

Motor learning theorists have concluded that the use of augmented feedback is very much dependent upon the individual learner and the skill (Magill, 1994b) being taught. There are some skills and some situations where a learner does not need a great deal of feedback and feedback may even create a dependency on the part of the learner. This dependency has the ultimate effect of reducing learner processing (Starkes and Allard, 1993). When a learner has a clear idea of the skill they are trying to perform and when they can access information on their performance, then teacher feedback may not be necessary. Where learners cannot access information on their performance and where they do not have a clear idea of what it is they are trying to do feedback may be essential. However, all learning is enhanced if teachers can get students to change aspects of their performance needing changing, and for many learners and many skills in physical education classes, appropriate feedback should improve learning. It is inappropriate to make the learner dependent upon teacher feedback to the extent that they do not learn to use information inherent in the task to guide their performance.

Feedback in a class instructional setting is important not only because of its potential to provide learners with critical information on performance. More than likely, feedback tends to improve learner processing and motivation. By helping students to maintain their focus on what they are doing, feedback should improve learner processing of what they are doing. By creating some kind of accountability for good performance, feedback can also serve to improve learner motivation to learn.

The Learning Environment

The issue for research on the learning environment from the perspective of learning theory is related to the kind of learning environment that facilitates learner processing and engagement. The early research on teacher management clearly illustrates the need for a well managed learning environment (Brophy and Good, 1986). What is new about the present discussion of learning environment, is the issue of whether learning is a social or an independent process. Much of the research on learning has taken place from the perspective of the individual learner and has been concerned with studying how individuals acquire knowledge and skills which may be facilitated by another or others. Learning from this perspective is primarily construed as an individual process. Research done from a social learning perspective is more concerned with the manner in which learning is actively constructed by a group of learners in particular environments (Salomon and Perkins, 1998; Vygotsky, 1978).

An active construction perspective and an individually acquired perspective on learning can coexist as explanations for different phenomena. Individuals can learn alone. They can acquire skills and knowledge from a facilitator whose role it is to help them acquire particular skills and knowledge (teacher or tutor). They can also learn in group environments devised to encourage interactive processes that help groups construct meaning. Physical education has been studied from the first two situations: individual learning and facilitated learning. Much of the work described in this chapter is from these perspectives. Some work on sport education and games for understanding approaches as a group learning situation and this work would indicate that group learning environments are effective in physical education (Hastie, 1996, 1998).

We know very little about the non-verbal and verbal interaction that takes place in a gymnasium where groups of learners are trying to acquire individual skills but have access to knowledge of the performance of others. We know less about the verbal interaction process between learners that might facilitate the process. Group learning environments are not without their problems and like most recommendations for pedagogy should not be considered universally effective for all students in all situations. For instance, less aggressive students (many girls) and the average student are more likely to not be as involved in the process as males and more highly aggressive students. When grouped heterogeneously these students are not likely to be as involved in the interactive process and therefore not likely to learn as much as other students (Salomon and Perkins, 1998).

There Is No Silver Bullet

So what is the point of this discussion. Put quite simply, there is no single theory of learning that would explain learning or the lack of it in all situations, and therefore, there can be no single approach to instruction. Each theory of learning is used to support an approach to instruction. Each has but a piece of a very complex phenomenon we call learning. Instructional processes are chosen that match instructional intent with likely outcomes with particular learners. There are times, particularly with beginning learners, when teachers do want students to gain some consistency in the execution of their motor responses and are more concerned with repetition, developing the ability to execute a motor response, and individual learning than they are with more complex or socially constructed learning. There are times when teachers are concerned that students learn to be decision makers involved in what skill to use, in the processes involved in creating new or adaptable responses, and in socially constructed learning. There are times when teachers would need to be concerned with assuring high levels of cognitive processing and times when teachers do not have to be as concerned about the level of cognitive activity as they do about getting students to engage in the process of what they are doing. Teachers of groups are largely put in the position of selecting processes that are likely to elicit particular processes and outcomes with most of the students.

A lot of the research done on instruction has been framed, not to establish theory or to understand learning, but rather, to establish direct links between what a teacher does and what a student learns. Often this research looks at a particular kind of learning, rather than viewing learning more holistically. Much of the process–product research on teaching that was part of the 1970s has become the research base for direct teaching as well as the research base for teacher instructional characteristics. As a result of the many studies done in a process–product paradigm, direct teaching was shown to be effective in producing learning with particular kinds of content. Most of the studies supporting direct teaching were done with elementary maths and reading which is easy to reduce to a step by step breakdown in content and explicit teaching. Because the teaching of motor responses lends itself well to step by step explicit teaching, there is more than ample support for the teaching of motor skills using direct instruction. Nevertheless, there is likewise support for the notion that limiting the teaching and learning of physical education to learning how to execute motor responses not only narrows our contributions but may have a negative effect on the manner in which students are able to use those motor responses in meaningful activity (see Chapters 3, 4, 5). Designing instruction to both give students the ability to execute a motor response as well as to use motor responses appropriately in meaningful and often complex activity environments would seem to be the challenge for physical education: a challenge that is likely to involve the need for a variety of instructional processes.

References

ALMOND, L. (1986) 'Reflecting on themes: A games classification', in THORPE, R., BUNKER, D. and ALMOND, L. *Rethinking Games Teaching*, Loughborough, UK: University of Technology, pp. 71–82.

ANDERSON, J., REDER, L. and SIMON, H. (1996) 'Situated learning and education', *Educational Researcher*, **25**, pp. 5–11.

ASHY, M., LEE, A. and LANDIN, D. (1988) 'Relationship of practice using correct technique to achievement in a motor skill', *Journal of Teaching in Physical Education*, **7**, pp. 115–20.

BANDURA, A. (1969) *Principles of Behavior Modification*, NY: Holt, Rinehart and Winston.

BROPHY, J. and GOOD, T. (1986) 'Teacher behavior and student achievement', in WITTROCK, M. (ed.) *Handbook of Research on Teaching* (3rd ed.), NY: MacMillan, pp. 328–75.

CHANDLER, T. and MITCHELL, S. (1991) 'Reflections on models of games education', *Journal of Teaching in Physical Education*, **14**, pp. 467–77.

FRENCH, K., RINK, J., RICKARD, L., MAYS, A., LYNN, S. and WERNER, P. (1991) 'The effects of practice progressions on learning two volleyball skills', *Journal of Teaching in Physical Education*, **10**, pp. 261–74.

FRENCH, K. and THOMAS, G. (1987) 'The relation of knowledge development to children's basketball performance', *Journal of Sport Psychology*, **9**, pp. 15–32.

GOULD, D. and ROBERTS, G. (1982) 'Modeling and motor skill acquisition', *Quest*, **33**, pp. 214–30.

GREHAIGNE, J. and GODBOUT, P. (1995) 'Tactical knowledge in team sports from a constructivist and cognitivist perspective', *Quest*, **47**, pp. 490–505.

HASTIE, P. (1996) 'Student role involvement during a unit of sport education', *Journal of Teaching in Physical Education*, **16**, pp. 88–103.

HASTIE, P. (1998) 'The participation and perceptions of girls within a unit of sport education', *Journal of Teaching in Physical Education*, **17**, pp. 157–71.

KENNEDY, J., CRUICKSHANK, D., BUSH, A. and MEYERS, B. (1978) 'Additional investigations into the nature of teacher clarity', *Journal of Educational Research*, **2**, pp. 3–10.

KIRK, D. and MACDONALD, D. (1998) 'Situated learning in physical education', *Journal of Teaching in Physical Education*, **17**, pp. 376–87.

KWAK, E. (1993) 'The initial effects of various task presentation conditions on students' performance in the lacrosse throw', Unpublished doctoral dissertation, The University of South Carolina.

LANDIN, D. (1994) 'The role of verbal cues in skill learning', *Quest*, **46**, pp. 299–313.

LEE, T., SWINNEN, P. and SERRIEN, D. (1995) 'Cognitive effort and motor learning', *Quest*, **46**, pp. 328–44.

LEPPER, M. (1988) 'Motivational considerations in the study of instruction', *Cognition and Instruction*, **5**, pp. 289–310.

MAGILL, R. (1993) *Motor Learning: Concepts and Applications*, Dubuque, IA: Wm. C. Brown.

MAGILL, R. (ed.) (1994a) 'Communicating information to enhance skill learning', *Quest*, **46**, pp. 267–368.

MAGILL, R. (1994b) 'The influence of augmented feedback during skill learning depends on characteristics of the skill and the learner', *Quest*, **46**, pp. 314–27.

MAGILL, R. (1998) 'Knowledge is more than we can talk about: Implicit learning in motor skill acquisition', *Research Quarterly for Exercise and Sport*, **69**, 2, pp. 104–10.

MARTENS, R., BURWITZ, L. and ZUCKERMAN, J. (1976) 'Modeling effects on motor performance', *Research Quarterly for Exercise and Sport*, **47**, pp. 277–91.

MASSER, L. (1985) 'The effect of refinement on student achievement in a fundamental motor skill in Grades K-6', *Journal of Teaching in Physical Education*, **6**, pp. 174–82.

MASSER, L. (1993) 'Critical cues help first grade students' achievement in handstands and forward roles', *Journal of Teaching in Physical Education*, **12**, pp. 301–12.

McCULLAGH, P., STIEHL, J. and WEISS, M. (1990) 'Developmental modeling effects on the qualitative and quantitative aspects of motor performance', *Research Quarterly for Exercise and Sport*, **61**, pp. 344–50.

METZLER, M. (1979) 'The measurement of ALT in Physical Education', Doctoral dissertation, The Ohio State University, University Microfilms No. 8009314.

Judith E. Rink

METZLER, M. (1989) 'A review of research on time in sport pedagogy', *Journal of Teaching in Physical Education*, **8**, pp. 87–103.

NEWELL, K. (1986) 'Constraints on the development of coordination', in WADE, H. and WHITING, H. (eds) *Motor Development Aspects of Coordination and Control*, Dordrecht: Martinus Nijhoff Publishers, pp. 341–61.

PARKER, M. and O'SULLIVAN, M. (1983) 'Modifying ALT-PE for game play contexts and other reflections', *Journal of Teaching in Physical Education*, Summer Monograph, pp. 8–10.

PETERSON, P. (1979) 'Direct instruction reconsidered', in PETERSON, P. and WALBERG, H. (eds) *Research on Teaching: Concepts, Findings, and Implications*, Berkeley, CA: McCutchan, pp. 57–69.

PINTRICH, P., MARX, R. and BOYLE, R. (1993) 'Beyond cold conceptual change: The role of motivational beliefs and classroom contextual factors in the process of conceptual change', *Review of Education Research*, **63**, 2, pp. 167–99.

RINK, J. (1994) 'Task presentation in pedagogy', *Quest*, **46**, pp. 270–80.

RINK, J. (1996) (ed.) 'Tactical and skill approaches to teaching sport and games', July Monograph, *Journal of Teaching Physical Education*, **15**, 4.

RINK, J. (1998) *Teaching Physical Education for Learning* (3rd ed.) Boston: McGraw-Hill.

RINK, J., FRENCH, K., WERNER, P., LYNN, S. and MAYS, A. (1992) 'The influence of content development on the effectiveness of instruction', *Journal of Teaching Physical Education*, **11**, pp. 139–49.

ROSENSHINE, B. (1987) 'Explicit teaching', in BERLINER, D. and ROSENSHINE, B. (eds) *Talks to Teachers*, NY: Random House, pp. 75–92.

ROSENSHINE, B. and STEVENS, R. (1986) 'Teaching functions', in WITTROCK, M. (ed.) *Handbook of Research on Teaching* (3rd ed.) NY: MacMillan, pp. 376–91.

SALOMON, G. and PERKINS, D. (1998) 'Individual and social aspects of learning', in PEARSON, P. and IRAN-NEJAD, A. (eds) *Review of Research in Education*, Washington, DC: American Educational Research Association, pp. 1–24.

SCHMIDT, R., YOUNG, D., SWINNEN, S. and SHAPIRO D. (1989) 'Support for the guidance hypothesis', *Journal of Experimental Psychology: Learning, Memory and Cognition*, **15**, pp. 352–9.

SIDAWAY, B., FAIRWEATHER, M., POWELL, J. and HALL, G. (1992) 'The acquisition and retention of a timing task: Effects of summary KR and movement time', *Research Quarterly for Exercise and Sport*, **63**, pp. 328–34.

SILVERMAN, S. (1990) 'Linear and curvilinear relationships between student practice and achievement in physical education', *Teaching and Teacher Education*, **6**, pp. 305–14.

SILVERMAN, S., DEVILLIER, R. and RAMMIREZ, T. (1991) 'The validity of ALT-PE as a process measure of student achievement', *Research Quarterly for Exercise and Sport*, **66**, pp. 32–40.

SOLMON, M. and LEE, A. (1996) 'Entry characteristics, practice variables, and cognition: Student mediation of instruction', *Journal of Teaching in Physical Education*, **15**, pp. 135–50.

SOLMON, M. and LEE, A. (1997) 'Development of an instrument to assess cognitive processes in physical education classes', *Research Quarterly for Exercise and Sport*, **68**, pp. 152–60.

STARKES, J. and ALLARD, F. (1993) *Cognitive Issues in Motor Expertise*, Amsterdam: Elsevier Science Publishers.

SWEETING, T. and RINK, J. (1998) 'Effects of direct instruction and environmentally designed instruction on the process and product characteristics of a fundamental skill', Paper submitted to the Journal of Teaching in Physical Education.

VYGOTSKY, L. (1978) *Mind in Society*, Cambridge, MA: Harvard University Press.

WERNER, P. and RINK, J. (1988) 'Case studies of teacher effectiveness in second grade physical education', *Journal of Teaching Physical Education*, **4**, pp. 280–97.

WIGFIELD, A., ECCLES, J. and RODRIGUEZ, D. (1998) 'The development of children's motivation in school contexts', in PEARSON, P. and IRAN-NEJAD, A. (eds) *Review of Research in Education*, Washington, DC: American Educational Research Association, pp. 73–118.

WULF, G. and WEIGELT, C. (1997) 'Instructions about physical principles in learning a complex motor skill: To tell or not to tell . . .', *Research Quarterly for Exercise and Sport*, **68**, pp. 362–7.

Part 4

The Teacher of Physical Education

9 Understanding Physical Education Teachers: A Focus on the Lived Body

Andrew C. Sparkes

Various researchers working from an interactionist perspective have made a convincing case regarding the importance of the self in teaching and the manner in which it is complex, differentiated and subject to change depending upon time and circumstance in the teacher's life. However, as Merleau-Ponty (1962) pointed out since perception is always from a vantage point, namely the body, the 'self' cannot be a disembodied agent. Likewise, Stevens (1996) argued that to be a person involves embodiment, or being related to a particular body. If this is the case then it would appear the part that the body plays in relation to the sense of self in teaching has been largely neglected. Indeed, teachers' bodies have been an absent presence in the literature (Sparkes, 1996a). That is, their bodies as part of the body-self complex are *everywhere* in terms of their gender, age, social class, ableness, sexual identity, race, ethnicity, career-decisions, tiredness, stress and emotional reactions to teaching episodes, critical events, and teacher burnout, yet their subjectively experienced bodies are *nowhere* in terms of being the direct focus for analysis. For Shilling (1993) this absence is symptomatic of a much wider underestimation of the importance of the corporeal in schooling and a more general neglect of the embodied nature of the educational enterprise.

This situation is echoed within the domain of physical education (PE). Here, the bodies of pupils and students have received critical attention in PE (e.g. see Delamont, 1998; Kirk, 1993; Kirk and Tinning, 1990, 1994; Page and Fox, 1997; Scraton, 1992; Shilling, 1993), but the part the body played in relation to the sense of self in PE teaching as it develops over time have been, with rare exceptions (e.g. see Dowling-Naess, 1996; Sikes, 1988), largely neglected. Indeed, much of my own life history work on the lives and careers of PE teachers has treated the body as an absent presence.[1]

When the body has been the focus of attention within PE, as Pronger (1995) pointed out, it has often been dealt with in a fragmented and mechanistic manner. That is, as something to be dissected, manipulated, treated, measured, or performance-enhanced, in ways that reflected the biomedical roots of this subject as it developed in schools and institutions of higher education. Regardless of discipline, the body has tended to be viewed as an object in an abstracted, theoretical manner. As Hall (1996) noted with regard to North America, the academic discipline and professional practice known as PE, 'has curiously disembodied the very focus of its discourse, the body' (p. 49).

The neglect of the *lived* body in attempts to understand PE teachers is surprising.[2] This is particularly so given Synnott's (1993) view that the body is both the prime symbol of the self, and the prime determinant of the self, which means that as the body changes so does the sense of self and associated identities. Accordingly, in this chapter, I attempt to place the embodied experiences of PE teachers centre stage so that the manner in which these operate to shape the teachers' senses of self over time can be explored. To accomplish this task I draw upon life history data from two PE teachers to highlight the dilemmas that some teachers face in maintaining a coherent sense of self and feeling at home in their bodies when their body projects are interrupted. By focusing upon selected moments from their lives I hope to raise questions about how they construct narratives, self images, and identities in relation to their role as teachers.

The data presented are offered as a rich resource and intended to be illuminative rather than definitive. It is hoped that the embodied reader, reading from their own subject positions, and drawing upon their own highly personal sedimentation of experience, will make connections to their own bodies and the bodies of others, so that insights are generated that operate across contexts. From a standpoint epistemology (see Harding, 1991; Stanley and Wise, 1993), the insights generated from the position of the two PE teachers in this paper are not exclusively about them or their occupational group. Rather the differences they share in relation to many other teachers with regard to, for example, the centrality and visibility of their performing body as a key definer of their sense of self, enables us to ask relevant theoretical questions and see things that might have otherwise been invisible to us about the body–self relationships of those who teach in other subject areas.

With these points in mind I will now begin to consider the experiences of Rachael and David (both pseudonyms). Rachael is a PE student in her early twenties who has competed as a horse rider at a very high level. After several years of a mysterious back pain she was diagnosed as having a large tumour at the base of her spine. This tumour was removed surgically but there were complications. The effect of the tumour on her hip girdle and lumbar spine makes it unlikely that she will ever ride again at the top level since a fall from the horse might result in a serious disability (see Sparkes, 1998). In contrast, David is middle aged and has not experienced such a traumatic event in relation to his body. However, he is experiencing the physical signs of ageing, has a nagging knee problem, and has now left teaching.

In what follows, moments from the lives of Rachael and David will be presented separately before a brief comment is made on each. Having reflected upon their experiences of their bodies in relation to teaching and their sense of self, I then consider how the views that Rachael and David hold of themselves as embodied beings are shaped and constrained by limited narrative resources. Finally, casting my net beyond the lives of these two teachers, some issues are raised about the kind of body stories that circulate within the PE community and the need to understand these in greater depth.

172

Moments from Rachael's Life History

Talking of the impact her illness has had on her life, Rachael commented:

> This has been the biggest thing in my life, although I am only just appreciating it now . . . Its no good just riding horses out and looking after them, it's just so tame . . . I feel like I have lost my identity. I was a horse rider through and through and I felt so at home when I was competing . . . I lived, ate, and breathed horses. Anything could go wrong and it just didn't seem to matter so long as I had the horse 'on the road' . . . It's no use pretending that life goes on, and there is more to life than horses, because in my opinion there isn't. (Reflective writing, September 1995)

This sense of loss needs to be located against Rachael's previous experiences as a very able performer in a variety of sports during her school career, and her experiences of high level performance in one particular sport. As her engagement with various sports increased when she was younger a *disciplined*, performing body emerged that, according to Frank (1991, 1995), becomes predictable through its regimentation.

Such predictability is an important feature of what Gadow (1982) called *primary immediacy*, a state of being when the body functions and performs tasks without conscious effort. In this state an overriding unity of the body–self relationship prevails where body and mind act in unison. Indeed, Leder (1990) argued that the body disappears from consciousness when it is functioning in this unproblematic state. As Rachael commented on her riding at big events, 'I don't actually think about what I'm doing when I'm going around it. It all happens so quickly. But you have got milliseconds if your horse makes a bit of a mistake at a jump, you've literally got a millisecond to throw your weight back so you don't fall over its head when it trips. You just do it. It's automatic.'

For athletes, as Kleiber, Brock, Youngkhill, Dattilo and Cadwell (1995) argued, this sense of primary immediacy is *cultivated* through the process of engagement with developmentally challenging incapacities in which a new unity of self and body is readily imagined and achieved. Once achieved, this cultivated immediacy is characterized by the feelings of 'flow' experienced in sporting or leisure situations where the consciousness of self disappears as ability matches challenges and action merges with awareness (Jackson, 1996). In this regard, Rachael spoke of the ecstasy of three day eventing and the feelings of control she gained from performing at a high level.

> It's just the feeling of power, of the horse, and the excitement . . . It's really indescribable because it feels so smooth and professional. Everything just comes together at once . . . It's a complete channelling of everything. I can remember tiny, tiny details as if it was slow motion, but in fact it's very fast. But it's like 'Boom', and you get in a rhythm. It's a very intrinsic sort of activity . . . It's a real buzz, incredible. (Interview transcript, March 1996)

Set against these previous peak experiences and feelings of control over a disciplined body, Rachael now experiences a sense of loss regarding these former body–self relations.

> My body has failed me because it can no longer perform the function I want it to. To ride horses in competition is for me the most meaningful expression of my body's special capabilities. This restriction has become the focus of my life; it has hit at the inner core of my being. (Reflective writing, April 1996)

With regard to this sense of loss, a piece of reflective writing undertaken by Rachael in August 1995 described herself on a strange imaginary journey in a Land Rover Discovery that encountered various diversions and obstructions that symbolized her confusions about who she was now and what the future held for her. She concluded one passage by saying, 'Nobody has given me any directions or map to follow. . . . The problem now though is that I don't seem to know where it is that I'm supposed to be going.'

During an interview in December 1995, Rachael and I discussed some of the meanings behind this piece of writing. She explained to me that the Range Rover represented her high performance body as it used to be when she was sponsored by this company. In contrast, Rachael stated that the car she would equate her body to now would be 'One that you have to pedal yourself [laughs]. A Sinclair 5. An old Fiesta that can't go up hills . . . I had one and I've just sold it. It was so crap. It was only 950 cc, it wouldn't go up any hills. That's me.' In total, Rachael felt like she was living without a map and these feelings were a source of anxiety that she had not expected, 'It's weird because I just didn't have any concept of how it would affect me mentally. Not a tiny little bit. I just thought "OK, just have the operation, get back and everything would be Hunky Dory." Instead, this is just a complete shock.' This complete shock related to the rapid demise of two key aspects of her sense of self.

The first of these revolved around the demise of the *disciplined body-self*. According to Frank (1995), 'The disciplined body-self defines itself primarily in actions of self-regimentation; its most important action problems are those of control. The disciplined body experiences its gravest crisis in loss of control' (p. 41). Rachael experienced just such a crisis as the following data indicated.

> I have always been in control of my body. I had always had great faith in my ability to control my body. I now realise that I have always felt a synchronisation of body and mind. It wasn't until after the complications that I fully appreciated the holistic feeling I had had previously between body and soul, but as with many things you don't even realise it is there until it has gone. (Reflective writing, February 1995)

Following her stay in hospital and on leaving hospital to recuperate, Rachael's words reflected a situation of *disrupted immediacy* in which the unity of the body–self relationship has been lost, control and predictability have diminished, and her sense of self has become defined in opposition to the body she now inhabited. Since the operation, issues of bodily control and predictability have become a central concern for Rachael. Emphasizing her concerns over losing a controlled and disciplined body, Rachael noted, 'The lack of control is a new experience for me. The whole thing has become an issue of control. I no longer have control over my physical body; I have no control over my life or destiny; I can't control my emotions.'

This loss of control has dramatically altered Rachael's feelings towards her own lived body. Rachael's body, like the body in multiple sclerosis described by Toombs (1992), was now inescapably embodied as it defined and presented itself to her as an oppositional force which curtailed activities, thwarted plans and projects, and disrupted her involvements in the surrounding world. Therefore, in contrast to former feelings of unity and harmony, her body was now experienced as something essentially alien, and as something that was Other-than-me. Indeed, as Leder (1990) commented, insofar as the body tends to disappear when functioning unproblematically, 'it often seizes our attention most strongly at times of dysfunction; we then experience the body as the very *absence* of a desired or ordinary state, and as a force that stands opposed to the self' (p. 4). On this issue, Rachael commented:

> I've just got no trust in my body whatsoever now [laughs]. For example, in the morning, the first thing I do out of habit, is to check to see if my left leg works. Just in case suddenly it's not working. Because that's the leg that's the problem. I check my left leg . . . I don't like my body any more. I think it's really let me down because I have been really good to it. It's just turned around and got this great big tumour . . . I don't like my body now because it just won't do the things that I want it to. It's frustrating. I'm still really annoyed with my body [laughs]. It's a bit weird, but I am, it's difficult to explain I think . . . I'd like to swap bodies with someone . . . One that can ride horses. That can do the things I want to do. At one stage I thought 'I quite like my body. It's all right. It's not too fat or too thin. It's all right. It suits riding. It's quite athletic.' I wouldn't have swapped it for any other body. But now, I'd swap it for someone fat and short, anything as long as it can ride. (Interview transcript, January 1995)

Rachael's words from some reflective writing in April 1996 echo this point, 'You develop a sense of self from the ability to perform required tasks associated with the self. The body must be able to physically carry out these tasks. I have lost an aspect of my self, a self that I wanted to be, a part of me that was the single most important aspect of my conception of self'.

There is another sense of self that Brock and Kleiber (1994) identified as being closely associated with the demise of the disciplined body and the loss of public recognition that comes with the inability to perform at a high level in major sporting events. This self is the *gloried self* as defined by Adler and Adler (1989). As the following comment indicates the demise of the gloried self was problematic for Rachael.

> I am a nobody at the moment. I have a desire to be someone. When I was riding I was someone. I was one of the best riders in the country of my age. It is a good

feeling to know that you are good at something. I had measured myself against others and come out on top, and that feels good. I don't want to slip into obscurity. I don't want to be normal. (Reflective writing, April 1996)

Adler and Adler (1989) noted that experiencing glory was exciting for the athletes involved and created or expanded various aspects of their sense of self. They pointed out that, characteristically, the gloried self is a greedy, intoxicating and riveting self, that seeks to ascend in importance and to cast aside other self-dimensions as it grows.

In statements like, 'It was my identity completely' Rachael also highlights how the gloried self encourages role engulfment or identity foreclosure to occur where energy and time are withdrawn from a variety of social roles in order to be focused upon the athlete role. This transformation involves various forms of self-narrowing or self-erosion. As both Adler and Adler (1989), and Brock and Kleiber (1994) pointed out, athletes can sacrifice both the multidimensionality of their current selves and the potential breadth of their future selves as various dimensions of their identities are either diminished, detached, or somehow changed as a result of their increasing investment in a gloried self.

In terms of self-immediacy Adler and Adler (1989) further noted that one of the first consequences of the ascent of the gloried self was the loss of a future orientation and long-term planning as the future became defined as a direct continuation of the present. For example, Rachael acknowledged that she invested little effort in her academic work at school because she assumed that her future career would be that of a professional horse rider. Likewise, Rachael's choice to study physical education as the main subject for her degree, and her choice of university, was haphazard and was motivated by her desire to maintain and develop her riding career. Indeed, in a piece of reflective writing in April 1996, Rachael noted the narrow internal focus and preoccupation she had previously with horse riding had resulted in, 'a lack of preparation, both for the state of being ill, and retirement from competition. I feel that I have put all my eggs in one basket and someone has come along and smashed them all. I don't even know who this someone is.'

It would appear that, for Rachael, via her socialization into the world of élite sport, a specific and strong athletic identity has emerged and ascended to a position of psychological centrality in her constellation of identities. As part of this process other identities have been relegated to a subordinate status. An example of this relegation was evident in an interview in December 1995 where Rachael and I discussed her thoughts about teaching as a future identity and career she might adopt now that becoming a leading horse rider was unlikely.

Rachael Yes, exactly, trying to make it [teaching] more important. Well, before, it was like I'd come away for 10 weeks [to university] and I'd go back and ride horses. It was just a bit of an interruption to my horse riding. It was like 'Yea'. But now it's like 'Oh my God, it's the whole thing. I'm going to be a teacher.' I find it really boring. I find teachers boring. I find the notion of teaching boring. It's terrible isn't it. But it's such a sort of non-thing to do.

Andrew   What, compared to the glamour of horse riding.

Rachael   Yes, in people's estimations, teaching is a non-event. It's not a very exciting thing to do. It hasn't got a lot of prestige. It doesn't earn a lot of money. It's a very sort of middle of the road affair. It's safe, that's the word I'm looking for. I don't like that.

Andrew   Could you stand teaching if you had the international riding to tag onto it. It's 'Rachael' an international horse rider and she teaches.

Rachael   Well, hopefully I'd just be riding full time but it would do. But yes. It's just the fact that I thought maybe I was going to make it and be, not famous, well known as a rider. I mean, I was well known anyway in the area. The people in your area always follow what you do. They send you good luck cards if you go into a big event. It's really nice. I don't think that I'm an attention seeker. But, it was nice [laughs] . . . But teachers, it's a kind of nobody thing to do.

As with the athletes described by Adler and Adler (1989), and Brock and Kleiber (1994), Rachael appears to receive less satisfaction from other available roles and has distanced herself from them in such a way she has lost both the desire and the ability to see the world through them. As a consequence, other roles and identities, such as teaching, have become more or less unavailable for alternative lines of action. This is because as Adler and Adler (1989) pointed out, 'The longer the gloried athletic self served as their master status, the harder the athletes found it to conceive of any other identity for themselves' (p. 308).

Comment

There are clearly many interpretations that could be made of these extracts (see Sparkes 1996a, 1998). However, the tumour, the operations on her body, and their combined effects have formed an epiphany in Rachael's life in terms of her sense of self. For Denzin (1989) epiphanies are interactional moments that leave their mark on people's lives in either positive or negative ways, and alter the fundamental meanings structures in a person's life. They can often be interpreted by the person and others as turning point experiences. In such moments, as the words of Rachael indicate, the normality and taken-for-grantedness of the body–self relationship is interrupted and the individual is forced to adopt a more reflexive stance towards this relationship. Often in these circumstances the lived body, or certain parts of it, emerge as an alien presence and is experienced as something foreign to the self. Likewise, the disruption and constriction of the individual's habitual world throws into sharp relief and destabilizes preferred identities and their place in the individual's identity hierarchy.

According to Brewer, Van Raalte and Linder (1993) high levels of commitment commonly accompany participation in sport and exercise activities, and many individuals ascribe a great deal of psychological significance to their involvement in sport and exercise. Accordingly, Brewer et al. (1993) defined athletic identity as the degree to which an individual identifies with the athlete role. The moments provided from Rachael's life history suggest that over time she has developed a very strong athletic identity that stands at the apex of her identity hierarchy. Even though events have undermined this identity by bringing about the demise of the disciplined body–self and the gloried self, it remains a powerful force in shaping her sense of self and how she reacts to, and interprets, past, current, and future events. The strength of this athletic identity is able to over-ride other possible identities, such as, being a teacher. As Knowles (1991) argued, personal biography seems to have a profound effect on the formation of a teacher role identity of 'image of teacher as self'. As the data suggested, the teacher role identity was not afforded a high position in Rachael's salience identity hierarchy and, therefore, any move towards this identity and career were resisted. Quite simply, despite the problems (some might say impossibility) of maintaining a strong athletic identity in the future, Rachael preferred this identity and its associated dilemmas over the possibility of adopting a teacher role identity.

For Rachael, the constriction of alternative selves under the choking pressures of a strong athletic identity has major implications for how, and if, she can reconstruct a life narrative that allows her to feel positive about the body she now inhabits. As Brock and Kleiber (1994) argued, although any future self imaginable has a body, the importance of that body and a concern for embodied performance will vary greatly from one life story to the next. Their own work involving injured college athletes who shaped their life narrative exclusively around the body's performance in sport led them to suggest the following:

> Being a celebrated athlete would likely be important in this illness process to the extent that the loss of that role would have implications for reconstructing a sense of self. Depending on the character and the life story of the athletes, on their idiosyncratic dreams of future sport attainment, the troubling effects on identity and self-esteem of an injury that ends their sport career are either severe or mild — but apparently unavoidable. (Brock and Kleiber, 1994, p. 416)

Identity issues and the narrative reconstruction of alternative selves and a new sense of body–self unity are clearly problematic for Rachael at the moment. Whether or not Rachael becomes a teacher on completing her course, and the kind of teacher she becomes should she choose this option, will very much depend of how she resolves her ongoing identity struggle. In this sense, a focus on epiphaneous moments or turning points in the lives of élite sport persons and/or PE teachers who become ill, get injured, and/or acquire a physical disability would seem to have a part to play in helping to understand the complexities of the many relationships of the body to the self in contemporary society, and the manner in which these relationships get constructed and reconstructed over time within educational institutions.

A specific focus upon PE teachers would be illuminative. Given the tendency of this occupational group, and their teaching colleagues, to define PE teachers in terms of the visible performance capabilities of their bodies, a range of general issues in relation to the lived body–self relationship and the world of schooling are raised by their plight. For example, many PE teachers have been, or aspired to be, élite performers at some stage in their career. Indeed, the socialization literature makes it clear that one of the major motivations for young people choosing PE as a career is their love of sport (usually because they are good at it), and a desire for an occupation that allows for sports continuance (Templin and Schempp, 1989). Once in this profession, PE teachers feel the reflected gaze of other teachers and students on their bodies and their performance capacities. For the most part, they are expected by others, and by themselves, to be fit, healthy and full of energy — and usually young! As a consequence the body is inscribed with a variety of meanings within the school context that provide a range of identity dilemmas for these teachers that relate not only to sudden interruptions to their body projects, but also to more gradual interruptions associated with the process of ageing. As Sikes (1988) pointed out with regard to career moves in PE, getting older and finding it physically more difficult to keep up the pace and the level of performance, and also suspecting that it would become even harder, were major concerns for many PE teachers.

> Some people do not enjoy the identity that goes with the ageing PE teacher. They do not like the physical implications of being outrun, out bowled and increasingly liable to be 'beaten'.... The situation is perhaps more difficult for ageing PE teachers who may find it increasingly difficult actually to do what is required of them and who cannot summon up the motivation and enthusiasm to go out on the field on a cold and damp winter morning. This was the spectre that haunted some of the teachers I spoke with, that and being the pathetic parody of a sportsperson. (Sikes, 1988, pp. 32–5)

To emphasize this point the following is an extended extract from an interview with a PE teacher called David (a pseudonym) just before he left the teaching profession.

David and His Lived Body As a PE Teacher

Andrew How old are you now?
David 36.
Andrew So what has brought on this decision to leave PE teaching?
David A lot of things really. Monetary was one of the considerations. I've been nearly 10 years in teaching and I'm only on about 16 grand. That was one thing. My wife, Helen [a pseudonym], is also a teacher, so we've developed a lifestyle which is based on two salaries. What's happened is that now the baby has come along, our first child, Helen has said 'Well, look, I'd like to pack up teaching or do something where at least I can work from home.' That obviously means a drop in income. I'm very supportive of this.

The other thing that worried me was the physical side of it, and also looking down the road at the PE teacher who has been in the job a fair while.
Andrew How do you mean the physical side?
David Well, look at someone like Mike [a pseudonym] down at [name of school], who had bad knees. They got so bad in the end that he couldn't do the job properly by the fact that he couldn't perform as well. Consequently, he tried to retrain, and the county has no money whatsoever for PE teachers to retrain as anything else. So he had to get out on a disability pension in the end at the age of 43. Now I'm 37 in September, so it's not that far away.

Andrew   So they just let him go and they wouldn't back him up. So he's out. Have you been injured?

David   You see, I'm the same in a way, in that I've got one slightly arthritic knee and the other one is sort of twinging a bit. I don't know, in five years time what is it going to be like? You just don't know. I looked at PE hard. The natural trend for PE teachers generally is to teach a full timetable up to sort of late 30s, early 40s, and then they start going into the pastoral. They start being odd-job men. Unless, they are actually specialists in another subject. My head of department is a specialist in History. He could transfer across quite easily. I'm not, I don't want to be. I didn't come into the game to be a classroom teacher. I came into be a PE teacher.

Andrew   Have you got a second subject?

David   Yes, I had to do it. So, I don't want to do that. I just don't want to go that way. I've seen too many of them. My old PE teacher at my old school was the same — early 40s playing rugby, couldn't perform as well, and he started to gradually drift into careers and all the other sort of paraphernalia. There is an awful lot of PE guys that go that way. They drift into the odd-jobs. They become the jack-of-all-trades. They become a bit of science, a bit of history, a bit of this and a bit of that. I just didn't want to go that way. The former head of PE at this place, he's retiring this summer. But for the last five years he's been looking forward to it. He couldn't wait to get out. Now I don't want to be like that.

Andrew   You say you have an arthritic knee. Has it actually troubled you over the last few years in terms of what you can do?

David   Yes, but it's only been the last sort of year, 18 months, that it's really become a problem. I've had knee injuries, that are now starting to play up. You know the theory, in the winter they start to hurt more.

Andrew   How did you get the injury?

David   Rugby. That was playing sport outside of teaching. That was a fair while ago.

Andrew   So how do you actually feel when you are injured and you are teaching?

David   Well, it's not a problem. What I'm saying is, looking down the road, it could be. What really brought it on was what happened to this fella. That's what got it from the back of my mind to the front, 'This could be you in five years time. What the hell are you going to do?.' It could be couldn't it. Why wait to find out when you can make a move now. I thought, let's just see if there is an alternative. It also came about as the teaching profession was going through, and still is going through a very rough patch as far as morale, pay, and status are concerned, and everything else. It all happened at the same time. I suddenly thought to myself, 'Hold on, I'm in the wrong job here because I'm not happy with where my career is going to be in 10 years time.'

Andrew   You mentioned the performance aspect of PE. Would that be something that worried you as you aged in PE?

David   Yes, of course. Essentially, I think that PE is a young man's game. I really feel that. My own personal opinion is that you've got to show them, by *doing* it. As opposed to not doing it. It's a case of lead by example here, isn't it. I think that another 10 years down the road, I don't think I could be doing it. As far as I'm concerned there is no worse scenario than an ageing PE bloke, who basically lives on what he's done 10 or 15 years ago. I've seen very few PE people teach on beyond 45 really.

Andrew   Let's say you couldn't demonstrate an activity in PE, how would you feel?

David   I wouldn't want to do it. I wouldn't want to do it. Purely on the fact, you know, to *me* it's something that you should do. I mean, how can you judge how kids can do it, unless you can do it yourself. I'm one of the sort of people that would say 'I wouldn't ask them to do anything that I wouldn't want to do, or be able to do.' I think it's still important that you are able to demonstrate things, to some extent. When you can't do them to any extent [laughs] it's time you weren't there [laughs].

Andrew   How do you think the kids view people who can't demonstrate. I mean, if they saw you at 45 or 50?

David   I don't know. I mean, that's it. That's something that I just don't want to think about really. I think they are always looking for you to show them. Even if they don't say it, they are looking for you to show them. It's alright saying 'Well, here's Johnny and he's great, and look at him doing that.' It's all fantastic isn't it. Don't show them because you might be giving a poor demonstration, but I don't you see. I never teach like that. I don't demonstrate myself. I do the classic way of getting the kid to demonstrate. But in my heart, I feel that if necessary I could do, just to show them that I could do it. Because it's that sort of game isn't it; it's a physical thing; it's all part and parcel of it. I think you should lead by example. You should be able to do the things that you are asking the kids to do in the end.

Comment

As with Rachael there are many interpretations that could be made of David's story. Even though his athletic identity does not appear to be as strong as Rachael's, it still plays a major part in how he views his lived body over time, and his sense of self as a teacher who can perform skills. In this sense, his teacher role identity has incorporated his athletic identity so that when the latter is threatened due to ageing and impairment, the teacher role identity also becomes problematic. Indeed, the tensions emerging between these two identities played a major part in David's decision to leave the teaching profession.

Also of interest is the manner in which David actively self-monitors his own body for signs of decay and reduced performance capacity. For him, the process of ageing coupled with impairment irrevocably creates a distance between a desired sense of self as a PE teacher who can perform, and one who cannot perform to the level he desires and the levels others expect of him. Talking of the *performing* self within consumer culture that latches onto the prevalent self-preservationist conception of the body, Featherstone (1991) noted:

> Within consumer culture individuals are asked to become role players and self-consciously monitor their own performance. Appearance, gesture and bodily demeanour become taken as expressions of self, with bodily imperfections and lack of attention carrying penalties in everyday interactions. Individuals therefore become encouraged to search themselves for flaws and signs of decay. (pp. 189–90)

Featherstone (1991) went on to argue that in consumer culture those who can get their body to approximate the idealized images of youth, health, fitness and beauty have a higher exchange value, 'Within this logic, fitness and slimness become associated not only with energy, drive and vitality but worthiness as a person; likewise the body beautiful comes to be taken as a sign of prudence and prescience in health matters' (p. 183). Therefore, rather than face a reducing exchange value coupled to an undesirable self (in his terms), David deliberately chooses to leave the teaching situation permanently. By leaving, he withdraws from a situation where he would constantly be reminded of his former body and self and enters, hopefully, a context where he might have the chance to develop different identities that are equally as satisfying. Having said this, as with Rachael, David's choice is constrained by his inability to let go of one identity in a specific context and reconstruct another around the body that he currently lives with, or thinks he might have to live with in the future.

Featherstone and Wernick (1995) believe that consumer culture offers a wide range of positive images of ageing. However, these are not evident in David's story of ageing in relation to PE. His story hints more of struggles with bodily betrayals, stigmatization and various modes of disempowerment that come with ageing in his chosen occupation. Here, as Featherstone and Wernick suggest 'the body is not only a masking device which conceals and distorts the self which others interact with, in addition the lack of mobility and functional capacity may make the body seem to be a prison' (p. 11). For both Rachael and David the body they inhabit in specific contexts has become a prison. These feelings about their lived body are, in part, shaped by their narrative resourcing in terms of the storylines they have lived by up till now, and the storylines available to them for their future development.

Closing Thoughts: Bodies and Narrative Resources

Having provided moments from Rachael's and David's story, it is important to locate these in a wider framework as a prelude to considering how the dilemmas they face (and perhaps other PE teachers like them) are shaped by their narrative resources. Their narratives are deeply embedded within and framed by a series of dominant scripts made available within our western culture in relation to gender, age, disability, social class, race/ethnicity, and sexuality (Sparkes, 1997b, Sparkes, in press). Some of these have been highlighted more than others in their stories. These inclusions and silences indicate how the occupation of certain social categories in relation to, for example, specific forms of gendered, performing, bodies have provided them with privileged access to certain storylines but denied them access to others in ways that have limited their potential to explore and change their sense of self. This is in keeping with the views of Denzin (1989) who noted that 'No self or personal experience story is ever an individual production. It derives from the larger group, cultural, ideological and historical contexts' (p. 73).

The narratives of Rachael and David also reveal an intriguing paradox. This revolves around the common absence and denial of vulnerability and fragility in the dominant narratives made available to men and women, and boys and girls, who have 'sporting bodies' within a patriarchal society. However, any narrative of self that centres upon specific forms of gendered athleticism in ways that alienate people from their own bodies and the bodies of others, is deeply ingrained with a host of insecurities, fragilities and vulnerabilities (Sparkes, 1996a). These vulnerabilities can intrude into a person's narrative at any time in the form of, for example, acute or chronic illness, serious injury or acquired physical disability.

The potential of a host of vulnerabilities to intrude into each and every person's narrative links the specific and highly self-conscious experiences of Rachael and David to those around them in the educational domain and the wider society in general. Here, the *inevitable fragility* of narratives in contemporary society identified by Shilling and Mellor (1994), along with the general problems of embodiment (control, body-relatedness, other-relatedness, and desire) signalled by Frank (1991, 1995), means that there is a constant need for identities to be reflexively created, recreated and sustained by the individual through flexible narratives of the self. Such flexibility, according to Gergen (1994), depends upon the cultural repertoire of stories that are available for synthesis into personal stories and the access people have to this repertoire. Accordingly, over the life course, people *may* develop greater sophistication in their potential for telling a variety of life stories and *may* develop the capacity to reconstrue their lives in ways that enhance their present situations, relationships and needs.

As the narratives of Rachael and David indicate, being able to restory a life is extremely difficult for many people. The problem relates to the availability of alternative narratives within specific cultures and sub-cultures on which to build alternative identities and notions of self that recognize and acknowledge, amongst other things, issues of vulnerability and fragility. It also raises questions about the willingness of individuals, in terms of their habitus and tastes, to approach and engage with different narratives should they become available.

In essence, people are not free to construct a life story in any possible way or from any template they might wish. This is because personal stories and life stories are part of larger interactional frameworks, embedded within a variety of social relationships, and are therefore open to sanction by those within the dialogic frame of the author. There must be some negotiated agreement among the relevant parties as to what is a suitable life story. Here, the narratives constructed by Rachael and David are connected to and powerfully shaped by other teachers around them, both in PE and those in other subjects, with regard to what is defined as an acceptable story for them to tell about their bodies within the teaching culture. In this sense, other teachers along with pupils and parents, act as a key resource that can either constrain or promote the development of different narratives and novel senses of self when teachers' body projects are interrupted. As McAdams (1985) pointed out, 'In art and in living, we cannot transcend our resources' (p. 19).

On this issue, Shotter (1993) noted that within the shifting terrain of the postmodern world, the narrative resources available to people in making sense of their lives has increased, thus expanding the genres available. These increased narrative resources provide greater space and opportunities for crafting who we want to be and who we can be. However, as Shotter went on to acknowledge, this increased resourcing is not equitably distributed. Some people have greater ease of access to some narratives than others within a political economy of developmental opportunities, that limits who or what people can become. As he comments 'We cannot just position ourselves as we please; we face differential invitations and barriers to all the "movements" (actions and utterances) we might try to make' (pp. 6–7).

In his exploration of the telling of sexual stories, Plummer (1995) further emphasized the interactive, social role of stories and the manner in which they get told and read in different ways depending upon the context. He pointed out that the consumption of any tale centres upon the different social worlds and interpretive communities who can hear the story in certain ways and not others due to their own location in wider habitual or recurring networks of collective activity. Accordingly, Plummer raised questions about the *making* of stories. For example: What strategies enable stories to be told, how are spaces created for them, and how are voices silenced? How do stories feed into wider networks of routine power? With regard to the *consuming* of stories he asks the following questions: Who has access to stories? What cultural and economic resources — literacy, knowledge, money, time, space — are needed to consume a story? How might the consumption of stories be extended? He acknowledges that although some stories may be told, they may not have the space to be told widely, and they may be told in ways that restrict them to narrow groups.

As the brief insights into the lives of Rachael and David suggest, the kinds of questions raised by Plummer (1995) regarding the social processes of producing and consuming of sexual stories, are equally as pertinent to the production and consuming of body stories within the teaching profession. For example, what kind of body–self stories about teachers circulate within the PE profession? Do these stories vary by subject specialism? How is the ageing, injured or ill teacher-body storied in PE and other practical subjects like music and drama as opposed to subjects such as English and mathematics? What part does gender, race, ethnicity, ableness, age and sexual identity play in this process? How are PE teachers differentially resourced in narrative terms when faced with interrupted body projects. Finally, how is the experience of the lived body shaped by, and in the telling of, these stories and what other possibilities exist for both the telling about and living within particular bodies?

Likewise, the questions raised by Plummer (1995) about the social role that stories play within communities needs to be explored in terms of the functions they might serve in the lives of teachers and the community. This would necessitate a consideration of the manner in which body stories in PE operate to serve both conservative functions that maintain the dominant order, and also how they might have the potential to act as sites of resistance so as to transform individual lives and cultures within teaching. Finally, following Plummer again, questions need to be considered regarding issues of change, history and culture so as to locate the body stories told by people like Rachael and David in the wider socioeconomic and political context that allows their stories to be told and received in specific ways at particular historical moments. Addressing such questions in the future would mean that the lived body would no longer be an absent presence but a central issue in any attempt to understand the lives and careers of PE teachers as embodied beings.

Notes

1 For examples of my work in which the body is an absent presence see Sparkes (1994a, 1994b), Sparkes and Templin (1992), Sparkes et al. (1990, 1993). I have begun to rectify this absence, in part, due to shifts in consciousness stimulated by my own interrupted body project and the need to write about these experiences in different ways. See Sparkes (1996b) for a fragmented narrative of self, and Sparkes (1995, 1997a, in press) for a theoretical standpoint on writing about lived experience using different genres.

2 The terms 'lived body' and 'embodiment' are difficult to define in the English language. In contrast, the Dutch and German language differentiates between the body as *lichaam* or *Körper* and the body as *lijf* and *Lieb*. That is, between the objective, exterior, instrumental and institutionalized body (*lichaam/Körper*) and the subjective, phenomenological, living, experiential body (*lijf/Lieb*). Thus, the lived body is simultaneously *lichaam/Körper* and *lijf/Lieb*. The work of Merleau-Ponty (1962) has been highly influential in this area and his ideas have been developed in relation to PE by Whitehead (1990, 1992).

References

ADLER, P. and ADLER, P. (1989) 'The gloried self: The aggrandisement and the constriction of self', *Social Psychology Quarterly*, **52**, 4, pp. 299–310.

BREWER, B., VAN RAALTE, J. and LINDER, D. (1993) 'Athletic identity: Hercules' muscles or Achilles' heel?', *International Journal of Sport Psychology*, **24**, pp. 237–54.

BROCK, S. and KLEIBER, D. (1994) 'Narrative in medicine: The stories of élite college athletes' career-ending injuries', *Qualitative Health Research*, **4**, 4, pp. 411–30.

DELAMONT, S. (1998) 'You need a leotard': Revisiting the first PE lesson', *Sport, Education and Society*, **3**, 1, pp. 5–17.

DENZIN, N. (1989) *Interpretive Biography*, London: Sage.

DOWLING-NAESS, F. (1996) 'Life events and curriculum change: The life history of a Norwegian physical educator', *European Physical Education Review*, **2**, 1, pp. 41–53.

FEATHERSTONE, M. (1991) 'The body in consumer culture', in FEATHERSTONE, M., HEPWORTH, M. and TURNER, B. (eds) *The Body*, London: Sage, pp. 170–96.

FEATHERSTONE, M. and WERNICK, A. (1995) 'Introduction', in FEATHERSTONE, M. and WERNICK, A. (eds) *Images of Aging*, London: Routledge, pp. 1–15.

FRANK, A. (1991) 'For a sociology of the body: An analytical review', in FEATHERSTONE, M., HEPWORTH, M. and TURNER, B. (eds) *The Body*, London: Sage, pp. 36–102.

FRANK, A. (1995) *The Wounded Storyteller*, Chicago: University of Chicago Press.

GADOW, S. (1982) 'Body and self: A dialectic', in KESTENBAUM, V. (ed.) *The Humanity of the Ill: Phenomenological Perspectives*, Knoxville, TN: University of Tennessee Press, pp. 86–100.

GERGEN, M. (1994) 'The social construction of personal histories: Gendered lives in popular biographies', in SARBIN, T. and KITUSE, J. (eds) *Constructing the Social*, London: Sage, pp. 19–45.

HALL, M. (1996) *Feminism and Sporting Bodies*, Champaign, IL: Human Kinetics Press.

HARDING, S. (1991) *Whose Science? Whose Knowledge?*, Milton Keynes: Open University Press.

JACKSON, S. (1996) 'Toward a conceptual understanding of flow experience in élite athletes', *Research Quarterly for Exercise and Sport*, **67**, pp. 76–90.

KIRK, D. (1993) *The Body Schooling and Culture*, Deakin: Deakin University Press.

KIRK, D. and TINNING, R. (eds) (1990) *Physical Education, Curriculum and Culture*, London: Falmer Press.

KIRK, D. and TINNING, R. (1994) 'Embodied self-identity, healthy lifestyles and school physical education', *Sociology of Health and Illness*, **16**, pp. 600–25.

KLEIBER, D. and BROCK, S. (1992) 'The effect of career-ending injuries on the subsequent well-being of élite college athletes', *Sociology of Sport Journal*, **9**, pp. 70–5.

KLEIBER, D., BROCK, S., YOUNGKHILL, L., DATTILO, J. and CADWELL, L. (1995) 'The relevance of leisure in an illness experience: Realities of spinal chord injury', *Journal of Leisure Research*, **27**, 3, pp. 283–99.

KNOWLES, D. (1991) 'Models for understanding pre-service and beginning teachers' biographies: Illustrations from case studies', in GOODSON, I. (ed.) *Studying Teachers' Lives*, London: Falmer Press, pp. 99–152.

LEDER, D. (1990) *The Absent Body*, Chicago: University of Chicago Press.

McADAMS, D. (1985) *Power, Intimacy, and the Life Story*, Homewood, IL: The Dorsey Press.

MERLEAU-PONTY, M. (1962) *Phenomenology of Perception*, London: Routledge and Kegan Paul.

PAGE, A. and FOX, K. (1997) 'Adolescent weight management and the physical self', in FOX, K. (ed.) *The Physical Self: From Motivation to Well-being*, Champaign, IL: Human Kinetics Press, pp. 229–56.

PLUMMER, K. (1995) *Telling Sexual Stories*, London: Routledge.

PRONGER, B. (1995) 'Rendering the body: The implicit lessons of gross anatomy', *Quest*, **47**, pp. 427–46.

SCRATON, S. (1992) *Shaping up to Womanhood: Gender and Girls' Physical Education*, Buckingham: Open University Press.

SHILLING, C. (1993) 'The body, class and social inequalities', in EVANS, J. (ed.) *Equality, Education and Physical Education*, London: Falmer Press, pp. 55–73.

SHILLING, C. and MELLOR, P. (1994) 'Embodiment, auto/biography and carnal knowing: The Protestant Reformation and modern self identities', *Auto/Biography*, **3.1**, **3.2**, pp. 115–28.

SHOTTER, J. (1993) 'Becoming someone: Identity and belonging', in COUPLAND, N. and NUSSBAUM, J. (eds) *Discourse and Lifespan Identity*, London: Sage, pp. 5–27.

SIKES, P. (1988) 'Growing old gracefully? Age, identity and physical education', in EVANS, J. (ed.) *Teachers, Teaching and Control in Physical Education*, London: Falmer Press, pp. 21–40.

SPARKES, A. (1994a) 'Life histories and the issue of voice: Reflections on an emerging relationship', *International Journal of Qualitative Studies in Education*, **7**, 2, pp. 165–83.

SPARKES, A. (1994b) 'Self, silence and invisibility as a beginning teacher: A life history of lesbian experience', *British Journal of Sociology of Education*, **15**, 1, pp. 93–118.

SPARKES, A. (1995) 'Writing people: Reflections on the dual crises of representation and legitimation in qualitative inquiry', *Quest*, **47**, 2, pp. 158–95.

SPARKES, A. (1996a) 'Interrupted body projects and the self in teaching: Exploring an absent presence', *International Studies in Sociology of Education*, **6**, 2, pp. 167–90.

SPARKES, A. (1996b) 'The fatal flaw: A narrative of the fragile body-self', *Qualitative Inquiry*, **2**, 4, pp. 463–94.

SPARKES, A. (1997a) 'Ethnographic fiction and representing the absent other', *Sport, Education and Society*, **2**, 1, pp. 25–40.

SPARKES, A. (1997b) 'Reflections on the socially constructed physical self', in FOX, K. (ed.) *The Physical Self: From Motivation to Well-Being*, Champaign, IL: Human Kinetics Press, pp. 83–110.

SPARKES, A. (1998) 'Athletic identity: An Achilles' heel to the survival of self', *Qualitative Health Research*, **8**, 5, pp. 628–48.

SPARKES, A. (in press) 'Exploring body narratives', *Sport, Education and Society*.

SPARKES, A. and TEMPLIN, T. (1992) 'Life histories and physical education teachers: Exploring the meanings of marginality', in SPARKES, A. (ed.) *Research in Physical Education and Sport: Exploring Alternative Visions*, London: Falmer Press, pp. 118–45.

SPARKES, A., TEMPLIN, T. and SCHEMPP, P. (1990) 'The problematic nature of a career in a marginal subject: Some implications for teacher education programmes', *Journal of Education for Teaching*, **16**, 1, pp. 3–28.

SPARKES, A., TEMPLIN, T. and SCHEMPP, P. (1993) 'Exploring dimensions of marginality: Reflecting on the life histories of physical education teachers', *Journal of Teaching in Physical Education*, **12**, 4, pp. 386–98.

STANLEY, L. and WISE S. (1993) *Breaking out Again: Feminist Ontology and Epistemology*, London: Routledge.

STEVENS, R. (ed.) (1996) *Understanding the Self*, London: Sage.

SYNNOTT, A. (1993) *The Body Social: Symbolism, Self and Society*, London: Routledge.

TEMPLIN, T. and SCHEMPP, P. (eds) (1989) *Socialization into Physical Education: Learning to Teach*, Indianapolis: Benchmark Press.

TOOMBS, K. (1992) 'The body in multiple sclerosis: A patient's perspective', in LEDER, D. (ed.) *The Body in Medical Thought and Practice*, Netherlands: Kluwer Academic Publishers, pp. 127–37.

WHITEHEAD, M. (1990) 'Meaningful existence, embodiment and physical education', *Journal of Philosophy of Education*, **24**, 10, pp. 3–13.

WHITEHEAD, M. (1992) 'Body as machine and body as self in teaching', in WILLIAMS, T., ALMOND, L. and SPARKES, A. (eds) *Sport and Physical Activity: Moving Towards Excellence*, proceedings of the AIESEP World Convention, July 20–25, Loughborough University, London: E. and F.N. Spon, pp. 376–82.

10 Knowledgeable Teachers in Physical Education: A View of Teachers' Knowledge

Tony Rossi and Tania Cassidy

Introduction

As a profession we remain unsure of the knowledge that distinguishes us as teachers. Teachers' knowledge in physical education is just as perplexing, even though it has received significant scholarly attention. There have been struggles to come to terms with what stands for discipline knowledge as well as what might be referred to as professional knowledge within the field (Kirk, 1990; MacDonald, 1992; Siedentop, 1989; Tinning, 1992; Whitson and Macintosh, 1990). The difficulties emerge through the uncertainty about what it is that we are referring to when we talk about teachers' knowledge in physical education. For example, is it the knowledge of movement and exercise sciences that are alleged to underpin teaching in physical education? Is it the knowledge of socio-cultural aspects of physical activity, within which physical education is alleged to take place? Is it knowledge of games or sports or is it knowledge of the teaching of such games and sports? Is it knowledge of the curriculum in physical education, official or otherwise? Is it all, or a combination of the above, or something else entirely?

Attempts to identify knowledge for teaching have attracted considerable effort in general terms (see Carr, 1989; Elbaz, 1991; Shulman, 1986, 1987; Smyth, 1987). In physical education also there have been attempts to identify important knowledge for teaching from a technical perspective (Mosston and Ashworth, 1986; Rink, 1985; Siedentop, 1989, 1991). These endeavours might be characterized as texts that deal with knowledge *for* teaching physical education. Other researchers have taken a more problematic view of physical education and these might be characterized as texts which deal with knowledge *about* teaching physical education (Kirk, 1986, 1988; Kirk and Tinning, 1990; Lawson, 1993; Templin and Schempp, 1989; Tinning, 1987, 1991; Tinning, Kirk and Evans, 1993). It is the latter approach that we take here since we believe that there are ample texts that talk about knowledge for teaching in absolute and final terms. We felt it is more productive to take a different view of teachers' knowledge in physical education.

To regard knowledge for teaching physical education as a composite of other knowledges and to talk of teachers' knowledge as though it was absolute or arbitrary is of limited use. We prefer to consider teaching to be a reflexive social practice and to explore the idea of dominant and alternative discourses using problem setting (Lawson, 1984, 1988, 1993; Tinning, 1991) as an analytical framework.

We discuss Shulman's (1986, 1987) notion of pedagogical content knowledge as a source of teachers' knowledge but argue it is more useful to talk about *knowledgeable teachers* in physical education, and in doing so draw upon a different theoretical framework informed by the work of Lusted (1986), and Giddens (1984, 1991). This requires us to make definite links between what it is to be a knowledgeable teacher of physical education and self identity.

To set the scene we discuss some of the traditions of research into physical education teachers' knowledge and what it has told us. We consider this work to represent ways in which pedagogy in general, and in physical education specifically, has been balkanized (Hargreaves, 1994) or broken up into discrete parts in order to be reassembled at a later date. In the second half of the chapter we take a holistic view of teachers' knowledge and discuss the concept of knowledgeable teachers. We feel that it is important not to repeat the work of others who have summarily written in this area (e.g. Bain, 1990; Lawson, 1990).

The Sum of the Parts Do Not Equal the Whole

What Research Has Told Us about Teachers' Knowledge

Linda Bain (1990) has composed a comprehensive summary of the research into what she refers to as 'sport pedagogy'. In doing so she identified three paradigms; the behaviourist, the socialization and critical theory paradigms. In our view, the first of these maintains an enduring dominance. The far reaching impact of scientific discourse then, has not left teaching untouched and the process–product research of the late 1970s and early 1980s generated a vast array of information related to discrete aspects of the pedagogical act. The overarching framework for such work is the concept of academic learning time (ALT) as a measurable outcome of teacher practice. ALT is in turn thought to be affected by a range of other variables many of which are researched using coded sets of tools and reduced to collections of numerical data. A text by Good and Brophy (1984) provides a good example of how the research process balkanizes knowledge about teaching. In physical education, the work of Daryl Siedentop (1991) is perhaps representative as is the collection by Darst, Zakrajsek and Mancini (1989, 2nd edition).

This work provides information on teacher practices that relate predominantly to *management*, which includes administration and organizational procedures, and to *instruction* which includes, instruction on skill technique, provision of practice opportunities and feedback on attempts at skill/movement patterns. Lawson (1990) argues that whilst this research has generated lots of what he calls information, it has, in his view, contributed little that is worthwhile to the stock of teachers' knowledge. Our argument is that whilst this information is important (e.g. Rossi, 1996), it is sometimes elevated to a level of significance perhaps out of proportion with its functional utility and reduces the teacher to little more than a technician or what Giroux and McLaren (1987) call pedagogical clerks. Giddens (1984) argues that much of our daily practice as humans is routinized and requires little reflective thought. We return to this discussion later in the chapter. What has emerged then, is a code of physical education teacher practice that is dominant, seemingly based on scientific rhetoric, extolling the virtues of performance and lauded as being professional.

Dominant Discourses

An assumption underpinning this analysis of the dominant discourses in physical education is that physical educators construct teachers' knowledge as a response to a problem. Using problem setting as a frame to view physical education is not new (e.g. Lawson, 1984, 1988, 1993; Tinning, 1991). Particular problems dominate physical education and as a consequence certain ways of viewing teachers' knowledge dominate the profession. According to Tinning (1991, p. 4) the process of problem setting: '. . . is a political act that is intimately linked with power, [and] control'.

Despite Tinning and Lawson using problem setting as a framework for analysing physical education they do not completely agree on the process through which problems are defined. One point of contention is Lawson's (1984) process of naming and framing problems. Tinning (1991) argues that Lawson was 'essentially talking about discourses' (p. 5). Lawson (1993) disagrees, though he does concede that 'it is timely to investigate approaches to problem setting, and linguistic or discourse analysis belongs in the protocols we need to develop' (p. 152). Heeding the concerns of Tinning (1991) and Lawson (1984, 1993) we view problems to be socially constructed as well as socially constituted. Furthermore, we recognize what is defined as a dominant problem is intimately connected with what is considered a problem by those whose discourses dominate the profession and by 'what counts as legitimate knowledge in the culture' (Tinning, 1991, p. 4). Our understanding of discourse is informed by Kirk's (1992) interpretation. He views discourse as not only what is said verbally, what is written and what is done, but also what is not said, written or done. Moreover he considers discourse to be

> . . . larger than language, because it embraces all forms of communicating rather than simply the verbal or written word. It refers to all meaning-making activity, whether this be intentional, conscious, unconscious, explicit, tacit, or reflexive . . .
> (p. 42)

Kirk's (1992) definition of discourse is useful for this present discussion of teachers' knowledge since it recognizes all aspects of 'meaning-making activity' and is compatible with Giddens's (1991) notion of knowledgeability. Discourses link together and when they do particular meanings are made and problems posed, resulting in certain ways of viewing that knowledge. This has consequences for teachers' knowledge in physical education because the 'arbitrary linking and fixing of formally separate discourses in ways that seem, or are made to seem, natural and necessary . . . have a range of effects on social relations and power' (Kirk, 1992,

p. 43). Failure to recognize that discourses can and do rearticulate and disarticulate leads to them being simply categorized erroneously as *the* dominant discourse.

In the following section of the chapter we focus on two problems that have dominated physical education and physical education teacher education (PETE). In response to these problems physical educators have constructed various discourses related to teachers' knowledge. To understand physical education teachers' knowledge, it is useful to examine how it is constructed in the context of PETE since in part, albeit small (e.g. Lortie, 1975), teachers' knowledge is shaped by their teacher education experiences. Tinning (1991) argues that 'there is little doubt that within PETE the dominant form of pedagogy . . . is based on structured discourses that foreground utility and that are concerned with the problem of *how* to teach physical education' (Tinning, 1991, p. 6). We therefore argue that one dominant problem relating to teachers' knowledge in physical education focuses on utility and how to teach. Another dominant and longstanding problem for physical educators according to Daryl Siedentop is the need to gain 'the respect and recognition of the educational world' (Siedentop, 1983, p. 47). Identifying this as a problem in physical education has ramifications for what is defined as worthwhile teacher knowledge.

Traditional discourses which seek to reproduce the status quo by focusing on the problems of utility and how to teach have dominated discourses in PETE. The hallmark and rationale of these discourses 'has its basis not in science or even theory, but in the unglamorous realities of life' (Hoffman, 1971, p. 100). Those whose teaching is framed by these discourses offer a 'methods-and-materials orientation. . . . Effectiveness and managerial efficiency are the primary evaluative criterion, and its indices are employment rates of graduates and their abilities to "hit the ground running" in schools' (Lawson, 1993, p. 155). This has implications for teachers' knowledge since it reinforces

> . . . a process of professional socialization and induction. On the job (that is, in school) reality is most highly valued, and skills, knowledge, and attitudes are passed on to prospective teachers by way of word of mouth. The dominant pedagogical knowledge in what might be called craft pedagogy (after Tom, 1984) is cast in such rules of thumb as 'start off firm, then you can relax later' and 'be consistent in your treatment of students.' Theory about teaching is little valued, and the main focus of methods courses is on tips for how to teach. Teacher education programs that champion this discourse favor long periods of practicum, with student teachers taking the role of apprentices. (Tinning, 1991, p. 7)

Kirk's (1986) analysis of the ways teachers' knowledges have traditionally been constructed support Lortie's (1975) claim that teacher education is a 'low impact' endeavour in comparison to the experiences gained in the 13,000 hours spent as a student in school (see also Graber, 1989; Schempp, 1989).

There has been a move away from 'on the job' induction approaches towards those that are perceived to be grounded in a science of education. This has been in response to an attack on the teaching profession where '. . . teachers' professional knowledge and judgement are being questioned' (Tinning, 1988, p. 85). One practice that has developed in response to the attack is to technologize teaching. According to

Tinning (1988, p. 86) it is easy to locate the work of physical educators who believe 'that a technology of teaching is necessary to solve the problems of practice' and therefore gain the respect of the educational world. Siedentop is a leading exponent claiming '. . . that it is to our advantage to pursue such technology goes without saying. Without it we will continue to suffer shadow status as a quasi-profession' (Siedentop, 1982, p. 49). Siedentop's commitment to pursuing technology has seen him focus on 'more experimental research to effect change in teacher behavior [which arguably is related to teachers' knowledge] and then to verify that changed teacher behavior results in greater student achievement' (Siedentop, 1983, p. 47).

In an attempt to address the problems of how to teach and how to gain credibility in the educational world, physical educators have articulated various discourses and have formed different alliances which appear natural and uncontestable (e.g. Crum, 1993). Two of the most dominant discourses, the traditional and scientific, have formed an alliance which appears natural and consequently uncontestable. This ideology has been termed technocratic. McKay, Gore and Kirk (1990, p. 52) claim that a technocratic ideology comprises of 'professionalism, scientism, and instrumental rationality' discourses. Understanding the 'ideological work' that occurs as a consequence of this discursive alliance provides insight into teachers' knowledge. McKay et al. (1990, p. 54) argue that this articulation of discourses results in physical educators being 'implicated in the scientization of politics and depoliticization of large portions of the citizenry'. They go on to argue that this has two consequences for understanding teachers' knowledge

> First, professionals disqualify the majority of citizens from the decision making process because professionals prescribe and proscribe how knowledge is defined to 'outsiders'. Second, by appealing to the purportedly neutral and benevolent aspects of professional knowledge, professionals have gradually translated questions about moral and political ends (What for? For whom?) into issues of technical, administrative, and managerial means (How to?). (McKay et al., 1990, p. 54)

Moreover, Tinning (1988) argues that teachers' knowledge, particularly practical knowledge,

> . . . is construed as knowledge of the relationship between means and ends. Moral questions such as 'How ought I act?' are essentially reduced to the instrumental question of which means are most efficient in achieving a desired end. Practical knowledge therefore has become defined in instrumental terms and practical problems as technical ones. (p. 86)

The Advent of Pedagogical Content Knowledge As a View of Teachers' Knowledge

A shift in paradigmatic orientation from quantitative to qualitative in education research has been central to the shift that has occurred in physical education pedagogy over the past decade. Rink (1993, p. 309) suggested that '. . . critical to the new way of thinking about teaching is the work of Lee Shulman.' His work became prominent in the physical education community after receiving exposure at the 1989 American Association of Health Physical Education Recreation and Dance preconvention symposium (Metzler, 1991). Shulman (1986) advocated a theoretical framework to understand the transmission of knowledge. In the framework he emphasized the notion of content knowledge which he subsequently broke into the following categories; subject matter content knowledge, pedagogical content knowledge and curricular knowledge. Subject matter content knowledge is more than just understanding the subject matter. It is the knowledge of 'why' the subject matter is so, on whose authority is it so and under what conditions could this change. Also the teacher must know why one topic is privileged over another. Pedagogical content knowledge is the 'subject matter knowledge for teaching' (Shulman, 1986, p. 9). This category of content knowledge is particularly important in understanding the teaching process and is considered to consist of:

> . . . the most useful forms of representation . . . the most powerful analogies, illustrations, examples, explanations and demonstrations — in a word, the ways of representing and formulating the subject that make it comprehensible to others. (p. 9)

Curricular knowledge consists of knowledge of the curriculum and its associated materials, as well as of alternative curriculum materials. Shulman emerged as one of the key researchers in the area of teachers' knowledge arguing that little research has been done on how teachers transform subject content into what he termed the content of instruction. He asks the questions: 'What are the sources of teacher knowledge? What does a teacher know and when did he or she come to know it? How is new knowledge acquired, old knowledge retrieved, and both combined to form a new knowledge base?' (Shulman, 1986, p. 8).

Shulman's conceptualization has been useful insofar as it enables an understanding of the knowledge base for teaching to develop. It serves as an impetus for acknowledging the link between subject content knowledge (or discipline knowledge) and knowledge for teaching. Some researchers have attempted to elaborate on Shulman's model. Geddis and Wood (1997) for example, argue that the transformation of subject matter into pedagogical reasoning requires a range of interactions which account for the children, the context, the time and place and in this sense, the knowledge becomes a representation upon which children's understanding is developed. Other attempts to reconceptualize Shulman's work includes Wilson, Shulman and Richert (1987) who suggested that for successful teachers, pedagogical content knowledge cannot simply be an intuitive understanding of subject matter. They argue

> . . . successful teachers cannot simply have an intuitive or personal understanding of a particular concept, principle, or theory. Rather, in order to foster understanding, they must themselves understand ways of representing the concept for students. They must have knowledge of the ways of transforming the content for the purposes of teaching. (p. 110)

For some, however, Shulman's conceptualization of pedagogical content knowledge remains inadequate. Cochran, DeRuiter and King (1993) regard it as neither complete or absolute but dynamic and ever evolving and therefore, prefer to refer to the knowledge for teaching subject content as pedagogical content *knowing* to emphasize the dynamic qualities of coming to know.

In many respects, the classic work by Berliner (1986) on 'experts' is similar to Shulman's (1986) work in that it identifies similar knowledge systems used in pedagogy, suggesting that it is helpful to conceptualize these as: knowledge of subject matter, and knowledge of organization and management of classrooms. In our view however, much of the above theorizing, with the exception of Cochran et al. falls into the trap of balkanizing the pedagogical act. Their ideas are perhaps closer to those of Lusted (1986) to whom we now turn for an alternative framework for considering teachers' knowledge. We argue for a theoretical framework that positions the work of Lusted and social theorist Anthony Giddens to form what we consider to be a productive alliance.

Considering the (W)hole: Knowledgeable Teachers in Physical Education

Pedagogical Process and Alternative Discourses

At the beginning of the chapter we made the claim that physical educators construct teachers' knowledge as a response to a problem and gave a brief overview of some of the discourses that dominate physical education teaching. We now consider it necessary to introduce the reader to problems in physical education and PETE which play a part in the construction of *alternative* discourses regarding teachers' knowledge.

McKay, Gore and Kirk (1990, p. 64) identify the lack of a critical consciousness in physical educators as a problem for physical education. They argue a critical consciousness is needed so questions relating to 'how and why physical education takes on its current form and content, which groups benefit from physical education and which groups are disempowered, and how physical education can be used for emancipatory purposes' are asked (McKay et al., 1990, p. 64). Linked to this is what Tinning (1991, p. 9) views as a central problem for PETE. He argues that the problem has three interrelated parts: the 'relationship of school to society; the way in which knowledge is created, disseminated, and legitimated; and the nature of teaching itself'. In this chapter we focus specifically on discourses associated with the way questions are asked about knowledge, specifically professional knowledge. Tinning (1988, p. 85) argues that professional knowledge is 'mismatched to the changing character of situations of practice . . . Moreover, the root of this professional problem lies in the history of professions themselves and in the dominant model of professional knowledge that they embrace'. In an attempt to address this problem a number of physical educators have utilized various discourse which draw upon Lusted's notion of pedagogy.

Lusted (1986) rejects the fractionation of the pedagogical act, instead he focuses on

> ... the *process* through which knowledge is produced. Pedagogy addresses the 'how' questions involved not only in the transmission or reproduction of knowledge but also in its production. ... How one teaches is therefore of central interest but, ... it becomes inseparable from what is being taught, and, crucially, how one learns. (pp. 2–3)

The relationship between the teacher, learner and content is a dynamic one and as such no one component of the relationship can ever be static. Hence as we have argued, teacher knowledge can never be absolute, it can only ever be contextual like ever shifting desert sands constantly shaped by competing and complementary elements. As Lusted says

> ... knowledge is produced not just at the researcher's desk nor at the lectern but in the *consciousness*, through the process of thought, discussion, writing, debate, exchange; in the social and internal, collective and isolated struggle for control of understanding; from engagement in the unfamiliar idea, the difficult formulation pressed at the limit of comprehension or energy; in the meeting of the deeply held with the casually dismissed; in the dramatic moment of realisation that a scarcely regarded concern, and unarticulated desire, the barely assimilated, can come alive, make for a new sense of self, change commitments and activity. And these are also *transformations* which take place across all agencies in the educational process, regardless of their title as academic, critic, teacher or learner. (Lusted, 1986, p. 4)

There is some overlap here between Lusted's ideas and Shulman's notion of content knowledge. Lusted, however, is specific about knowledge *production*. It is this which is the key for us and the vital separator between Lusted's ideas and others who theorize about teachers' knowledge. However, in our view, one of the weakness of Lusted's work is his failure to consider the identities of the actors in the pedagogical process. Just as a paradigmatic shift was instrumental in Shulman's work being adopted by physical educators, a shift within the qualitative paradigm has also been instrumental in recognizing the agency, subjectivity or identity of the actors in the pedagogical process in physical education.

In an attempt to address the problem of the way professional knowledge is created, disseminated and legitimated physical educators have articulated various discourses and formed alliances. O'Sullivan, Siedentop and Locke (1992) call the authors of these discourses radicals. They collectively call the discourses radical even though they recognize 'the variety of perspectives within this discourse, including critical theorists, feminists, postmodernists, and poststructuralists' (p. 267). Failing to recognize that the discourses rearticulate and disarticulate to form different alliances, O'Sullivan, Siedentop and Locke do not see the range of ideological work that is possible and therefore erroneously consider there to be one radical discourse. Below we have focused on only two discourses we have loosely called 'social responsible' represented by the work of Hellison (1978, 1985, 1988),

Fernandez-Balboa (1995) and Hickey (1995, 1997) and 'Foucauldian', represented by the work of Gore (1990). We acknowledge that this work is not exhaustive but we believe that these discourses have formed a theoretical and ideological alliance and are underpinned by a socially critical ideology therefore providing valuable insight into teachers knowledge. In particular what they do is foreground notions of identity or subjectivity within the pedagogical act.

One of the first discourses that advocated recognizing the subjectivities of those involved in the pedagogical process stemmed from the work of Don Hellison. In 1978 he problematized physical education pedagogy by focusing on at-risk youth (Hellison, 1978) and later used social problems as the basis for a physical education programme (Hellison, 1985). A decade after he first problematized physical education pedagogy he called for more attention to be given to 'the subjectivity of the experience, social problems, reflection and empowerment of teachers and students . . .' (Hellison, 1988, p. 88). He does this by using issues of self-development and social conscience in designing instructional strategies. Hellison views his work as personal 'theory-in-action' and offers his work

> . . . as an alternative that may serve to affirm you, give you a new idea or two, or cause you to reflect on what you are doing with students. It is an in-process model; I'm sure I will be in a different place a year from now so please don't etch this in stone. (Hellison, 1978, p. vi) (Hellison, 1988, p. 87)

Fernandez-Balboa (1995) identifies how the unequal power sharing that occurs between teachers and students in traditional pedagogy reproduces the inequalities in society. Consequently, he attempts to implement alternative procedures with his co-learners believing the 'responsibility of the learning should be shared by the teacher and students as much as possible' (p. 104).

Hickey (1995) draws on a classroom based physical education programme, underpinned by an action research model, where primary school teachers attempted to address issues associated with gender, elitism and violence. The teachers did not want to preside over the students' knowledges, instead they invited the children to critique behaviours and attitudes using open discussion, narrative and counter narrative, with the aim of it being a conscious raising exercise. In another study, Hickey (1997) focuses on the ways teacher education students engage socially critical discourses in a physical education course of study. Hickey was the teacher educator involved in the course and he encouraged the students to 'examine and (re)construct their pedagogy through their interactions with critical discourses' (p. v).

Another physical educator uses the notion of 'pedagogy as text' as the foundation for her approach to PETE (Gore, 1990, p. 103). Despite its acknowledged weakness, using pedagogy as text enables Gore to offer a possible critical pedagogy without it being viewed as *the* answer. In her study Gore did not want the students to see the university lecturer as the fount of all knowledge, rather she was keen to have them *produce* knowledge through a self reflective journal based on their practical engagement in the course. Knowledge was viewed as contestable and its meaning was a site of struggle in which she found her PETE students 'far from passive in their own construction of meaning' (Gore, 1990, p. 134). Gore admits to being disappointed with some of the outcomes, particularly the unwillingness of some to participate. One can see the attraction for Gore in her pedagogy-as-text notion. We believe there is great promise in an approach to pedagogy which positions all players as learners. It certainly places teachers knowledge in physical education in a transitory mode. We can never say 'this is how to organize a class', 'this is how to teach high jump', 'this is when to provide feedback'. Such utilitarian statements have only relevance for the here and now and are superseded by questions such as 'why should I teach the high jump?', what happens if I organize the class this way? and so on. If teachers of physical education can think in this way then the learner is explicitly involved in pedagogical decisions and a democratized form of pedagogy then becomes possible.

The above scholars have made the difficult but arguably vital step of integrating teachers' knowledge into pedagogical process. There are two distinct issues that emerge. First, these scholars confirm that teachers' knowledge in physical education is neither absolute or complete and second as we have said there is no one pedagogy that fits all (Lawson, 1990) rather there are only pedago*gies* and these tend to compete for legitimacy in the broader profession. What this does mean however, is that just as there is no one pedagogy, then similarly there can be no one teachers' knowledge.

Considering the Relationship between Teacher's Identity and Knowledgeability

Another way of considering the identities of the actors in the pedagogical process is to adopt a framework based on the notion of knowledgeability as proposed by Giddens (1991). In this period of late or reflexive modernity Giddens (1991) argues what we know is based on how we recursively reproduce our behaviour or mediate it in the light of other experience or knowledge. This emphasizes the redundancy of the notion that there is an arbitrary thing called teachers' knowledge.

Giddens (1991) premises his model of self-identity on the assumption that 'to be a human being is to know' (p. 35). He argues that actors reflexively monitor daily social action and can describe discursively the 'nature of, and the reasons for, the behaviour in which they engage' (p. 35). Giddens divides this rationalization of action into three levels; discursive consciousness, practical consciousness and unconscious cognition. In this chapter we focus on the first two levels. Discursive consciousness is evident when an actor can give an account of particular issues. But many of our day to day social practices occur at the level of practical consciousness which is non-conscious rather than unconscious and are 'characteristically simply done' (Cassell, 1993, p. 94). Giddens (1991) argues that many aspects of being able to 'go-on' are communicated through the practical consciousness which has 'taken-for-granted' qualities. It is practical consciousness which enables us to simply 'do' things while concentrating on activities we deem to require conscious effort.

Most physical education teachers can give an account of what they are doing in their classes (i.e. their discursive consciousness). Ask any PE teacher why they did this or that and they will be able to provide an answer. However as we have argued, much of our practice in teaching physical education occurs at the level of practical consciousness and is therefore simply done. We argue that if we are to become knowledgeable teachers we must somehow inform ourselves about what we simply do in class.

Practical consciousness is associated with day to day routines and allied regimes. Routines are connected to the ability of being able to 'go-on' in social life (Giddens, 1991) and play a part in emotionally anchoring feelings of what Giddens calls ontological security. By this he means a 'protective cocoon' (Giddens, 1991), a device by which we maintain a personal equilibrium in our day to day lives. Routines provide us with 'a sense of continuity and order of events, including those not directly within the perceptual environment of the individual' (Giddens, 1991, p. 243). Furthermore, they are 'constitutive of an emotional acceptance of the reality of the "external world"' (Giddens, 1991, p. 42). Regimes are those actions in which we engage partially to conform to social conventions and partially by personal dispositions and inclinations. Regimes differ from routine because they relate to personal habits. They are important in understanding self-identity because 'they connect habits with aspects of the visible appearance of the body' (Giddens, 1991, p. 62).

If we look at the routines and regimes of physical education teachers, we can see that they are imbued with a sense of investment. This is another term that is used to define the sense of continuity. It is considered to be 'the emotional commitment, involved in taking up positions in discourses which confer power and are supportive of our sense of our continuity, confirming ourselves . . . in accordance with frames of reference which are themselves socially produced' (Henriques, Hollway, Urwin, Venn and Walkerdine, 1984, p. 205). This forces us to ask what messages does the physical educator convey by the way they are dressed, their body shape, their approach to teaching, their expectations of children? These things cannot be separated from the way a physical educator goes on with things, those social and professional practices that reside in the practical consciousness — the things that are simply done. This in turn cannot be separated from teachers' knowledge in physical education. Our argument is that the ideological alliances formed between the dominant discourses in physical education have become part of the practical consciousness of the teacher. They do so because they represent the routines and regimes of individuals that provide the protective cocoon. In this sense, the discourses are inextricably linked with a teacher's identity. If we recall what Kirk (1992) said about discourses, they include all that is said and written, but also includes what is not said or written. Hence the way a physical education teacher is, is inherently linked to what they do and these recursively reproduce themselves.

Security provided by conforming to convention has a tendency to guide teacher practice. The social constructionist Ken Gergen (1991) describes this as a 'community of agreement'. In other words, those conventions become acceptable as knowledge because they fit with the conventions of the community of which one is a part. The alliance of certain discourses then, both frame and reinforce what is accepted as knowledge and the day to day actions of individuals recreate the conditions for that knowledge to maintain its sovereignty. It is not difficult to understand therefore why a technologized form of pedagogical practice in physical education is dominant. We argue that the role of teacher education and the broader critical community is to disturb the ontological security and cast the conventions of teacher knowledge to critical scrutiny. Questioning such conventions as the first school term being traditionally based on athletics and swimming (in the southern hemisphere) does not win friends in the staffroom or in the profession for that matter. However, we believe it is at this point that knowledgeable teachers of physical education can emerge — by acting upon the awareness of what is simply done rather than simply doing it. The taken for granted routines then can be changed by recognizing the regimes under which we operate. This then can lead to structures *not* reproducing themselves and giving rise to recursively reproduced practices. Rather, changed structures will require new and innovative practices. This is dangerous however, as it can create a situation that Giddens (1991) refers to as 'existential anxiety'. This is where the protective cocoon is disturbed and Giddens suggests that actors seek to re-establish equilibrium as quickly as possible. It is at this juncture however, that we believe that new discourses and new alliances can be formed. We argue that as a consequence, the balkanized forms of physical education teacher knowledge that dominate physical education practice can be transformed into a seamless form of knowledge that is not bounded by the conventions of expertise.

Concluding Comments

We have not taken a conventional position with this chapter, we saw no point in replicating what has been well done by others. Rather we have argued that the sum of the parts of physical education teachers' knowledge do not equal the whole. We have argued that this is because certain discourses in alliance with other discourses dominate both what is taught in physical education and how it is taught. We feel that Lusted's (1986) notion of pedagogy provides a better framework within which to consider knowledge. In our view, this leads us towards considering knowledge in much broader terms. Using the work of Giddens, we have shown that this too is incomplete and that teachers' knowledge is inextricably linked to teacher identity. Hence in our view, identity is a crucial feature in teachers' knowledge. We are unwilling to suggest that our position offers a complete view of teachers' knowledge in physical education. We would claim, however, that it provides a more secure basis upon which we can begin to talk of knowledgeable teachers in physical education.

References

BAIN, L. (1990) 'Research in sport pedagogy: Past, present and future', in *Sport and Physical Activity: Moving Towards Excellence*, Proceedings of the AIESEP world convention, Loughborough University, UK, 20–25 July.

BERLINER, D.C. (1986) 'In pursuit of the expert pedagogue', *Education Researcher*, **15**, 7, pp. 5–13.

CARR, W. (ed.) (1989) *Quality in Teaching: Arguments for a Reflective Profession*, Lewes, UK: Falmer Press.

CASSELL, P. (1993) *The Giddens Reader*, London: Macmillan Press.

COCHRAN, K.F., DERUITER, J.A. and KING, R.A. (1993) 'Pedagogical content knowing: An integrated model for teacher preparation', *Journal of Teacher Education*, **44**, 4, pp. 263–72.

CRUM, B. (1993) 'Conventional thought and practice in physical education: Problems of teaching and implications for change', *Quest*, **45**, 3, pp. 339–57.

DARST, P., ZAKRAJSEK, D. and MANCINI, V. (1989) *Analyzing Physical Education and Sport Instruction* (2nd ed.), Champaign, IL: Human Kinetics.

ELBAZ, F. (1991) 'Research on teacher's knowledge: The evolution of a discourse', *Journal of Curriculum Studies*, **23**, 1, pp. 1–19.

FERNANDEZ-BALBOA, J.-M. (1995) 'Reclaiming physical education in higher education through critical pedagogy', *Quest*, **47**, 1, pp. 91–114.

GEDDIS, A. and WOOD, E. (1997) 'Transforming subject matter and managing dilemmas: A case study in teacher education', *Teaching and Teacher Education*, **13**, 6, pp. 611–26.

GERGEN, K. (1991) *The Saturated Self*, New York: Basic Books.

GIDDENS, A. (1984) *The Constitution of Society*, Berkeley: University of California Press.

GIDDENS, A. (1991) *Modernity and Self-identity: Self and Society in the Late Modern Age*, Cambridge: Polity Press.

GIROUX, H. and MCLAREN, P. (1987) 'Teacher education as a counter public sphere: Notes towards a redefinition', in POPKEWITZ, T.S. (ed.) *Critical Studies in Teacher Education: Its Folklore, Theory and Practice*, London: Falmer Press, pp. 266–97.

GOOD, T. and BROPHY, J. (1984) *Looking in Classrooms* (3rd ed.), New York: Harper and Row.

GORE, J.M. (1990) 'Pedagogy as text in physical education teacher education: Beyond the preferred reading', in KIRK, D. and TINNING, R. (eds) *Physical Education, Curriculum and Culture: Critical Issues in the Contemporary Crisis*, Basingstoke: Falmer Press, pp. 101–38.

GRABER, K. (1989) 'Teaching tomorrow's teachers: Professional preparation as an agent of socialization', in TEMPLIN, T. and SCHEMPP, P. (eds) *Socialization into Physical Education: Learning to Teach*. Indianapolis: Benchmark press, pp. 59–80.

HARGREAVES, A. (1994) *Changing Teachers, Changing Times*, London: Cassell.

HELLISON, D. (1978) *Beyond Balls and Bats: Alienated (and Other) Youth in the Gym*, Washington, DC: AAHPERD.

HELLISON, D. (1985) *Goals and Strategies for Teaching Physical Education*, Champaign, IL: Human Kinetics.

HELLISON, D. (1988) 'Our constructed reality: Some contributions of an alternative perspective to physical education pedagogy', *Quest*, **40**, pp. 84–90.

HENRIQUES, J., HOLLWAY, W., URWIN, C., VENN, C. and WALKERDINE, V. (eds) (1984) *Changing the Subject: Psychology, Social Regulation and Subjectivity*, London and New York: Methuen.

HICKEY, C. (1995) *Can Physical Education Be Physical Education?*, ACHPER Healthy Lifestyles Journal, **42**, 3, pp. 4–7.

HICKEY, C. (1997) 'Critical intellectual resources for praxis in physical education: The limits to rationality', Unpublished doctoral thesis: Deakin University, Geelong, Australia.

HOFFMAN, S.J. (1971) 'Traditional methodology: Prospects for change', *Quest*, **15**, pp. 51–7.

KIRK, D. (1986) 'Beyond the limits of theoretical discourse in teacher education: Towards a critical pedagogy', *Teaching and Teacher Education*, **2**, 2, pp. 155–67.

KIRK, D. (1988) *Physical Education and Curriculum Study: A Critical Introduction*, London: Croom Helm.

KIRK, D. (1990) 'Knowledge, science and the rise and rise of human movement studies', *Australian Council for Health, Physical Education and Recreation National Journal*, **127**, pp. 8–11.

KIRK, D. (1992) 'Physical education, discourse, and ideology: Bringing the hidden curriculum into view', *Quest*, **44**, pp. 35–56.

KIRK, D. and TINNING, R. (eds) (1990) *Physical Education, Curriculum and Culture: Critical Issues in the Contemporary Crisis*, London: Falmer Press.

LAWSON, H.A. (1984) 'Problem-setting for physical education and sport', *Quest*, **36**, pp. 48–60.

LAWSON, H.A. (1988) 'Occupational socialization, cultural studies and the physical education programs', *Journal of Teaching in Physical Education*, **7**, pp. 265–88.

LAWSON, H.A. (1990) 'Sport pedagogy research: From information-gathering to useful knowledge', *Journal of Teaching in Physical Education*, **10**, 1, pp. 1–20.

LAWSON, H.A. (1993) 'Dominant discourses, problem setting, and teacher education pedagogies: A critique', *Journal of Teaching in Physical Education*, **12**, pp. 149–60.

LORTIE, D. (1975) *Schoolteacher. A Sociological Study*, Chicago: University of Chicago Press.

LUSTED, D. (1986) 'Why pedagogy', *Screen*, **27**, 5, pp. 2–14.

MACDONALD, D. (1992) 'Knowledge, power and professional practice in physical education teacher education: A case study', Unpublished doctoral thesis: Deakin University, Geelong, Australia.

MCKAY, J., GORE, J. and KIRK, D. (1990) 'Beyond the limits of technocratic physical education', *Quest*, **42**, pp. 52–75.

METZLER, M.W. (1991) 'Bringing the teaching act back into sport pedagogy', *Journal of Teaching in Physical Education*, **11**, 2, pp. 150–60.

MOSSTON, M. and ASHWORTH, S. (1986) *Teaching Physical Education*, OH: Charles Merrill.

O'SULLIVAN, M., SIEDENTOP, D. and LOCKE, L. (1992) 'Toward collegiality: Competing viewpoints among teacher educators', *Quest*, **44**, pp. 266–80.

RINK, J. (1985) *Teaching Physical Education for Learning*, St Louis: Times Mirror Mosby.

RINK, J.E. (1993) 'Teacher education: A focus on action', *Quest*, **45**, pp. 308–20.

ROSSI, T. (1996) 'Pedagogical content knowledge and critical reflection in physical education', in MAWER, M. (ed.) *Mentoring in Physical Education: Issues and Insights*, London: Falmer Press, pp. 176–93.

SCHEMPP, P. (1989) 'Apprenticeship of observation and the development of physical education teachers', in TEMPLIN, T. and SCHEMPP, P. (eds) *Socialization into Physical Education: Learning to Teach*, Indianapolis: Benchmark Press, pp. 13–37.

SHULMAN, L. (1986) 'Those who understand: Knowledge growth in teaching', *Educational Researcher*, **15**, 2, pp. 4–14.

SHULMAN, L. (1987) 'Knowledge and teaching: Foundations of the new reform', *Harvard Educational Review*, **57**, 1, pp. 1–22.

SIEDENTOP, D. (1982) 'Teaching research: The interventionist view', *Journal of Teaching in Physical Education*, **1**, 3, pp. 46–9.

SIEDENTOP, D. (1983) *Physical Education: Introductory Analysis*, Dubuque, IA: Brown.

SIEDENTOP, D. (1989) *Content Knowledge for Physical Education*, Address to the C and I Academy Conference on the Implications of the Knowledge for Teaching for Teacher Education, Boston, AAHPERD.

SIEDENTOP, D. (1991) *Developing Teaching Skills in Physical Education*, Mayfield, CA: Mountain View Press.

SMYTH, J. (1987) (ed.) *Educating Teachers: Changing the Nature of Pedagogical Knowledge*, Lewes, UK: Falmer Press.

TEMPLIN, T. and SCHEMPP, P. (1989) (eds) *Socialization into Physical Education: Learning to Teach*, Indianapolis: Benchmark Press.

TINNING, R. (1987) *Improving Teaching in Physical Education*, Geelong: Deakin University Press.

TINNING, R. (1988) 'Student teaching and the pedagogy of necessity', *Journal of Teaching in Physical Education*, 7, 2, pp. 82–9.

TINNING, R. (1991) 'Teacher education pedagogy: Dominant discourses and the process of problem setting', *Journal of Teaching in Physical Education*, **11**, pp. 1–20.

TINNING, R. (1992) 'Teacher education and the development of content knowledge for physical education teaching', Keynote address prepared for the Conference on The Place of Subject Specific Teaching Methods in Teacher Education, Santiago de Compostela, Spain.

TINNING, R. and KIRK, D. (1990) (eds) *Physical Education, Curriculum and Culture: Critical Issues in the Contemporary Crisis*, Lewes, UK: Falmer Press.

TINNING, R., KIRK, D. and EVANS, J. (1993) *Learning to Teach Physical Education*, Sydney: Prentice Hall.

TOM, A. (1984) *Teaching as a Moral Craft*, New York: Longman.

WHITSON, D. and MACINTOSH, D. (1990) 'The scientization of physical education: Discourses of performances', *Quest*, **42**, 1, pp. 40–51.

WILSON, S.M., SHULMAN, L.S. and RICHERT, A.E. (1987) '"150 different ways" of knowing: Representations of knowledge in teaching', in CALDERHEAD, J. (ed.) *Exploring Teachers Thinking*, London: Cassell, pp. 104–24.

11 Teacher Thinking and Decision Making in Physical Education: Planning, Perceiving, and Implementing Instruction

David C. Griffey and Lynn Dale Housner

Teacher cognition and decision making emerged as a topic of interest in the middle 1970s at the National Conference on Studies in Teaching (National Institute of Education, 1975). Up until that time, research on teaching had been focused on behaviour in classrooms. Particularly the relationship of teacher behaviour to student achievement. Teacher thinking was seen as an important topic of study because it was not known how good teachers accomplished the things that they did. In other words, we knew what good teachers did but not how they did it. Numerous studies of teacher cognition, decision making, and belief have been conducted since that time. Interesting and useful results have been produced.

We have gained insight into teachers' belief systems and how those beliefs presage thinking and action that teachers take in working with students in classrooms. We now know something about how teachers plan for instruction and their thinking while interacting with students. We have learned how they perceive the instructional environment; that is, what kinds of things they look for, and how they allocate their attention during instructional episodes. We have learned how management issues are framed by teachers as they consider alternatives for their action during instruction. The study of teacher thinking has helped us understand how teachers conceptualize pedagogical knowledge — how teachers structure information in ways that can be understood and used by students. We have seen how pedagogical heuristics, metaphor, simile, and other representational forms are created by teachers in the course of their work. Further, we are beginning to understand how teachers assign value to the work that they do — how they evaluate the success of their work and the performance of their students. The findings from research on teacher thinking, decision making, and belief have implications for teacher education, the ongoing development of teachers, and for future studies on effective teaching.

Much of the study of teacher thinking and belief has been conducted in a context of comparing beginning, or novice, teachers with experienced, or more fully developed, teachers. Results of that work suggest strongly that teachers have different capacities for thinking about their work at different stages of their careers. That confuses any straightforward, unidimensional, consideration of teacher thinking. Clearly, we must bear in mind that suitable models of cognition for beginners on the one hand and more mature teachers on the other will differ.

Beliefs

Presumably, all thinking and decision making that teachers do is premised on a set of beliefs about schools as institutions, the role of children in those organizations, and the purposes of education in culture. A teacher's sense of purpose — their notion of what they are trying to accomplish with their curriculums and during instruction — is premised on a set of beliefs about children and schooling. If teachers hold a warrant (a set of beliefs) that suggest to them that recreation is important, then recreation is the kind of activity that we are likely to see in their gymnasiums. If they hold a strong commitment to fitness, then we are likely to see that warrant realized in the tasks they require of students. If they believe that sport is central to physical education, then we will be likely to see an emphasis on sporting activities in their physical education programme. In these ways, beliefs will attenuate all other thinking, planning, and decision making that attends a teacher's work.

Beliefs condition teachers' perceptions. If teachers hold a strong custodial orientation to the work of teaching, and the role of children, then their perceptions are inclined to be parochial with regard to children's behaviour and management decisions. They might have, for example, limited tolerance for accepting differences in students' behaviour, abilities, or personalities. Because of their beliefs, teachers will see certain situations in classrooms as important or unimportant. For example, a set of beliefs about adhering to strict behaviour standards, which might emerge from a custodial perspective, might precondition a teacher to be very aware of a child chewing gum in class. A teacher's set of beliefs, or sense of purpose, will also dictate how they allocate attention during class. As Doyle (1986) has pointed out, the act of teacher thinking involves selectively focused attention. The issues that receive teachers' attention are those deemed important. Importance is based wholly in belief.

Many studies have been done showing that teachers rarely comply with standardized curriculums or other prescriptive suggestions for their work (Hollingsworth, 1989; McDiarmid, 1990). Rather, curriculums are interpreted through the matrix of a teacher's beliefs about schooling. In describing teachers' adoption of a new mathematics curriculum, Morine-Dershimer and Corrigan (1997) point out that 'teachers had adapted the new concepts and procedures to conform to their own belief systems and techniques of practice, drastically transforming the mandated curriculum in the process (p. 298).' Studies we have done looking at teachers' beliefs about curriculum in physical education, suggest that beginning teachers seem to be focused on physical education as a way of teaching children about acceptable standards for their behaviour (Boggess, 1985; Griffey and Housner, 1983). We found very few instances among early teachers where any curricular intent about sport, fitness, dance, play, or movement development emerged in their beliefs. Rather, they told us their job was to enforce rules and gain compliance from students to a set of behavioural standards.

It is only when we studied teachers who had ten or more years of experience that teachers started to tell us that they had a sense of purpose about goals that had to do with physical education outcomes, such as sport, fitness, or play. Further, beliefs about children elaborate with time and experience in the classroom. Berliner (1987) showed that the kinds of things that beginning teachers see in the classroom tend to be literal and superficial. Such superficial understanding of classroom phenomena are formed by their own personal experience, or apprenticeship (Lortie, 1975) as students, in classrooms. Teachers with extensive experience working with children in classrooms, on the other hand, have deep and propositional knowledge about events that occur during instruction. So beliefs can become elaborated.

There are recent studies that show it is possible to affect the beliefs that teachers have, and consequently affect their actions in classrooms. Changing beliefs occurs gradually over a long period of time. Asking teachers to directly consider images and metaphors about teaching has been show to be a productive approach to belief change. Another way to promote change in beliefs is to directly confront preconceptions when those notions are contradicted in actual teaching practice. In other words, highlight and emphasize situations where prior beliefs do not serve intended outcomes. Finally, beliefs can be revealed and changed in the light of case studies. Asking teachers to wrestle with critical cases has resulted in the elaboration and change of belief systems. For an excellent discussion of teacher beliefs and their impact on practice, the interested reader is referred to Morine-Dershimer and Corrigan (1997).

Planning for Instruction

The things that teachers value result in them choosing activities for students they feel are important or worthwhile. Their planning involves selecting units for instruction, the duration of activities, and the specific structure of a day's lesson. Differences in approaches to planning are associated with teachers' years of experience. Once again, as with beliefs, the pattern of thinking and decision making appears to be related to expertise. In the realm of planning for instruction, we found teachers at all levels of development able to generate numerous activities in preparing for lessons. Experienced teachers seem no better able to generate activities for students in physical education classes than are beginning teachers. However, when we look at the pattern of planning, we find the approach to planning quite different for experienced teachers than for beginners. When beginners are asked to plan, they enumerate a series of activities in linear fashion. They schedule the list of activities with respect to sequence and duration. They do not consider student ability or student preference, or managerial issues that may arise during a lesson. That is, they plan in a linear way to use activities regardless of student responses during the lesson. Experienced teachers, on the other hand, plan by considering the kinds of things that might happen during instruction. Their plans form a branching set of activities that are linked to contingencies — anticipated student reactions, student success, managerial issues. Each point in their plan represents a decision where the teacher will assess how well students are performing on the task. From that point, alternate activities are selected based on the information that has been gathered. The activities chosen by master teachers are not ends in themselves, as in the beginning teacher's lesson. Rather, activities in the expert's plan are intended as opportunities for assessment. That assessment forms the basis for deciding when to move along, backtrack, or abandon an activity entirely. Experienced teachers report they use activities as means for gathering information about student performance and preference.

In addition to having an understanding of contingencies that might occur during instruction, master teachers are also sensitive to environmental factors that can influence lesson success. We have found that teachers with many years of experience are anxious to know, in detail, about the environment where they will be teaching. They require information about the kinds of equipment available to them, as well as the demographic characteristics of students — their ages, prior experience, and ability levels. Teachers with experience require a great deal of information about the setting and about the task before they are willing, or even able to plan for instruction. Novices ask relatively fewer questions about the instructional setting before producing a sequence of activities that they will expect students to participate in during class.

All of this points to a dilemma, or paradox, in the matter of planning among beginning teachers. How is it that we can expect beginners (novices or teachers-in-training) to plan for situations that they are not familiar with? They have limited knowledge of the context of classrooms from the perspective of teacher — because it is something that they have not yet experienced. In other words, if the task of planning entails sequencing activities contingent on the responses of students, the beginner has no such contingent-rich knowledge. It is particularly difficult, if not impossible, for the beginner to develop mature plans for instruction. When pressed to plan for instruction, novice teachers prepare sequences of activities that are unrelated to the needs or potential responses of students. Their plans are thus superficial — focused solely on content. And, when those plans are implemented in the instructional environment, teaching takes the form of imparting information, rather than working with individual students, nurturing their success. It is probably this deficit in planning that results in beginning teachers' focusing on student compliance, conformity, and the overwhelming tendency to impart discursive and factual information to students. Since beginners cannot plan for contingencies they do not know about, they naturally rely on didactic instruction. Further, their approach to students is typically custodial; demanding that students conform to the plan that they have prepared rather than altering the plan to accommodate students.

Perceiving the Instructional Environment

All decisions teachers make, and all of the actions that they take while working with children in classrooms are, presumably, based on the information that they gather while teaching. Their perceptions of the instructional environment presage the actions that they take in teaching. In using a mediational-process description for classroom management as a way of thinking about the work of teaching, Walter Doyle (1986) pointed out that the cognitive demands of teaching are extreme. Teachers have to focus on many students — each of whom has their own intentions, their own volition, their own abilities, talents, and interests. Add to the demands of monitoring large numbers of students the complexity of the school curriculum and the uncertainty of events during the school day. The environment is a complicated one, indeed. In time, teachers learn to selectively attend to issues in the classroom that are salient, or potentially important to maintaining the instructional environment and helping children learn. It is practically impossible to attend to all the various things that transpire during instruction. And, it is certainly impossible to attend to more than one issue at a time. One of the salient characteristics of experienced teachers is the economy in the way they attend to instructional events. They are not prone to respond to every individual, or every request that students might make. Rather, they have learned over time that certain events occuring during instruction are important to attend to, and that others are less significant. In this way a refinement occurs in the allocation of limited attention to the very complex environment of classrooms.

The beginning teacher, on the other hand, lacks a seasoned understanding of the instructional environment. Such a deficit results in allocating attention to many issues that are insignificant to the success of the lesson. One can readily observe beginning teachers being taken off track by student requests and other unimportant events. Beginners have not yet learned what contingencies to attend to and what ones to ignore. Not surprisingly, beginners also report extreme exhaustion at the end of a day of such intense work.

We have carried out studies of teachers' allocation of attention during instruction in Physical Education classes (Housner and Griffey, 1985). Those studies have revealed that experienced teachers attend to a different constellation of issues than beginning teachers do. And, we have found that certain student characteristics are the key to teacher monitoring individual children. Further, more experienced teachers seem to be able to attend to students as individuals. Beginning teachers, on the other hand, tend to focus on classes as a whole, being relatively unaware of the individual students that comprise the class.

Using stimulated recall as a way of accessing teachers' attention, we have learned that there is a range of student behaviour cues and context cues that are salient to teachers. The categories of teacher attention that have been observed included:

1 student performance in cognitive and psychomotor tasks;
2 student involvement in the task at hand;
3 student interest and enjoyment in a particular activity;
4 the kinds of verbal requests and statements that students make to the teacher;
5 interactions between and among students;
6 the moods and feeling that children express.

With respect to the instructional environment, we accessed:

1 teachers' awareness of their own moods and feelings during instructional episodes;
2 the amount of time available/remaining during a lesson;
3 the condition of the facility and equipment that is available;
4 awareness that the teacher has of how their own actions might be affecting students.

Experienced teachers are markedly more concerned about attending to student performance and the student's involvement/engagement with prescribed activities than are inexperienced teachers. Conversely, inexperienced teachers focus most on cues related to student interest in activities. Beginning teachers are also quite sensitive to student requests for changes in activities or class procedures — being subject to such requests virtually all the time. The pattern emerging from this work suggests that experienced teachers are attending to students' progress in a course while inexperienced teachers are more focused on cues related to student affect.

In another study of teachers' perceptions and how those perceptions influence managerial decision making, we focused on student temperament as it might mediate teacher decision making (Boggess, Griffey and Housner, 1986). Teachers were asked to rate each student in third and fourth grade physical education classes on a number of factors including: how well the student worked up to their potential, the student's overall ability in physical education activities, the student's interest and motivation in physical education, and the social and behavioural skills of the student. Teachers were then asked to describe how well each student would perform in different physical education settings including: working independently at learning stations, moving from one activity to another, waiting for a turn to perform an activity, working cooperatively at problem solving and group activities, and capacity for working well in a competitive sport environment.

We found that teachers' perceptions about students could be summed up with three factors:

1 The child's reactivity — could the child sit quietly without supervision; how easily were they distracted; would they stay on task for long periods of time; and how easily the child might be distracted by other children in the room.
2 The child's adaptability — how long it takes the student to become comfortable in new situations, whether the student is comfortable working with other children, and whether or not the child enjoys working in collaborative environments.
3 The third factor that teachers focused on was children's physical sensitivity: their sensitivity to temperature, light, sound, or pain.

When these factors of temperament were related to various kinds of activity in the gymnasium a consistent pattern of attention by teachers was revealed for all, typical physical education environments. In station activity, during transitions, while waiting for a turn, working cooperatively, and when participating in competitive sports, the student characteristics that were most salient to teachers were the child's motor ability, the child's reactivity/task orientation, and their realization of potential. Only in competitive environments was the pattern of teacher attention slightly different, with teachers allocating some attention to the students' adaptability. Teachers allocate attention most to students of high ability, those that are unusually reactive and frequently off-task, and those who are achieving below their potential.

We have also studied the relationship of teachers' perceptions of classroom events and subsequent decisions to implement changes in a lesson. We found experienced teachers more apt to adjust lesson flow when they perceived certain cues in the environment. In particular, experienced teachers were likely to make adjustments to a lesson as the result of their perceptions that a student's performance or involvement were unacceptable. And, experienced teachers were found to be sensitive to students' moods and feelings and the quality of interactions that students were having with one another. They frequently altered lesson structure because of such perceptions. Experienced teachers tended to be sensitive to individual student performance, resulting in lesson adjustments like working with individual students or altering tasks. To the contrary, inexperienced teachers tended to have perceptions about the entire class, with their decisions to intervene resulting in changes at the class level. That is, their perception of classroom cues results in changes to the lesson structure for the entire class. It is important to note, that while we saw substantial links between teachers' perceptions and their decisions to change instructional activities, this sequence only happened about one third of the time. Usually, when teachers reported perceptions about classroom events, they subsequently took no action to change the instructional environment, lesson, or task at hand. So, teachers are cognitively aware of what they see, they are thinking about it, but often their decision is to leave the instructional episode unchanged.

When experienced teachers did decide to make changes in a lesson, their inclination was to shorten an activity, or drop it all together. They also frequently restructured activities so that children might be more successful. On the other hand, inexperienced teachers acted on their perceptions by prolonging activities or moving on to another activity without resolving the problem that they had perceived. When teachers perceived a need for making a managerial or disciplinary decisions, experienced teachers tended to restate their expectations for students, adjust the amount of praise or criticism that they give to students, find a new way to model appropriate behaviour or performance, ask students to demonstrate correct performance, ask more questions, and to give higher levels of individual attention. Beginning teachers were almost never observed using these kinds of behaviours to address the perceptions they were having about a lesson.

Novice teachers seem to be perceiving a different set of cues than the experienced teacher. They are focused on whole-groups of students, they are particularly sensitive to the comments that students make, and they have a keen awareness of students' affect. When noting these matters, beginning teachers have few strategies at hand for mediating the problems and situations that they perceive. Novices do not seem to possess the broad palette of pedagogical actions that the expert might use for altering student success or engagement rates in their classes.

David C. Griffey and Lynn Dale Housner

These issues imply an important objective for teacher education programmes: focusing beginning teachers on student performance and engagement, while encouraging beginners to ignore student affect. Beginners must also be prepared to implement specific remedial strategies like: giving more individual attention, asking more questions, using students to demonstrate, giving more praise, using modelling as an adjunct to their teaching. In general terms, what the beginner must learn to do is alter an activity in order to enhance student success, rather than discarding activities, moving on to subsequent preplanned tasks.

Pedagogical Knowledge

Studies of teacher concerns, beliefs, instructional interventions, and students' perceptions of teacher talk during instruction have led us to an understanding of how teachers might be helpful to students who are having difficulty in physical education activity (Boggess, 1985; Fahleson, 1985; Griffey, Housner and Williams, 1986; McBride, Griffey and Boggess, 1986). Understanding teachers' decision making during instruction is premised on some conception of a teacher's function. In our work, the working definition of instruction has been: those teacher behaviours that help individual students who are trying to master a concept or skill. Simply put, we have been trying to understand how teachers assist students who need help. The traditional and behavioural approach to this issue has been to relate rates and categories of teacher feedback to student achievement. While important and productive results have come from that work, a fuller understanding of helping students can be achieved by accessing teachers' thoughts about providing assistance to students. What we have been after is understanding how teachers conceptualize, perceive, and remediate student difficulties. We want to know what kinds of talents teachers employ to assist students who are experiencing difficulty acquiring skill and knowledge. How do teachers think about pedagogical interventions? How do they interact with students when trying to help them?

We have discovered that teachers have a reservoir of knowledge that they employ when helping students. These resources, however, do not seem to be present in beginning teachers. Only after years of experience do these abilities begin to surface. With less than a decade of experience, teachers seem to be more focused on issues other than helping students master material. As Francis Fuller (1969) postulated, beginning teachers are predominantly concerned with the impressions that they are leaving with their students, colleagues, and supervisors. Early career teachers are concerned that they appear competent to others. These early concerns with the perceptions of others give way to a concern about the demands of the management of the instructional environment and the complex environment of the schools. Mid-development concerns are focused on keeping records, developing assignments, reporting grades, managing classrooms, and other logistical issues and demands. It is not until a relatively mature stage of teaching that teachers become concerned about the effect their work is having on children's learning and development.

We conducted a series of studies on teachers' concerns (McBride, Griffey and Boggess, 1986) and found that Fuller's conception of a developmental hierarchy of concerns was substantiated among physical education teachers. Early career physical education teachers are focused on how others are perceiving them. In time, physical education teachers report that their most important concerns are those of the demands of the job — the routine logistical tasks that are necessary for supporting instruction in schools. It is not until teachers have a substantial amount of experience that they begin to report strong levels of concern about student achievement and performance in physical education.

Taking another approach to studying teachers thinking about the instruction, we employed Construct Grid Analysis as a way of accessing the curricular beliefs and intentions of teachers. We found that early career teachers are focused on gaining student cooperation. Often early career/beginning teachers would report to us that their main purpose in class was getting students to understand standards of comportment and gaining their adherence to these standards. Only when teachers had achieved a substantial amount of experience (10–15 years) did they begin to report intentions for developing students' fitness, motor ability, sportsmanship, and other substantial, physical education objectives. It became clear that understanding how teachers think about helping students would require focusing our studies on mature, seasoned teachers.

Subsequently we studied national level and Olympic coaches (Griffey, Housner and Williams, 1986). We followed them throughout a sport season, recording the kinds of things that they said to their students/athletes both during practice and contest situations. We were surprised to find these coaches made use of language in very specific ways. These expert teachers relied on non-literal uses of language. They employed metaphor, simile, and other indirect forms of language when helping athletes improve at a skill. Some coaches relied on non-literal language exclusively in working with athletes. The question then became, 'why do coaches use language in this way when communicating with performers?' What might this mean for understanding effective teaching? Studying these non-literal uses of language carefully, we found that experienced teachers/coaches focus student attention on either visual cues or kinesthetic sensations that are related to successful performance. The power of their language choice resided in its usefulness in conjuring vivid visual and physical sensations in the minds of students. We observed little use of kinematic explanations among expert teachers and coaches. (Kinematic explanations are that type of teacher utterance that tells students how they are supposed to look while performing a task.) Numerous studies of the effect of kinematic information on performance have assured us that this type of information is all but useless to the student who is having difficulty. Expert teachers rarely used such kinematic information. Rather, they would tell students about how to perceive the environment or what specific physical (kinesthetic) sensations they ought to rely on while practising.

Following on from these results, an intervention was designed. We employed an experienced, elementary physical education teacher, providing her with specific verbal interventions. She was constrained to particular verbal interactions when working with children. These verbal cues were designed to focus student attention on visual and kinesthetic information while learning a novel, scoop-ball task. Classes were intact, third, fifth, and seventh grade students. The teacher was constrained to using the scripted lessons and cues. Following lessons, we carefully interviewed each child in those classes, asking them to tell us if they had listened to what the teacher was saying, if they had thought about the cues the teacher related, and whether or not they had found those comments useful for helping their perform-ance. An interesting interaction was revealed. Younger children, and those with lower ability, reported that cues about kinesthetic sensation were the most helpful to them. Their reports of such an interaction were supported by actual performance scores on post-tests that measured the students' skill at the tasks (Fahleson, 1985).

On the other hand, we noted that high ability and older students tended to benefit most from teacher utterances and cues that focused those students on visual information in the movement environment. High ability and older students improved most when they concentrated on visual perception. There are particu-lar ways of verbally interacting with students that can help them to improve performance.

In summary, we have found that experienced teachers are concerned about the curricular outcomes of physical education. Expert teachers use specific kinds of pedagogical interventions as they help students learn. Further, the kinds of inter-ventions that teachers use vary in their effectiveness depending on the aptitudes of students. This provides a good beginning to understanding how teachers think about, and make decisions about, helping students in physical education. Such pedagogical content knowledge will certainly be at the heart of future studies of effective teaching and teacher thinking in physical education.

Evaluation

Recent inquiry has revealed that the ways teachers think about successful teaching may differ dramatically from the ways that researchers studying teaching and teacher thinking have conceptualized effectiveness (Kagan, 1993). While *our* notion of teaching has caused us to focus on teachers helping students achieve in the realm of physical education, teachers may have very different ideas about effectiveness. Kagan points out that teachers hold core beliefs about their work that characterize teaching as an idiosyncratic form of self-expression. This is in opposition to the empirically derived view that action in teaching is a science based on theory and research (pp. 128–9).

Further, teachers judge themselves to be successful when they are able to achieve rapport with students, rather than upon successfully employing specific pedagogical techniques. Teachers are pleased when they are able to communicate affection, respect, and dedication to students. Teachers feel successful when they help students prepare psychologically and socially for life. Teachers see small, personal interactions with students as the key to achieving such ends.

Finally, Kagan tells us that teachers are comfortable when maintaining a status quo with respect to governance of schools and society. This certainly is at variance with teacher preparation programmes that regularly advocate critical perspectives and reflective practice. Surprisingly, teachers feel that the work of teaching cannot be taught directly. Rather, mastery accrues in time, with the experience of working with children.

Conclusion

Perhaps the greatest value of studying teacher thinking and decision making is to the teacher educator. We have learned that there are differences in the thinking processes of beginners compared to experienced teachers at all points in the instructional process. Many of these differences seem related to actual, practical experience, or 'time on the water' as a seasoned sailor once remarked.

Facing these findings always call up the question, 'what is reasonable to do and expect in a three-month-long student teaching experience, or four year teacher education programme, or the first year of teaching . . . ?' The answer, to us, seems to be, 'not as much as we once thought possible'. Learning to teach takes a long time. Perceiving the complex environment of classrooms accurately and efficiently takes many years. Developing routines that are responsive to the contingencies that occur when working with students takes a long, long time. Routinizing the work of teaching so that durable and important curricular goals can be addressed takes a decade, or more, for most teachers!

The study of teacher thinking and decision making in physical education has more about long-range goals for our teacher education programme and less about short-range and technical issues. We have grown in patience, since much of what we hope to achieve in educating teachers takes a long time to accomplish. And, we have had to become more tolerant as we have learned that the work of teaching, in itself, precipitates beliefs that are quite different from those espoused by our teacher education programmes.

The study of teacher thinking, decision making, and belief has helped us begin to understand the cognitive aspects of teaching. Such understanding has grounded prior, behavioural research by explaining what goes on behind the actions that teachers take.

Continued study of teacher cognition will surely be a productive and interesting pursuit. We have discussed elsewhere the kinds of tools necessary for such inquiry (Griffey and Housner, 1996). Knowing what teachers value, how they perceive the classroom, how they make instructional decisions, and how they assess the work of teaching will allow us to be more effective and realistic in improving instruction in the gymnasium.

References

BERLINER, D.C. (1987) 'Ways of thinking about students and classrooms by more and less experienced teachers', in CALDERHEAD, J. (ed.) *Exploring Teachers Thinking*, London: Cassell, pp. 60–83.

BOGGESS, T.A. (1985) 'A study of the implicit beliefs about curriculum and instruction of physical education teachers with varying years of experience', Unpublished Doctoral Dissertation, University of Texas, *Dissertation Abstracts International*, pp. 47-02A, 0462.

BOGGESS, T.E., GRIFFEY, D.C. and HOUSNER, L.D. (1986) 'The influence of teachers' perceptions of student temperament on managerial decision-making', *Journal of Teaching in Physical Education*, **5**, pp. 140–8.

DOYLE, W. (1986) 'Classroom organization and management', in WITTROCK, M.C. (ed.) *Handbook of Research on Teaching* (3rd ed.), New York: Macmillan, pp. 392–431.

FAHLESON, G.A. (1985) 'Imagery orientation effects associated with students' cognitions during instruction of a novel Jai Alai-like skill', Unpublished Doctoral Dissertation, University of Wyoming, *Dissertation Abstracts International*, pp. 47-01A, 0118.

FULLER, F.F. (1969) 'Concerns of teachers: A developmental conceptualization', *American Educational Research Journal*, **6**, pp. 207–26.

GRIFFEY, D.C. and HOUSNER, L.D. (1983) 'Beliefs and values of physical education teachers: An exploration of implicit theories', *Proceedings of the Third Curriculum Conference of NASPE*: The University of Georgia, Athens.

GRIFFEY, D.C. and HOUSNER, L.D. (1991) 'Differences between experienced and inexperienced teachers' planning decisions, interactions, student engagement, and instructional climate', *Research Quarterly for Exercise and Sport*, **62**, pp. 196–204.

GRIFFEY, D.C. and HOUSNER, L.D. (1996) 'The study of teacher cognition in sport pedagogy', in SCHEMPP, P.G. (ed.) *Scientific Development of Sport Pedagogy, German and American Sport Studies*, New York: Waxmann, pp. 103–22.

GRIFFEY, D.C., HOUSNER, L.D. and WILLIAMS, D. (1986) 'Coaches use of non-literal language: Metaphor as a means of effective teaching', in PIERON, M. and GRAHAM, G. (eds) *Sport Pedagogy: Proceedings of the 1984 Olympic Scientific Symposium*: Human Kinetics Press, pp. 131–7.

HOLLINGSWORTH, S. (1989) 'Prior beliefs and cognitive change in learning to teach', *American Educational Research Journal*, **26**, 2, pp. 160–89.

HOUSNER, L.D. and GRIFFEY, D.C. (1985) 'Teacher cognition: Differences in planning and interactive decision making between experienced and inexperienced teachers', *Research Quarterly for Exercise and Sport*, **56**, pp. 45–53.

KAGAN, D.M. (1993) *Laura and Jim and What They Taught Me about the Gap Between Educational Theory and Practice*, Albany, NY: SUNY Press.

LORTIE, D. (1975) *Schoolteacher: A Sociological Study*, Chicago: University of Chicago Press.

McBRIDE, R., GRIFFEY, D.C. and BOGGESS, T.E. (1986) 'Concerns of inservice physical education teachers as compared to Fuller's concern model', *Journal of Teaching in Physical Education*, **5**, 3, pp. 149–56.

McDIARMID, G.W. (1990) 'Challenging prospective teachers' beliefs during early field experience: A quixotic undertaking?', *Journal of Teacher Education*, **41**, 3, pp. 12–20.

MORINE-DERSHIMER, G. and CORRIGAN, S. (1997) 'Teacher beliefs', in WALBERG, H.J. and HAERTEL, G.D. (eds) *Psychology and Educational Practice*, Berkeley, CA: McCutcheon, pp. 297–319.

NATIONAL INSTITUTE OF EDUCATION (1975) *Teaching As Clinical Information Processing* (Report of Panel 6, National Conference on Studies in Teaching), Washington, DC: National Institute of Education.

Part 5

The Future of Research in Physical Education

12 Silver Bullets, Golden Visions, and Possible Dreams: A Wish List for the Future of Research in Physical Education

Patt Dodds

Introduction

This chapter suggests that sport pedagogy researchers, that is, those interested in teaching and learning in physical education, constitute a loosely structured social organization called a research learning community. Researchers in a learning community are bound together by social customs through sharing their conceptions of the research enterprise, ethics and principles governing appropriate behavior (e.g. toward their participants), ways of conducting their business (e.g. within paradigms, researchers share methodologies), and their results. This chapter presents an adaptation of Rosenholtz's (1991) work on schools as social organizations, drawing out three important values that differentiate learning-enriched from learning-impoverished organizations. For researchers, these values can facilitate progress toward greater sophistication and more powerful payoffs in understanding the practices of teaching and the conditions for learning. Much future research on learning and teaching in physical education can be built profitably on the research reviewed earlier in this book. This chapter offers analysis of how our research community might work better to insure such profits.

Historical and Present Context

Over a quarter century has passed since the serious emergence of sport pedagogy scholarship on teaching and learning in physical education. In the early 1970s, doctoral programs in the US began specializing in the study of teaching (and the close corollary of teacher education), and sport pedagogy researchers produced enough work to be recognized as a legitimate field of inquiry within physical education (Nixon and Locke, 1973). Now the sport pedagogy research community has reached early maturity and must now set its future directions to enhance its present contributions to teaching and learning.

Many reasons exist for celebrating current accomplishments. At least three research paradigms are strong and lively: not only do positivists, interpretive, and critical pedagogy researchers contribute to our body of research-based knowledge, but they engage each other in lively debates about research as well (O'Sullivan, Siedentop and Locke, 1992). Several national and international conferences provide venues for presentation of research. The American Alliance of Health, Physical Education, Recreation and Dance (AAHPERD) annual meeting now produces annually an entire issue Supplement to the *Research Quarterly for Exercise and Sport* (*RQES*) to accommodate abstracts of the research presented, and sport pedagogy typically has the longest sections in that issue. The Association Internationale des Ecoles Supérieures d'Education Physique (AIESEP) generally sponsors more than one annual meeting for research presentations, and publishes research abstracts from its annual World Sport Science Congress.

Sport pedagogy scholars have won two of the *RQES* Research Writing Awards, Pat Griffin the very first with her portrayal of middle school teachers wrestling with sex equity problems in the gymnasium (Griffin, 1985), and Kate Barrett and Sarah Collie the 1997 award for their study of physical educators developing pedagogical content knowledge through observing their own students learning lacrosse (Barrett and Collie, 1996). The first sport pedagogy researcher to give the McCloy Lecture at AAHPERD, Daryl Siedentop (1998), centered his address on what has been learned from students and teachers about effective teaching. From these examples in the US alone, it is clear that the research community focused on teaching and learning in physical education is healthy and robust. Now, how do we stay this way? What conditions will sustain our viability? And where might we go from here?

Values of Learning-enriched Social Organizations

A central obligation of a research community is to influence the practice with which it is associated. In our case, the products of sport pedagogy researchers should influence how physical education is learned and taught in schools. To frame the salient conditions under which the sport pedagogy research community might prosper, the work of Susan Rosenholtz, *Teachers; Workplace: The Social Organization of Schools* (1991) is useful. Rosenholtz's thesis is that some social organizations exhibit particular values that facilitate change. Her study of schools characterizes some as *learning-enriched* and others as *learning-impoverished*. The teaching staff at learning-enriched schools shared school-wide goals, collaborated well, created many opportunities for their own learning and professional development, had high individual and collective teaching efficacy (they *knew* they were making differences in kids' lives), and were strongly committed to their students and to the continual improvement of their own work. In contrast, learning-impoverished schools were characterized by teaching staffs whose dispositions were at the opposite ends of these value dimensions.

Three of these values are particularly relevant to the changes required of our sport pedagogy research community at this point in the development of our loosely structured social organization in order to better influence improvement in the learning and teaching of physical education:

1   Creating sufficient meaningful and challenging individual and collective learning opportunities to improve research practice;
2   Supporting a sustained, long-term view of learning about and how to do research;
3   Sharing *practice*-oriented goals based on divergent yet complementary conceptions of research.

Creating Learning Opportunities to Improve Research Practice

Rosenholtz (1991) maintains that in learning-enriched schools teachers have multiple, diverse opportunities, both individually and collectively, to develop their teaching skills. Regular access to such opportunities, along with expectations that these are used wisely, differentiate learning-enriched schools from learning-impoverished ones.

Our research community, in order to remain healthy and productive, deserves equal opportunities to engage in the study of our work, individually and together. This activity represents metacognitive processing of how well we do research, allowing for refinement of research strategies, formulation of more elegant research questions, and better articulation of results with those of other researchers. Already, important practices have been systematized among sport pedagogy researchers for this kind of ongoing learning about and learning to do research.

More program spaces and spontaneous opportunities are available for formal and informal exchange of research ideas at the periodic meetings of professional organizations such as AERA, the Canadian Association of Health, Physical Education, Recreation, and Dance, or AIESEP. Formal presentations now take more interactive alternate forms such as poster sessions, round tables, or panel discussions to promote interchange of ideas and more detailed discussions of research. *RQES* and the *Journal of Teaching in Physical Education* (*JTPE*) sometimes include tutorial features to improve reflections on research practice, to refresh the memories of experienced researchers, and to instruct neophytes.

Technological enhancements to communications (email, faxes, Internet websites, list-servs, distribution lists) offer faster means of moving research projects along and better ways to communicate and collaborate across distance. Many researchers now realize the value of including graduate students in joint research projects with faculty as a way to socialize them into research productivity. A much-needed recent development to strengthen communication has been 'research-in-progress' conferences in the US (Paul Schempp at the University of Georgia initiated these). Their key feature is the chance, through detailed conversations with colleagues, to consider alternative designs and to refine methods before studies unfold completely. More regularized conferences with this focus could prevent many researchers from receiving rejection reviews in a project after it already has been completed. Because many sport pedagogy researchers are 'singles' in university departments with scholars in other subdisciplines of physical education, it is even more critical to create frequent, regular occasions to communicate, to 'talk the talk' of scholarship, in order to become a more mature, learning-enriched research community.

Taking a Life-long View of Learning Research

A second feature Rosenholtz (1991) found in schools that support change is a long-term, sustained view of learning. Equally, our research community should understand that research skills and capabilities are learned over a lifetime of practice. Learning to do good research is parallel in several ways to learning to teach well — it takes time, and reflection, and feedback, and practice.

Doctoral programs do not turn out expert researchers fully formed, nor capable of contributing their best work to the research community early in their career. Just as newly graduated induction period teachers are not yet polished, proficient professionals, neither are newly-hooded EdDs or PhDs finished with learning about research; they've only just begun.

Although systematic study of the socialization and career development of sport pedagogy researchers is warranted, no one to my knowledge has taken on this task. It is probable that researchers' career trajectories mirror those now well-documented in the literature about the lives and careers of teachers (Templin and Schempp, 1989). It is clear from most of that research that teachers need support, facilitation of learning, and nurturance over their entire careers (Galvez-Hjornevik; Little, 1990). If that is the case, sport pedagogy scholars will require the same support, which could be provided through inservice for ourselves. At the very least, this might translate to the following strategies:

1   Mentoring researchers carefully through their first few years
This can be done at the same institution by peers (who themselves may or may not be sport pedagogy specialists), or long distance by colleagues at other institutions. Such mentoring may include more colleagues than the major dissertation advisor in a mentoring mosaic (Galvez-Hjornevik, 1986; Little, 1990). Several scholars have made the point that our closest sport pedagogy colleagues are often those in other colleges and universities rather than the faculty down the hall with different specializations. With technology and a reasonably strong network of professional meetings on our yearly calendar, this strategy is already in place.

Mentoring should begin in graduate school but all is not lost if it does not happen there. Mentoring might take such forms as incorporating clear expectations and support for pre-dissertation writing for publication to build confidence in one's writing under guidance from more experienced (and even peer) scholars; or, instead of the traditional lengthy chaptered document as dissertation, writing a competent, stand-alone literature review and two journal articles prepared for submission for publication; or even explicit contracts for single-authored or joint publications with major advisors before or after graduation from doctoral study.

2   Supporting researchers who, like teachers, take different career trajectories
Researchers should recognize signs of stagnation or burnout in their mid-career (or other career stage) colleagues, helping them redirect their careers away from research or revitalize their enthusiasm and commitment to research (see Huberman, 1993).

3   Holding each other accountable with clear expectations of continued learn-
    ing and development in our researcher roles

Although this comes partially through peer review for publication, complementary
professional development opportunities (e.g. half- or full-day workshops prior to
AERA) such as workshops and peer tutorials are necessary as well. These may be
especially beneficial to early- and mid-career scholars.

Making such strategies a regular part of their commitment to scholarship, researchers can do much to support each other through particularly vulnerable times
in their careers.

Sharing Practice-oriented Goals

The phrase '*practice*-oriented goals' which recurs throughout Rosenholtz's analysis
of schools as social organizations, is particularly important to researchers because it
foregrounds the most immediate, most significant, and most difficult problem facing
our research community today: that our research has *not* yet influenced the majority of school physical education practice to any satisfying extent, except perhaps
in the immediate vicinity of particular researchers and doctoral programs. One of
the reasons frequently given for not influencing teaching practice to the extent
researchers envision is that our research questions do not provide answers to the
same questions that teachers have about teaching and learning (Lawson, 1990;
Martinek and Hellison, 1997). To this end, Tanner (1998) warns researchers that
they must '. . . help solve practical problems of social significance' (p. 348). He
goes on to say,

> The capacity to build and draw from the knowledge base requires that our theory
> be tested continually for its power for generalizability and practicability in a wide
> range of situations. In social research, theory must have the generative power for
> revealing useful pathways to solutions of social significance. (Tanner, 1998, p. 349)

Socially significant research questions can help us reach practice-oriented
goals. The first value of our learning-enriched research community, if we follow
Rosenholtz's (1991) work, is the degree to which we influence teaching practice.
To implement this value, a broadly shared, collective goal for setting research questions is needed: one broad enough to enlist the enthusiasms of the diversity of sport
pedagogy researchers, possible enough to reach to sustain commitment over time to
doing relevant research in the small steps of cumulative studies, and sufficiently
complex to engage our best collective intellectual efforts over the long haul.

We could share the following broad goal as a social contract among sport
pedagogy researchers:

> We agree to investigate socially significant problems such that small- and large-
> scale changes in school- and community-based physical education are made and
> lifetime activity habits in children, youth, adults, and families are intentionally
> cultivated and supported.

Without such a shared goal, we will continue to wildcat like the West Texas oil barons, with independent individual research agendas and little inclination (or reinforcement) to coordinate our research or collaborate with other researchers (and dare I also suggest, practitioners?) in powerful, exponentially cumulative ways.

This goal is not intended to become a collective national or international research agenda in any restrictive way, nor to be used as a litmus test of politically correct research. Nonetheless, keeping this broad goal in mind as we design and implement individual studies should afford us as a research community more opportunities to make significant and real differences in teachers' and students' lives in the gym (see Martinek and Hellison, 1997).

But don't we already hold this goal? Yes, but it's how researchers define social significance that's important. I have argued elsewhere (Dodds, 1998) that in order to achieve social significance researchers must begin to include many subordinate groups who are now absent presences (see Sparkes, Chapter 9) in our world as well as in research ventures: people with disabilities, those who live in poverty, and many others.

Imbedded in any social contract for a maturing sport pedagogy research community are two significant questions:

- Why, as scholars, are we so keen to influence teaching and learning practice, anyway?
- Whose interests are ultimately being served by our research and scholarship?

Whether and how we engage in finding workable answers to these questions will be perhaps the most important measure of our maturity as a research community. One way to frame the debates and discussions of these questions is to consider that the answers lie partly in our own histories as educators. Another is to name the research–practice gap as a problem. Yet a third is to reframe the questions in terms of power and resistance.

Our Histories

Examining our own histories as educators uncovers at least four motivations for doing research focused on teaching and learning in physical education. First, *we were there*. Almost all of us have been K-12 teachers, and then have left, drawn away to pursue other intellectual interests in physical education (mostly though graduate degrees and subsequently into different teaching positions in colleges or universities). Perhaps we feel guilty when school teachers ask us, 'How long did you teach?' (implying that we no longer do so) to gauge our credibility when interacting with them about research-based ideas.

Second, *we care about kids and teachers*. After all, our research agendas focus on questions about teaching and learning, we generate new ideas about how things work in gyms and on playing fields, we seek deeper understandings of the phenomena that make those learning environments tick, and we want to share what we learn with other teachers, particularly those in most direct contact with our own former students.

We also care about vigorous physical activity and play. This is the stuff we're intellectually curious about and in which we engage ourselves, along with kids, teachers, and those who teach teachers. Finally, *we want our work to be socially significant.* As educators, we want to see payoffs in people's learning through our work, we want to see some impact from our new ideas and deeper understandings of how physical education is conducted and how it might be improved even further.

Thus, researchers have many reasons to value influencing the course of physical education as carried out in the public schools most of us left in our past, as well as in the college and university (teacher education) programs we now operate. Jointly committing our research community to the shared goal of influencing practice, however, will not automatically provide the means for doing so, as will be seen when we move to the second frame for our lack of influence on practice, the research–practice gap.

The Research–practice Gap

Sometimes the lack of impact of research on teaching is framed as the 'research–practice gap'. Numerous sport pedagogy researchers over the years have analysed and lamented this gap in various ways (Lawson, 1990; Metzler, 1994). It frequently is framed as a problem in communication between researchers and practitioners, that is, researchers rarely make their work available to teachers in user-friendly ways. The reasons, therefore, that teachers pay little attention to research are legion:

1 Access to research is too difficult (teachers can't readily find it);
2 Researchers' language is too esoteric (teachers can't understand it easily if they can find it);
3 Researchers' questions are not teachers' questions (teachers need to do their own problem-setting and problem-solving, not rely on someone else's view);
4 Teachers are not partners in research (teachers frequently feel exploited, not valued by researchers);
5 Teachers think it's for researchers, not them (teachers feel left outside researchers' elite intellectual community);
6 Teachers may not think they have time for or value reflection on practice (the daily press of the multidimensional, simultaneous, typical frenzy of teaching leaves little time or inclination to think);
7 Teachers are far more likely to be *context*-driven than *concept*-driven, and researchers are just the opposite.

Given these reasons for teachers not being impressed by research, what ought researchers to do? New visions for addressing the research–practice gap are in order if the work of this research community will truly benefit that of practitioners, and vice versa. This reciprocal view of research and teaching practices influencing each other is critical. If the sport pedagogy research community operates as a social organization, sharing the goal of influencing practice, then long and serious conversations must occur — with teachers, exploring a 'research of the possible', relationships between research and practice. What should these be? What might these be? What kinds of relationships could we develop — and how — to be of mutual benefit to all parties? Questions like these have no easy answers, but are well worth asking. Raising such questions and being willing to engage in serious dialogue is another sign of a maturing research community.

Issues of Power and Resistance

A third alternative for framing the debates about why researchers are interested in teaching practice and whose interests are being served by research — not as one to which the answers lie in researchers' own histories, and not as a research–practice gap or communication problem — is to consider the issue one of power and resistance, or politics. Taking this view requires examining the power relationships among researchers and practitioners. Power relationships typically involve who influences whom, when, how, and under what circumstances, as well as the outcomes resulting from power in use.

As mindful and respectful as researchers usually try to be when working in schools, practitioners often perceive a power differential (they have less, researchers have more) that plays out in various forms of resistance, in itself a method of exerting power. Practitioners see researchers as the ones who left their more difficult school settings. Researchers don't teach multiple classes per day but a few seminars per week. Researchers don't deal with literally hundreds of students per week, but far fewer. Researchers can sit in their offices to plan classes and do other work, some practitioners don't even have offices. Researchers' salaries are higher, practitioners' income is generally lower and lock-stepped with small increments. Researchers escaped the dreary dailyness of school routines, but return for other purposes, while practitioners never got — or took — opportunities to change work contexts. And most practitioners are savvy enough to understand that what researchers learn in their gyms will eventually, somehow, in some way, be turned into advice about doing their jobs better — and at bottom, some practitioners simply may not wish to change at all what they do in constructing learning environments.

The perceived power differential affects researchers as much as practitioners. Researchers select carefully the teachers with whom they work: who is most likely to volunteer for the study? Ideally we choose teachers who are interested in how research might help them change their practice. If such practitioners are not accessible, researchers settle for those willing to tolerate their presence but clearly not interested in what those researchers find out, and certainly not in using it. And some schools and practitioners are never considered as sites or participants by researchers who surmise that they either won't let them in or are so awful that studying their work would not increase understanding of teaching and learning in physical education. To borrow from Siedentop (1998), each of these researcher options involves 'making treaties' with teachers.

Taking such a political view forces researchers to acknowledge differently why practitioners may not be eager to use research and provides opportunities to approach teachers more equitably. Discussing what might be positive outcomes for teachers, students, and researchers from a study is far different from swooping in and, even gently, coercing agreements to participate from teachers that they may not wish to make but may be too polite to refuse.

Those who take seriously the development of a social contract for the sport pedagogy research community will examine their own histories for appropriate intentions for doing research, will search for strategies to make results from their studies available in palatable forms to practitioners, and will continually examine the political dimensions of their own practice and work for equity with their participants.

Improving Research Practice: My Wish List

As important as are the values shared by a research community, equal attention should be given to improving how research is conducted to allow its full potential for creating useful and interesting outcomes. Sport pedagogy researchers might consider increasing our use of the following strategies for enriching our present contributions to teaching practice and the establishment of positive, productive learning environments for students in school-based physical education: replication, synchronization, and integration.

Replication

Most sport pedagogy research now consists of single studies, with researchers asking interesting questions that may change considerably from one investigation to their next. Some sport pedagogy researchers, however, have strong, clearly delineated research programs. Programmatic lines of research, that is, tightly connected, ever progressing series of studies focused on the same phenomenon in which research questions quite profitably lead from one investigation to the next and what is known about a topic is gradually expanded in systematic ways over time, represent a kind of systematic replication (Sidman, 1960). In the US for example, Catherine Ennis's work on value orientations and the effects of context on teachers' values and beliefs (e.g. Ennis, 1994, in press; Ennis and Chen, 1993), Peter Hastie's studies of the sport education model and classroom ecologies (e.g. Hastie, 1995, 1996), Rovegno's investigations of teachers' pedagogical content knowledge (e.g. Rovegno, 1993), Rink's research on teaching from a learning perspective (see Rink chapter this volume for review), or Silverman's explorations of student characteristics interacting with practice and achievement variables (e.g. Silverman, 1993).

Direct replication, in contrast, involves repeating the same study (methods) with different participants in order to discover whether unknown variables might function to prevent successful repetition of results (not to ascertain the reality of the initial findings). Arguably, we could learn much from deliberate replication across activities and across age groups. Rink (email) once lamented that we know a lot about how middle school students participate in volleyball but little about their performances in other movement activities.

Several advantages accrue in a replicative research program of action (see Doyle, 1986). First, scholars might pursue differentiated research responsibilities: some researchers might choose to follow the paths of others, spending their time replicating studies after someone else has demonstrated an initial set of interesting results rather than exploring brand new territory with original research questions. And our research community ought to honor 'good replicators' as well as 'good originators' (though this presently is not the case). While journal space is limited, short research notes based on replications could be quite enlightening.

Second, faster and deeper accumulation of knowledge about the activities and participant contexts of our research through successive replications will tell us far more precisely under which conditions particular learning and teaching phenomena work or don't work. Understanding systematically, for instance, how the same students learn successful tactics in lacrosse, soccer, or rugby, as well as netball tells us much more than simply assuming that they transfer tactical skills from one game context to another. A tactical approach to teaching games (Griffin, Mitchell, and Oslin, 1997) exemplifies this kind of replication. Other such careful, deliberate replications could do much to enrich and expand our present knowledge about factors that promote or inhibit physical education teaching/learning.

Synchronization

Our rapidly expanding accumulation of research-based knowledge often makes it difficult even to 'keep up' thoroughly with the publications of colleagues within a subdiscipline of physical education. The increasing pressures to publish exacerbate the knowledge explosion. Sport pedagogy researchers may not take time to read related literature from motor learning, motor development, or sport psychology, all of which might inform their own work. Synchronization of researchers' interests from different disciplinary perspectives within the same investigations could enhance our research community. For example, Rink, French, and others at the University of South Carolina have produced studies which clearly demonstrate strong, linked influences of sport psychology, motor development, motor learning, and sport pedagogy in the methods as well as findings (see Rink chapter this volume).

A second kind of synchronization obtains when studies within different paradigms are sequenced to add to the knowledge base on a topic or integrated within a single mixed methods study. For example, Ennis's work has segued from a positivist orientation in development and validation of a psychometric instrument for measuring teachers' value orientations (e.g. Ennis and Chen, 1993) to interpretive studies examining how teacher and student values and beliefs are influenced by school context (Ennis, in press). Advantages of sequencing different paradigmatic approaches to a topic (by the same or different researchers) center on generating different kinds of information about the topic of interest. A disadvantage is that individual researchers sometimes don't have the range of research skills necessary to conduct sound studies across paradigms or methodologies.

Integration

Our continually expanding research base demands deliberate integration of the bits and pieces of knowledge accumulated across time and by multiple researchers. Thus a market exists for excellent *research reviews*, that is, papers in which accumulated studies on the same topic are compared, contrasted, and organized so readers get a 'big picture' sense of what is presently known about that topic. Unfortunately, single research reports have space restrictions resulting in short or poorly articulated reviews of research. In contrast, the larger scope and different purpose of research reviews provide an excellent entry point to the study of a topic or major clarification of a topic by bringing together the work of different researchers and taking a reflective, and in many instances metacognitive (see Luke and Hardy's chapter) perspective on that body of work.

Conclusion

My plan in this chapter has been to raise issues about the values that will sustain our continuing maturation as a sport pedagogy research learning community. I believe we are presently doing well on each of Rosenholtz's (1991) qualities of learning-enriched social organizations — and we can do even better in the future if we reflect carefully and share clear visions of what research might be. One quality is creating appropriate learning opportunities for each researcher to grow as a scholar. Another is to make life-long commitments to learning about research. A third is to figure out how to better influence teaching and learning and then work hard to make that happen. All researchers must find their place in this loosely structured social organization based on individual dispositions and capabilities and on our collective responsibilities to influence the practice of physical education. Our research community has always endeavored to promote changes in schools and other learning environments. Whatever strategies we choose to maintain our community will require changes in ourselves and in how we relate to each other as scholars. Sarason (in Locke, 1995) reminds us how difficult change can be in his comment that new regularities we desire must replace old ones, and that we must understand the social contingencies that held the old ones in place before we are able to sustain the new. Or as Boyer noted (1996),

> We sit back and pretend that change is going to happen outside us. The truth is that it will happen within us. We are the transformers or our own academy, and if there is to be change, it will be in this group. . . . (p. 139)

Most researchers secretly harbor a desire to find a 'silver bullet', but in the gradual accumulation of research-based knowledge, rarely if ever are results from a single study or even a line of research so profound that large-scale, significant changes occur in the practice to which they apply. Nevertheless, regardless of practical outcomes, something drives researchers to pursue their quests to understand teaching and learning in physical education more deeply — to chase their silver bullets for interventions to improve practice, their golden visions of how such practice might look, and their possible dreams of a better world of physical education for both teachers and students. The extent to which the sport pedagogy research community is willing to change will determine how much we will contribute to physical education practice.

References

BARRETT, K. and COLLIE, S. (1996) 'Children learning lacrosse from teachers learning to teach it: The discovery of pedagogical content knowledge by observing children's movement', *Research Quarterly for Exercise and Sport*, **67**, 3, pp. 297–309.

BOYER, E. (1996) 'From scholarship reconsidered to scholarship assessed', *Quest*, **48**, 2, pp. 129–39.

DODDS, P. (1998) 'Dismal prospects for "new times" in US physical education', paper presented at the AIESEP World Science Congress, July, Garden City, New York.

DOYLE, W. (1986) 'Classroom organization and management', in WITTROCK, M. (ed.) *Handbook of Research on Teaching* (3rd ed.), pp. 392–431.

ENNIS, C. (1994) 'Urban secondary teachers' value orientations: Delineating curricular goals for social responsibility', *Journal of Teaching in Physical Education*, **13**, pp. 163–79.

ENNIS, C. (in press) 'The theoretical framework: The central piece in the research plan', *Journal of Teaching in Physical Education*.

ENNIS, C. and CHEN, A. (1993) 'Domain specifications and content representativeness of the revised Value Orientation Inventory', *Research Quarterly for Exercise and Sport*, **64**, pp. 436–46.

GALVEZ-HJORNEVIK, C. (1986) 'Mentoring among teachers: A review of the literature', *Journal of Teacher Education*, **37**, 1, pp. 6–11.

GRIFFIN, P. (1985) 'Teachers' perceptions of and responses to sex equity problems in a middle school physical education program', *Research Quarterly for Exercise and Sport*, **56**, 2, pp. 103–10.

GRIFFIN, L., MITCHELL, S. and OSLIN, J. (1997) *Teaching Sport Concepts and Skills: A Tactical Games Approach*, Champaign, IL: Human Kinetics.

HASTIE, P. (1995) 'An ecology of a secondary school outdoor adventure camp', *Journal of Teaching in Physical Education*, **15**, pp. 79–97.

HASTIE, P. (1996) 'Student role involvement during a unit of sport education', *Journal of Teaching in Physical Education*, **16**, pp. 88–103.

HUBERMAN, M. (1993) *The Lives of Teachers*, London: Falmer Press.

LAWSON, H.A. (1990) 'Sport pedagogy research: From information-gathering to useful knowledge', *Journal of Teaching in Physical Education*, **10**, pp. 1–20.

LITTLE, J. (1990) 'The mentor phenomenon and the social organization of teaching', *Review of Research in Education*, **16**, pp. 297–351.

LOCKE, L. (1995) 'An analysis of prospects for changing faculty roles and rewards: Can scholarship be reconsidered?', *Quest*, **47**, 4, pp. 506–24.

LUKE, I. and HARDY, C. (in press) 'Pupil learning and meta-cognition', in HARDY, C. and MAWER, M. (eds) *Learning and Teaching in Physical Education*, London: Falmer Press.

MARTINEK, T. and HELLISON, D. (1997) 'Service-bonded inquiry: The road less traveled', *Journal of Teaching in Physical Education*, **17**, 1, pp. 107–21.

METZLER, M. (1994) 'Scholarship reconsidered for the professoriate of 2010', *Quest*, **46**, 4, pp. 440–5.

NIXON, J. and LOCKE, L. (1973) 'Research on teaching physical education', in TRAVERS, R. (ed.) *Second Handbook of Research on Teaching*, pp. 1210–42, Chicago: Rand McNally and Co.

O'SULLIVAN, M., SIEDENTOP, D. and LOCKE, L. (1992) 'Toward collegiality: Competing viewpoints among teacher educators', *Quest*, **44**, 2, pp. 266–80.

RINK, J. (in press) 'Instruction from a learning perspective', in HARDY, C. and MAWER, M. (eds) *Learning and Teaching in Physical Education*, London: Falmer Press.

ROSENHOLTZ, S. (1991) *Teachers' Workplace: The Social Organization of Schools*, New York: Teachers College Press.

ROVEGNO, I. (1993) 'Content knowledge acquisition during undergraduate teacher education: Overcoming cultural templates and learning through practice', *American Educational Research Journal*, **30**, pp. 611–42.

SIDMAN, M. (1960) *Tactics of Scientific Research: Evaluating Experimental Data in Psychology*, New York: Basic Books Inc.

SIEDENTOP, D. (1998, April) *In Search of Effective Teaching: What We Have Learned from Teachers and Students*, McCloy Lecture presented at the AAHPERD Annual Meeting, Reno, NV.

SILVERMAN, S. (1993) 'Student characteristics, practice and achievement in physical education', *Journal of Educational Research*, **87**, pp. 54–61.

TANNER, D. (1998) 'The social consequences of bad research', *Phi Delta Kappan*, pp. 345–9.

TEMPLIN, T. and SCHEMPP, P. (1989) *Socialization into Physical Education: Learning to Teach*, Indianapolis: Benchmark Press.

Notes on Contributors

Stuart Biddle is Professor of Exercise and Sport Psychology in the Department of Physical Education, Sports Science and Recreation Management at Loughborough University. His research interests are in the area of sport and exercise psychology with particular reference to: motivational and social cognitive approaches, including attribution theory, attitudes, goals, and self-determination theory; motivational influences on health-related exercise; emotion and other psychological outcomes of exercise and sport. Stuart has delivered many Keynote papers at international conferences, edited and authored books, published numerous academic papers in his area of expertise and acted as editor for sport science journals.

Tania Cassidy lectures in the School of Physical Education at the University of Otago, Dunedin, New Zealand. Before this she studied for her PhD at Deakin University, Geelong, Australia. Tania has taught physical education in primary and secondary schools in New Zealand and England. Her research interests are in pedagogy, tertiary and school physical education and the physical education curriculum.

Brian Davies is Professor of Education at University of Wales, Cardiff. He was formerly Professor of Education at King's College London, and a lecturer in Sociology at the University of London Institute of Education and at Goldsmith's College, London. He has written widely on the sociology of education and is author of *Education and Social Control* (1986), editor of an issue of *Educational Analysis* which dealt with *The State and Schooling*, and co-editor with Paul Atkinson and Sara Delamont (1995) of *Discourse and Reproduction: Essays in Honour of Basil Bernstein.*

Patt Dodds is a Physical Education Teacher Education (PETE) Professor, University of Massachusetts. Her research publications are broadly within teacher socialization, more specifically about teacher recruits, pre-service teachers, and teacher educators. She is currently senior co-editor of the *Journal of Teaching in Physical Education*, and has served as Pedagogy Section Editor of the *Research Quarterly for Exercise and Sport*, Chairperson of the Physical Education Special Interest Group of the American Educational Research Association, and as Chairperson of the Curriculum and Instruction Academy of the American Alliance for Health, Physical Education, Recreation, and Dance.

John Evans is Professor of Physical Education and Head of the Department of Physical Education, Sports Science and Recreation Management at Loughborough University. His research interests centre on the study of policy, teaching and equity issues in the secondary school curriculum, and he is currently researching the relationships between physical education and nationalism in England and Wales. John has published widely in the sociology of education and physical education and he has authored and edited standard texts in the area. He is co-editor of the international journal *Sport, Education and Society*.

Richard Fisher is currently Assistant Principal at St Mary's University College, Twickenham, having been Head of the Department of Sport, Health and Exercise Science for ten years. He is also President of The European Physical Education Association and an Executive Board Member of The International Council of Sport Science and Physical Education. His work in physical education has been mainly in the field of international and comparative studies, with particular interests in aspects of children's and young people's participation in physical education and sport, and in the selection and development of the talented. Richard has published widely in these fields and he has worked with a number of governing bodies of sport in the development of curriculum materials for physical education.

David C. Griffey is Professor of Physical Education in the College of Education at The University of Arizona, USA. Dave is the former editor of the *Journal of Teaching in Physical Education*, and serves on editorial/review boards of JOPHER *Journal* and *Research Quarterly for Exercise and Sport*. He is a former middle school physical education and science teacher. He has worked in the area of teacher education physical education for the past 20 years.

Colin A. Hardy is a senior lecturer in the Department of Physical Education, Sports Science and Recreation Management at Loughborough University. His main research interests are on how pre-service teachers learn to teach, the mentoring process in schools and how pupils learn in physical education settings. Colin has authored and edited books in the area of physical education and he has published widely in professional and academic journals. He is co-editor of the international journal *Sport, Education and Society*.

Lynn Dale Housner is currently Professor and Assistant Dean in the School of Physical Education at West Virginia University, USA. Lynn has served as Chair of the AAHPERD Curriculum and Instruction Academy, President of the New Mexico AAHPERD, as Professional Preparation Chair of the Southwest District AAHPERD, and as an editorial board member for the *Journal of Teaching in Physical Education*, and was the 1994–5 Southwest District AAHPERD Scholar.

Christopher Laws is Head of the School of Physical Education at University College Chichester, having previously taught in schools for 14 years. He is currently President of the Physical Education Association of the United Kingdom. He serves on a number of consultative groups for the English Sports Council, the Qualifications Curriculum Authority, Office for Standards in Education and the Department for Education and Employment as well as on Education Committees for several National Governing Bodies of Sport. His work in physical education has been mainly concerned with teacher education curriculum development, teaching and learning and pupils' responses. He has worked with a number of national governing bodies of sport developing curriculum materials and, most recently, co-authored the *Football Association Curriculum Guide*.

Ian Luke has recently completed his PhD at Loughborough University on the topic of 'metacognitive ability in physical education'. He is a qualified teacher who has gained experience in British and Australian schools. Ian is a talented gymnast who represented Great Britain in Sports Acrobatics between 1986 and 1994, winning medals at both European and World Championships.

Mick Mawer is Programme Director of degrees in Physical Education and Sports Science at the University of Hull, and is a Fellow of the Physical Education Association of the UK. His research interests are in the area of Sports Pedagogy and the mentoring of pre-service teachers of PE, and his publications include: *The Effective Teaching of Physical Education* and *Mentoring in Physical Education: Issues and Insights*.

Dawn Penney is a Senior Research Fellow in the Department of Physical Education, Sport and Leisure at De Montfort University, Bedford. Since 1990 Dawn has been involved in research that has pursued the politics and processes of policy and curriculum development in education and of equity in physical education and sport. Dawn was previously a Research Fellow at the University of Queensland and at Loughborough University, and she has published widely for professional and academic journals in physical education and the sociology of education.

Judith E. Rink is the department Chair and Professor in the Department of Physical Education, University of South Carolina. She is the author of several textbooks dealing with curriculum and instruction in physical education, including *Teaching Physical Education for Learning*, and has been co-editor of the *Journal of Teaching in Physical Education*. Her research interests are primarily in investigating relationships between what teachers do and what students learn.

Tony Rossi teaches in the Faculty of Education at the University of Southern Queensland, Australia. Before this he taught physical education in secondary schools in England including several years as a head of department. His current interests are in knowledge, identity and dilemmas of self in physical education teacher education. He is about to complete his PhD at Deakin University.

Andrew C. Sparkes is Professor of Social Theory in the School of Postgraduate Medicine and Health Sciences at Exeter University. His research interests are eclectic and currently include: interrupted body projects, identity dilemmas, and the narrative (re)construction of self; organizational innovation and change; the lives and careers of marginalized individuals and groups. Each of these interests is framed by a desire to develop interpretive forms of understanding and a postmodern aspiration to represent lived experience using a variety of genres.

Index